ESSENTIALS for design

XHTML

level one

Kelly L. Valqui

PEARSON

Prentice Hall

Prentice Hall
Upper Saddle River, New Jersey 07458

Library of Congress Cataloging-in-Publication Data
Valqui, Kelly.
XHTML, level one/[Kelly L. Valqui]
    p.cm. — (Essentials for design)
Includes index.
ISBN 0-13-146645-3 (alk. paper)
1. XHTML (Document markup language). I. Title. II. Series

QA76.76.H94V358 2004
006.7'4—dc22   2004044744

Publisher and Vice President: Natalie E. Anderson
Executive Editor: Jodi McPherson
Acquisitions Editor: Melissa Sabella
Editorial Assistant: Alana Meyers
Senior Media Project Manager: Cathleen Profitko
Senior Marketing Manager: Emily Knight
Marketing Assistant: Nicole Beaudry

Senior Managing Editor: Gail Steier de Acevedo
Project Manager, Production: Vanessa Nuttry
Manufacturing Buyer: Vanessa Nuttry
Interior Design: Thistle Hill Publishing Services, LLC
Cover Design: Blair Brown
Cover Printer: Coral Graphics
Printer/Binder: Von Hoffman Press

Credits and acknowledgments borrowed from other sources and reproduced, with permission, in this textbook appear on the appropriate page within the text.

The fonts utilized in these training materials are the property of Against The Clock, Inc., and are supplied to the legitimate buyers of the Against The Clock training materials solely for use with the exercises and projects provided in the body of the materials. They may not be used for any other purpose, and under no circumstances may they be transferred to another individual, nor copied or distributed by any means whatsoever.

A portion of the images supplied in this book are copyright © PhotoDisc, Inc., 201 Fourth Ave., Seattle, WA 98121, or copyright ©PhotoSpin, 4030 Palos Verdes Dr. N., Suite 200, Rollings Hills Estates, CA. These images are the sole property of PhotoDisc or PhotoSpin and are used by Against The Clock with the permission of the owners. They may not be distributed, copied, transferred, or reproduced by any means whatsoever, other than for the completion of the exercises and projects contained in this book.

Against The Clock and the Against The Clock logo are trademarks of Against The Clock, Inc., registered in the United States and elsewhere. References to and instructional materials provided for any particular application program, operating system, hardware platform, or other commercially available product or products do not represent an endorsement of such product or products by Against The Clock, Inc.

Photoshop, PageMaker, Acrobat, Adobe Type Manager, Illustrator, InDesign, Premiere, and PostScript are trademarks of Adobe Systems Incorporated. Macromedia Flash, Generator, FreeHand, Dreamweaver, Fireworks, and Director are registered trademarks of Macromedia, Inc. QuarkXPress is a registered trademark of Quark, Inc. Macintosh is a trademark of Apple Computer, Inc. CorelDRAW!, procreate Painter, and WordPerfect are trademarks of Corel Corporation. FrontPage, Publisher, PowerPoint, Word, Excel, Office, Microsoft, MS-DOS, and Windows are either registered trademarks or trademarks of Microsoft Corporation.

Other product and company names mentioned herein may be the trademarks of their respective owners.

10 9 8 7 6 5 4 3 2 1

ISBN 0-13-146645-3

ABOUT THE SERIES EDITOR

Ellenn Behoriam is president and founder of Against The Clock, Inc. (ATC), one of the nation's leading content providers. Ellenn and her staff have successfully produced many of the graphic arts industry's most popular and well-received books and related series. These works include the *Electronic Cookbook*, *Workflow Reengineering*, *Teams and the Graphic Arts*, *Adobe Photoshop Creative Techniques*, *Adobe Illustrator Creative Techniques*, and *QuarkXPress 6: Creating Digital Documents*, the foundation for the QuarkXPress Trainer certification programs. The Against The Clock Series, published in concert with Prentice Hall/Pearson Education, includes more than 26 titles that focus on applications for the graphic and computer arts industries.

Against The Clock also worked with Pearson to develop the *Companion for the Digital Artist* series. These titles focus on specific and fundamental creative concepts, including design, Web site development, photography, typography, color theory, and copywriting. The concise and compact works provide core concepts and skills that supplement any application-specific education, regardless of which textbooks are being used to teach program skills.

Under Ellenn's leadership and direction, ATC is currently developing more than 20 titles for the new *Essentials for Design* series. Her staff and long-established network of professional educators, printers, prepress experts, workflow engineers, and business leaders add significantly to ATC's ability to provide current, meaningful, and effective books, online tutorials, and business-to-business performance and workflow-enhancement programs.

ABOUT THE AUTHOR

Kelly Valqui has been writing and teaching about Web development for over eight years. As senior Web developer for Triskelion Concepts Corporation, Kelly has designed and built sites for many local companies in the Miami area.

Kelly has also developed online courses for the University of Miami, Miami Dade Community College, and Craven Community College. In addition, Kelly has authored *Web Design and Development*, the *Web Site Creation Kit*, and the *HTML Template Master* for Charles River Media.

Currently, Kelly is teaching a variety of courses at the Broward Community College.

ACKNOWLEDGMENTS

We would like to thank the professional writers, artists, editors, and educators who have worked long and hard on the *Essentials for Design* series.

Special thanks to Deborah Zerillo, Editorial Assistant, for her help in keeping us all together. And thanks to the dedicated teaching professionals: Kara Hardin; Michele Ebert, Allentown Business School; and Janice Potter, Ph.D., Albuquerque Technical Vocational Institute. Your insightful comments and expertise have certainly contributed to the success of the *Essentials for Design* series.

Thank you to Laurel Nelson-Cucchiara, copy editor and final link in the chain of production, for her help in making sure that we all said what we meant to say.

And to Melissa Sabella, Jodi McPherson, and Vanessa Nuttry, we appreciate your patience as we begin this new venture together.

CONTENTS AT A GLANCE

TABLE OF CONTENTS

HOW TO USE THIS BOOK

Essentials courseware from Prentice Hall is anchored in the practical and professional needs of all types of students. The *Essentials* series presents a learning-by-doing approach that encourages you to grasp application-related concepts as you expand your skills through hands-on tutorials. As such, it consists of modular lessons that are built around a series of numbered step-by-step procedures that are clear, concise, and easy to review.

Essentials books are divided into projects. A project covers one area (or a few closely related areas) of application functionality. Each project consists of several lessons that are related to that topic. Each lesson presents a specific task or closely related set of tasks in a manageable chunk that is easy to assimilate and retain.

Each element in the *Essentials* book is designed to maximize your learning experience. A list of the *Essentials* project elements, and a description of how each element can help you, begins on the next page. To find out more about the rationale behind each book element and how to use each to your maximum benefit, take the following walk-through.

WALK-THROUGH

Project Objectives.   Starting with an objective gives you short-term, attainable goals. Each project begins with a list of objectives that closely match the titles of the step-by-step tutorials. ▶

OBJECTIVES

In this project, you learn how to

- Identify key differences between HTML and XHTML
- Create hypertext documents
- Apply document tags
- Format text into paragraphs

- Align paragraphs
- Create line breaks
- Add headings
- Align headings
- Indent sections of text

◀ Why Would I Do This?   Introductory material at the beginning of each project provides an overview of why these tasks and procedures are important.

Visual Summary.   A series of illustrations introduces the new tools, dialog boxes, and windows you will explore in each project. ▼

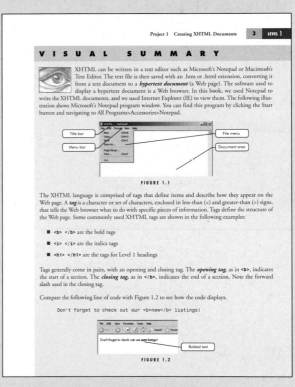

◀ Step-by-Step Tutorials.   Hands-on tutorials let you learn by doing and include numbered, bold, step-by-step instructions.

If You Have Problems. These short troubleshooting notes help you anticipate or solve common problems quickly and effectively.

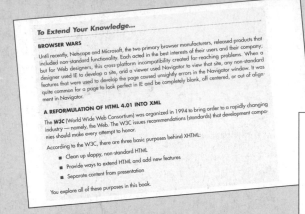

To Extend Your Knowledge. These features provide extra tips, alternative ways to complete a process, and special hints about using the software.

Careers in Design. These features offer advice, tips, and resources that will help you on your path to a successful career.

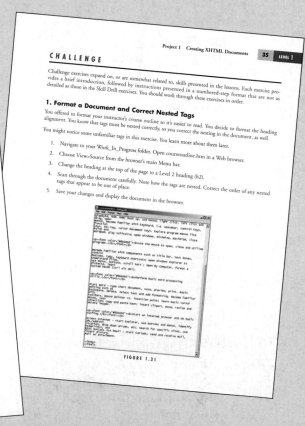

End-of-Project Exercises. Extensive end-of-project exercises emphasize hands-on skill development. You'll find two levels of reinforcement: Skill Drill and Challenge.

Portfolio Builder. At the end of every project, these exercises require creative solutions to problems that reinforce the topic of the project. ▶

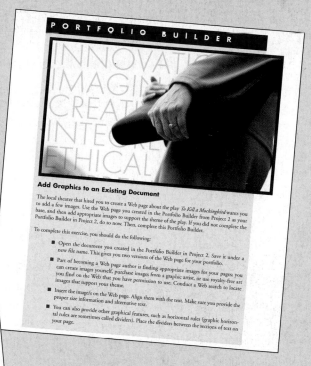

Add Graphics to an Existing Document

The local theater that hired you to create a Web page about the play *To Kill a Mockingbird* wants you to add a few images. Use the Web page you created in the Portfolio Builder from Project 2 as your base, and then add appropriate images to support the theme of the play. If you did not complete the Portfolio Builder in Project 2, do so now. Then, complete this Portfolio Builder.

To complete this exercise, you should do the following:

- Open the document you created in the Portfolio Builder in Project 2. Save it under a new file name. This gives you two versions of the Web page for your portfolio.
- Part of becoming a Web page author is finding appropriate images for your pages; you can create images yourself, purchase images from a graphic artist, or use royalty-free art images that support your theme. Conduct a Web search to locate images that you have permission to use.
- Insert the image/s on the Web page. Align them with the text. Make sure you provide the proper size information and alternative text.
- You can also provide other graphical features, such as horizontal rules (graphic horizontal rules are sometimes called dividers). Place the dividers between the sections of text on your page.

LEVEL 1

INTEGRATING PROJECT

This Integrating Project is designed to reflect a real-world XHTML programming job, drawing on the skills you learned throughout this book. The files you need to complete this project are located in the RF_XHTML_L1>IP folder.

Build the Backwater's Web Site

In this Integrating Project, you create a three-page Web site for a restaurant. The home page includes information about the restaurant; the menu page allows viewers to see the variety of foods offered at the restaurant; and the form page allows users to submit inquiries to the owner of the restaurant. Once the site is complete, you prepare it for publishing by providing meta information for search engines, as well as validate the document.

◀ **Integrating Projects.** Integrating projects are designed to reflect real-world graphic-design jobs, drawing on the skills you have learned throughout this book.

XHTML TAG REFERENCE					367 LEVEL 1	
Element	Strict	Transitional	Frameset	Basic	XHTML1.1	Empty
a	x	x	x	x	x	
abbr	x	x	x	x	x	
acronym	x	x	x	x	x	
address	x	x	x	x	x	
applet		x	x			
area		x	x			x
b	x	x	x		x	
base	x	x	x		x	x
basefont		x	x		x	x
bdo	x	x	x		x	
big	x	x	x			
blockquote	x	x	x		x	
body	x	x	x		x	
br	x	x	x	x	x	
button	x	x	x		x	
caption	x	x	x		x	x
center		x	x		x	
cite	x	x	x		x	
code	x	x	x		x	
col	x	x	x		x	
colgroup	x	x	x		x	
dd	x	x	x		x	
del	x	x	x		x	
dfn	x	x	x		x	
dir		x	x			
div	x	x	x		x	
dl	x	x	x		x	
dt	x	x	x		x	
em	x	x	x	x	x	
fieldset	x	x	x		x	
font		x	x		x	
form	x	x	x	x	x	
frame			x		x	x

Task Guides. These charts, found at the end of each book, list alternative ways to complete common procedures and provide a handy reference tool. ▶

STUDENT INFORMATION AND RESOURCES

Companion Web Site (www.prenhall.com/essentials). This text-specific Web site provides students with additional information and exercises to reinforce their learning. Features include: additional end-of-project reinforcement material, online Study Guide, easy access to *all* resource files, and much, much more!

Before completing the projects within this text, you need to download the Resource Files from the Prentice Hall Companion Web site. Check with your instructor for the best way to gain access to these files or simply follow these instructions:

1. From an open Web browser, go to http://www.prenhall.com/essentials.

2. Select your textbook or series to access the Companion Web site. We suggest you bookmark this page, as it has links to additional Prentice Hall resources that you may use in class.

3. Click the Student Resources link. All files in the Student Resources area are provided as .exe files. These files do not require any additional software to open.

4. Click the Start Here link.

5. Once you have downloaded the proper file, double-click that file to begin the self-extraction process. You will be prompted to select a folder location specific for your book; you may extract the file to your hard drive or to a removable disk/drive.

   The Start Here file contains three folders:

   - **Fonts.**
   - **RF_XHTML_L1.** You can place this folder on your hard drive, or on a removable disk/drive.
   - **Work_In_Progress.** You can place this folder on your hard drive, or on a removable disk/drive.

6. Locate the project files you need from the list of available resources and click the active link to download. There is a separate file for each project in this book (e.g., Project_01, Project_02, etc.).

7. Once you have downloaded the proper file, double-click that file to begin the self-extraction process. You will be prompted to select a folder location specific to your book; you should extract the project-specific folders into the RF_XHTML_L1 folder that was extracted from the Start Here file.

Resource CD.   If you are using a Resource CD, all the files you need are provided on the CD. Resource files are organized in project-specific folders (e.g., Project_01, Project_02, etc.), which are contained in the RF_XHTML_L1 folder. You can either work directly from the CD, or copy the files onto your hard drive before beginning the exercises.

Before you begin working on the projects or lessons in this book, you should copy the Work_In_Progress folder from the Resource CD onto your hard drive or a removable disk/drive.

Resource Files.   Resource files are organized in project-specific folders. Words are separated by an underscore, and all file names include a lowercase three-letter extension. For example, if you are directed to open the file "mysite.htm" in Project 2, the file can be found in the RF_XHTML_L1> Project_02 folder. We repeat these directions frequently in the early projects.

The Work In Progress Folder.   This folder contains individual folders for each project in the book (e.g., WIP_01, WIP_02, etc.). When an exercise directs you to save a file, you should save it to the appropriate folder for the project in which you are working.

The exercises in this book frequently build upon work that you have already completed. At the end of each exercise, you will be directed to save your work and either close the file or continue to the next exercise. If you are directed to continue but your time is limited, you can stop at a logical point, save the file, and later return to the point at which you stopped. In this case, you will need to open the file from the appropriate WIP folder and continue working on the same file.

Typeface and Code Conventions.   Computer programming code appears in a monospace font that **looks like this**. In many cases, you only need to change or enter specific pieces of code; in these instances, the code you need to type or change appears in a second color and `looks like this`.

Rather than include every line of code in the exercises in Projects 2-8, we use ellipses (...) to show you where we truncated the code. We show you three or more lines of code before and after each section of code that you should modify in the step. This ensures that you place the new code in the correct location within the script.

INSTRUCTOR'S RESOURCES

Customize Your Book (www.prenhall.com/customphit). The Prentice Hall Information Technology Custom PHIT Program gives professors the power to control and customize their books to suit their course needs. The best part is that it is done completely online using a simple interface.

Professors choose exactly what projects they need in the *Essentials for Design* series, and in what order they appear. The program also enables professors to add their own material anywhere in the text's presentation, and the final product will arrive at each professor's bookstore as a professionally formatted text.

To learn more about this new system for creating the perfect textbook, go to www.prenhall.com/customphit, where the online walk-through demonstrates how to create a book.

Instructor's Resource Center. This CD-ROM includes the entire Instructor's Manual for each application in Microsoft Word format. Student data files and completed solutions files are also on this CD-ROM. The Instructor's Manual contains a reference guide of these files for the instructor's convenience. PowerPoint slides with more information about each project are also available for classroom use.

Companion Web site (www.prenhall.com/essentials). Instructors will find all of the resources available on the Instructor's Resource CD-ROM available for download from the Companion Web site.

TestGen Software. TestGen is a test generator program that lets you view and easily edit test bank questions, transfer them to tests, and print the tests in a variety of formats suitable to your teaching situation. The program also offers many options for organizing and displaying test banks and tests. A built-in random number and text generator makes it ideal for creating multiple versions of tests. Powerful search and sort functions let you easily locate questions and arrange them in the order you prefer.

QuizMaster, also included in this package, enables students to take tests created with TestGen on a local area network. The QuizMaster utility built into TestGen lets instructors view student records and print a variety of reports. Building tests is easy with TestGen, and exams can be easily uploaded into WebCT, Blackboard, and CourseCompass.

Prentice Hall has formed close alliances with each of the leading online platform providers: WebCT, Blackboard, and our own Pearson CourseCompass.

OneKey.   OneKey lets you in to the best teaching and learn- ing resources all in one place. OneKey for *Essentials for Design* is all your students need for out-of-class work conveniently organized by chapter to reinforce and apply what they've learned in class and from the text. OneKey is all you need to plan and administer your course. All your instructor resources are in one place to maximize your effectiveness and minimize your time and effort. OneKey for convenience, simplicity, and success.

WebCT and Blackboard.   Each of these custom-built distance-   learning courses features exercises, sample quizzes, and tests in a course management system that provides class administra- tion tools as well as the ability to customize this material at the instructor's discretion.

CourseCompass.   CourseCompass is a dynamic, inter- active online course management tool powered by Blackboard. It lets professors create their own courses in 15 minutes or less with preloaded quality content that can include quizzes, tests, lecture materials, and interactive exercises.

Performance-Based Training and Assessment: Train & Assess IT. Prentice Hall offers performance-based training and assessment in one product — Train & Assess IT.

The Training component offers computer-based instruction that a student can use to preview, learn, and review graphic design application skills. Delivered via Web or CD-ROM, Train IT offers interactive multimedia, and computer-based training to augment classroom learning. Built-in prescriptive testing suggests a study path based not only on student test results but also on the specific textbook chosen for the course.

The Assessment component offers computer-based testing that shares the same user inter- face as Train IT and is used to evaluate a student's knowledge about specific topics in software including Photoshop, InDesign, Illustrator, Flash, and Dreamweaver. It does this in a task-oriented, performance-based environment to demonstrate students' proficiency and comprehension of the topics. More extensive than the testing in Train IT, Assess IT offers more administrative features for the instructor and additional questions for the stu- dent. Assess IT also enables professors to test students out of a course, place students in appropriate courses, and evaluate skill sets.

INTRODUCTION

HyperText Markup Language, better known as HTML, has come a long way since it was first standardized in the early 1990s. Unlike earlier hypertext systems that required authors to possess programming skills, this scripting language allows people who have little or no programming experience to successfully create Web pages. HTML "programmers" can use different programs, operating systems, and file formats to exchange information.

Tim Berners-Lee is the visionary programmer who developed the theory behind HTML and the Web. His idea was to create a global information system that would be available to anyone with a computer. His system would allow people to link information on disparate systems using a common addressing method, which is what we know as the Uniform Resource Locator (URL), or Web address.

As the Web evolved and gained commercial popularity, Web authors began to express the desire for more than simple methods of structuring content; they wanted presentational control, as well. This gave rise to new HTML formatting techniques that delivered more design capabilities — as well as frustrating compatibility issues.

To resolve those compatibility issues, and to satisfy the content and presentational require-ments of Web authors, a new scripting language was developed: the eXtensible HyperText Markup Language. XHTML begins the migration from non-compatible hypertext documents to Web pages that contain both structural and presentational elements, while offering universal accessibility across platforms.

This book is designed to introduce you to the tools and features of XHTML, as well as teach you how to produce professional-looking documents for the Web. We encourage you to look at the big picture — what you're actually creating — and make design decisions based on that reality, rather than establishing a blanket rule for production. You can apply the skills you learn to virtually any document, from a one-page gallery, to a multi-tiered corporate site.

As you progress through this book, pay attention not only to the step-by-step tasks within the projects, but also to the principles behind them. Most hands-on exercises and Skill Drills demand absolute attention to detail; but many of the Challenges and Portfolio Builders provide opportunities to express your personal creativity. In addition, we encour-age you to go beyond the projects and experiment on your own, rather than limit yourself solely to the ideas presented in this book.

Creating XHTML Documents

OBJECTIVES

In this project, you learn how to

- Identify key differences between HTML and XHTML

- Create hypertext documents

- Apply document tags

- Format text into paragraphs

- Align paragraphs

- Create line breaks

- Add headings

- Align headings

- Indent sections of text

WHY WOULD I DO THIS?

Part of the reason the Web gained popularity so quickly was that virtually anybody could use HTML to build a Web page. Non-programmers and programmers alike were able to build and post sites on the Web — and you will, too, after you complete the lessons and exercises in this book. Before you begin the lessons on XHTML, it's important that you know a bit about the Hypertext Markup Language (HTML), the framework upon which XHTML is built.

HTML is a simple scripting language that instructs a Web browser how to display a Web page. A *scripting language* is a type of programming language that typically does not need to be *parsed* (interpreted by the computer) or executed as a full-blown programming language. Scripting languages run from or within other programs; they are not stand-alone applications. HTML was designed to run with different programs (such as the various Web browsers) and operating systems to exchange information through a large heterogeneous network (the Internet).

HTML 4.01 is likely the final version of HTML. The new recommended language for Web page development is XHTML 1.1 (eXtensible Hypertext Markup Language). *XHTML 1.1* is essentially HTML 4.01 that includes minor code changes, as well as stricter structural rules and syntax. The *syntax* of a programming language is the structure of its strings and characters. A *string* is a line of code that instructs the program to complete a specific task. A *character* is a part of the code, such as a semicolon (;), which ends a string of code.

When XHTML 1.0 was standardized, it was designed to offer *backward compatibility*, which is the ability to support older technology and browsers, even though it was designed for newer technology and browsers. A new standard is on the horizon, however, called XHTML 2.0. This newer version does not offer support for older browsers. (You'll learn more about browser compatibility issues as you work through this book.)

The focus of this book is on XHTML 1.1 and how you can use it to create compelling content for the Web. When necessary, we note specific examples of when it makes better sense to use HTML. As you complete the exercises and build Web-based content, you receive sneak peeks at what's new in XHTML 2.0.

V I S U A L   S U M M A R Y

XHTML can be written in a text editor such as Microsoft's Notepad or Macintosh's Text Editor. The text file is then saved with an .htm or .html extension, converting it from a text document to a ***hypertext document*** (a Web page). The software used to display a hypertext document is a Web browser. In this book, we used Notepad to write the XHTML documents, and we used Internet Explorer (IE) to view them. The following illustration shows Microsoft's Notepad program window. You can find this program by clicking the Start button and navigating to All Programs>Accessories>Notepad.

FIGURE 1.1

The XHTML language is comprised of tags that define items and describe how they appear on the Web page. A ***tag*** is a character or set of characters, enclosed in less-than (<) and greater-than (>) signs, that tells the Web browser what to do with specific pieces of information. Tags define the structure of the Web page. Some commonly used XHTML tags are shown in the following examples:

- **`<b> </b>`** are the bold tags

- **`<i> </i>`** are the italics tags

- **`<h1> </h1>`** are the tags for Level 1 headings

Tags generally come in pairs, with an opening and closing tag. The ***opening tag***, as in **`<b>`**, indicates the start of a section. The ***closing tag,*** as in **`</b>`**, indicates the end of a section. Note the forward slash used in the closing tag.

Compare the following line of code with Figure 1.2 to see how the code displays.

```
Don't forget to check out our <b>new</b> listings!
```

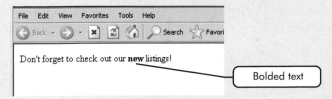

FIGURE 1.2

As you see, only the word "new" is bold because it is the only word inside the tags. XHTML also allows you to use nested tags. A ***nested tag*** is contained within another tag. For instance, you could italicize the entire sentence using the following tags:

```
<i>Don't forget to check out our <b>new</b> listings!</i>
```

This line of code displays as follows:

FIGURE 1.3

In HTML, it doesn't matter how you order the nested tags. For example, if you opened with a **<b>** tag and followed it with an opening **<i>** tag, you could choose to close the **<b>** tag first, or the **<i>** tag — either way, you would achieve the same result. For example:

```
<i><b>Content here.</i></b>
```

creates the same result as

```
<i><b>Content here.</b></i>
```

In XHTML, however, you must close nested tags in the reverse order you opened them:

```
<i><b>Content here.</b></i>
```

The above examples are simple illustrations, but you can begin to see how XHTML instructs elements to display on a Web page. An ***element*** is an object that can contain text, such as a paragraph or an image. We examine elements in more detail throughout this book.

LESSON 1   Understanding a Hypertext Document

On the most basic level, a Web page is simply a text file that refers to other files (text and images). The browser knows how to interpret a hypertext document because it understands the system of tags that describes the content. Tags describe each string of text, whether the string represents a headline, an image, a name rendered in bold typeface, or the overall body of content. Every page uses the same standard structure.

don't need to buy an expensive layout program to create Web pages. All you need to know is how to apply HTML scripting language to your content. A text editor and browser are all you need to get started.

Create a Web Page

1   **Create a folder named "Work_In_Progress" on your hard drive. Copy the RF_XHTML_L1 folder from your Resource CD-ROM to the Work_In_Progress folder.**

The RF_XHTML_L1 folder contains the files you need to complete the exercises in this book.

2   **In the Work_In_Progress folder, create a subfolder named "WIP_01".**

Save all of the files in this project to your WIP_01 folder.

3   **Open a simple text editor, such as SimpleText or Notepad.**

The text-editing program launches. Do not use a word-processing program, such as Microsoft Word or Corel WordPerfect. Using a word-processing program causes unpredictable results.

4   **Type the following on the first line of the document:**

```
Hello World!
```

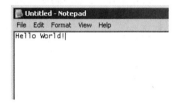

FIGURE 1.4

5   **Save the document as "hello.htm" in your WIP_01 folder. Make sure to choose Save as type all files *.* from the Save As dialog box.**

This ensures that the .txt extension is excluded from the file name. Web browsers recognize .htm and .html extensions as Web pages. The difference between the two extensions dates back to Windows 3.x, which only recognized three-letter extensions, and the Macintosh, which used the four-letter extension. Today's platforms recognize both extensions. Remember to always save your documents in lowercase letters. This prevents any issues with case sensitivity and linking.

❓ If you have problems...

You want this to be a text file, but you want it to include the .htm extension — not .txt. Occasionally, Windows adds .txt to a file name, which would rename the file hello.html.txt. If this happens, manually rename the file, and then reopen it.

6   **Open your browser.**

We used Microsoft Internet Explorer (IE) for the illustrations in this book. If you use another browser, there may be slight differences in button names and/or how the page renders.

7   **Choose File>Open (or Open File) in the browser window.**

The Open dialog box displays. If you do not see a hypertext file in the Open dialog box, pull down the Files of Type menu and choose All Files. By default, the browser opens .htm or .html files. If you do not see the file you saved in the Open dialog box, pull down the Files of Type menu.

FIGURE 1.5

8   **Click the Browse button in the Open dialog box. Navigate to WIP_01>hello.htm.**

9   **Double-click hello.htm.**

The path to hello.htm displays in the Open dialog box.

To Extend Your Knowledge...

BROWSER WARS

Until recently, Netscape and Microsoft, the two primary browser manufacturers, released products that included non-standard functionality. Each acted in the best interests of their users and their company; but for Web designers, this cross-platform incompatibility created far-reaching problems. When a designer used IE to develop a site, and a viewer used Navigator to view that site, any non-standard features that were used to develop the page caused unsightly errors in the Navigator window. It was quite common for a page to look perfect in IE and be completely blank, off centered, or out of alignment in Navigator.

A REFORMULATION OF HTML 4.01 INTO XML

The **W3C** (World Wide Web Consortium) was organized in 1994 to bring order to a rapidly changing industry — namely, the Web. The W3C issues recommendations (standards) that development companies should make every attempt to honor.

According to the W3C, there are three basic purposes behind XHTML:

- Clean up sloppy, non-standard HTML
- Provide ways to extend HTML and add new features
- Separate content from presentation

plore all of these purposes in this book.

10	**Click OK.**

The Web page displays in the browser. Even though you created a Web page, it is not considered an XHTML document. In the next lesson, you learn some of the requirements for creating a valid XHTML document.

FIGURE 1.6

11	**Leave the file open in both windows.**

LESSON 2 Document Tags and Elements

Tags are the underlying foundation of Web pages. Tags tell the browser what to do with specific pieces of information and define the structure of a Web page. ***Document tags*** specify each section of an XHTML document. HTML did not require the use of all document tags, but the stricter XHTML requires that opening and closing document tags must be applied to every document. Additionally, *all* tags must be written in lowercase.

Document tags are as follows:

- **`<html></html>`**. The html tags define the beginning and end of an XHTML document. A requirement for a valid XHTML page is that all other tags (including document tags) are contained between the **`<html>`** and **`</html>`** tags.

- **`<head></head>`**. The head section of a page is where you place information that is not generally displayed on the page, but is still important to the page. For instance, ***meta data*** (information about the author, date) is placed in the **`<head>`** section. In other situations, the **`<head>`** section may include scripts that will be run by the browser.

- **`<title></title>`**. The title, which is included in the head of the document, doesn't actually appear on the page, but typically controls the text that displays in the Title bar of the browser window.

- **`<body></body>`**. You place the content of your page between the **`<body>`** tags. All text, images, and other items the user sees are located in this section of the document.

Elements

As you learned earlier, an element is a type of object that can contain text or other objects. For example, a Web page might consist of an HTML element that contains many other elements, including a body element. The body element might contain text. When one element (such as the above body element) is contained with another element, it is called a nested element. The text element is nested within the body element, and the body element is nested within the html element.

Add Document Tags to a Web Page

1 Continue working in the open text editor window that contains hello.htm.

2 Place your cursor before the words "Hello World!" Press the Enter/Return key three times.

This positions "Hello World!" three lines farther down in the window, allowing you to type the first document tag at the top of the page (above "Hello World!").

3 Reposition your cursor at the top of the page and type the following tag:

```
<html>
```

The **<html>** document tag (element) defines the entire page as an HTML document. All of the page's content must be placed within the **<html>** and **</html>** elements.

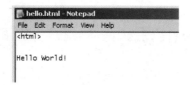

FIGURE 1.7

4 Press Enter/Return. Type the following:

```
<head>
```

Remember that important information about the document is placed in the head section of a page. This information does not display in the browser.

5 Press Enter/Return. Type the following:

```
<title>This is my first Web page.</title>
```

The title typically displays in the Title bar of the browser window. The **<title>** tag is also used when indexing your Web page with search engines. You learn more about search-engine indexing later in this book.

6 Press Enter/Return. Type the following:

```
</head>
```

This closes the head section of the document.

7 Press Enter/Return. Type the following:

```
<body>
```

The content of the page is contained within the body section of the document. Content can include text, images, and any other items the user sees.

8 | **Position your cursor after the words "Hello World!" Type the following:**

```
</body>
```

This closes the body section of the document.

9 | **Press Enter/Return and type the following:**

```
</html>
```

This ends the XHTML document.

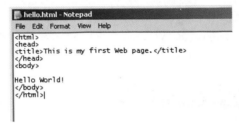

FIGURE 1.8

10 | **Choose File>Save from the main Menu bar in the text editor.**

This saves your XHTML file.

11 | **Click your browser window to activate it. Click the Refresh button on the browser toolbar.**

The document refreshes in the browser. The only visual change you see is the addition of a Title bar. Even though you can't see it on your screen, the document tags added more structure to the XHTML document.

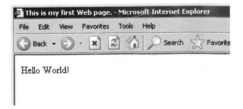

FIGURE 1.9

12 | **Close hello.htm in your text editor.**

To Extend Your Knowledge...

XHTML VALIDATION

Unlike HTML documents, XHTML documents must be validated. *Validating* an XHTML document confirms that the document adheres to one of the three Document Type Definitions (DTDs) defined by the W3C. You can use this process to ensure that you didn't make any structural or typing mistakes in the content of a page.

The three types of XHTML are:

1. *XHTML Strict*. To comply with this recommendation, you must not only follow the XML rules that prevent you from creating sloppy code, you must also remove any HTML that is focused on presentation. Instead, you must rely on Cascading Style Sheets.

    Cascading Style Sheets (CSS) allow Web designers to control the style and layout appearance of multiple Web pages at the same time, without making individual page adjustments.

    XML (eXtensible Markup Language) is a markup language designed specifically for the Web. It allows Web page authors to create customized tags, enabling the definition, transmission, and validation of data between applications.

2. *XHTML Transitional* is literally a reformulation of HTML 4.01. Virtually every tag is reproduced in entirety, but all of the loopholes for which browsers have been compensating have been removed. Some pages require minor modifications to conform to the new rules; some *deprecated* features (those marked for extinction) must be removed. It should take a short amount of time to bring any properly written page into conformance with this standard. XHTML Transitional documents are closest in form and function to the vast majority of Web pages that already exist. XHTML Transitional is sometimes needed to compensate for browsers that don't fully support CSS. We use and discuss this version of XHTML throughout this book, with certain noted exceptions.

3. *XHTML Frameset*. HTML frames enable you to create a window-in-a-window effect on a Web page.

LESSON 3   Creating Paragraphs

White space, the empty area on a page that makes it easier to read, is an important design element, one that is often taken for granted when working with word-processing or page-layout programs. With those programs, you can press the Enter/Return key to add as many blank lines as you prefer, and immediately see the result on the screen.

In XHTML, however, adding a blank line is not such a simple matter. Browsers ignore the white space in the HTML file. If you want to display white space in the final document, you must instruct the browser to do so. You use several methods to add white space to a Web page. Adding a new paragraph, for example, creates space between the preceding paragraph and the new one. To create a paragraph, you enclose a section with the `<p>` and `</p>` tags.

Work with Paragraphs

1   **Create a new file in your text editor.**

A new blank document displays on your screen.

2   **Type the document tags, as follows:**

```
<html>

<head>

<title>Creating Paragraphs.</title>

</head>

<body>

</body>

</html>
```

3   **Type the following copy in the text editor after the <body> tag.**

When typing your code into the text editor, choose Format>Word Wrap from the text editor menu bar to turn on the word wrap feature. As an alternative, you can manually wrap your code by pressing the Enter/Return key when you want to advance to a new line.

```
White space is an important element of design, and one that we often take
for granted when working with word-processing or page-layout programs. With
those types of programs, if we want to add several blank lines to the page,
we just do it and see the results immediately. Want to break a line of
text? Just add a hard return to the text.

Things are not quite so simple in XHTML. White space in our file is ignored
by the browser, so if we want to see it in our final document, we're going
to have to add it specifically using tags.
```

? If you have problems...

Throughout this book, you will find several sections that may require significant typing. To save time, we provide some of these lengthy files on the Resource CD-ROM. These files are organized by project; you can find them in the RF_XHTML_L1 folder.

4 Save the document as "paragraph.htm" in your WIP_01 folder. Display the file in your browser.

The Web page displays in your browser without the blank space between the two sections of text, because there are no instructions to separate the text into paragraphs.

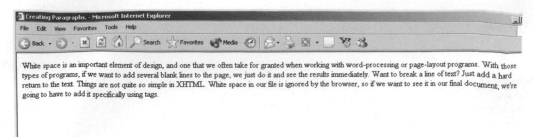

FIGURE 1.10

5 Return to the document in the text editor. Enclose the two sections of text with the `<p></p>` tags, as follows:

```
<p> White space is an important element of design, and one that we often
take for granted when working with word-processing or page-layout programs.
With those types of programs, if we want to add several blank lines to the
page, we just do it and see the results immediately. Want to break a line
of text? Just add a hard return to the text. </p>

<p> Things are not quite so simple in XHTML. White space in our file is
ignored by the browser, so if we want to see it in our final document,
we're going to have to add it specifically using tags. </p>
```

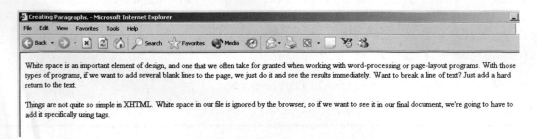

FIGURE 1.11

6 Save the changes to the document. Refresh paragraph.htm in your browser.

The `<p></p>` tags separate the sections of text into paragraphs.

7 Leave paragraph.htm open in your text editor.

To Extend Your Knowledge...

CLOSING CONTAINER TAGS

One of the changes from HTML to XHTML is stricter coding. For instance, HTML 4.01 states that paragraph (**<p></p>**) tags should be placed at the beginning and end of a block of text to set it off from the text around it. Both major browsers, however, allow developers to leave off the ending **</p>** tag, effectively using the **<p>** tag as a double line break. In XHTML however, the **<p>** tag must be accompanied by a closing **</p>** tag. All container tags have a similar requirement.

LESSON 4   Aligning Paragraphs

Before you learn how to align paragraphs on a Web page, it's important to understand that there is more to a tag than the command itself. For instance, the paragraph element (**<p>**), which adds a blank line before and after a section of text, can offer more instruction than the basic command; it can also contain attributes. *Attributes* are pieces of information in the opening tag that provide information about the tag and what it is supposed to do. For example:

```
<p align="center">
```

In this case, you have a **<p>** element. The element contains an align attribute, which has a *value* (option) of center. This is known as an *attribute-value pair* (also called *name-value pair*). The value is enclosed in double quotes so the browser knows where it begins and ends. In XHTML, name-value pairs must be surrounded by quotes; quotes are not required in HTML. The align attribute offers three value options: right, left, or center.

The align attribute for the paragraph tag has been deprecated (replaced with a newer method) in the current XHTML standard; style sheets are now the preferred method of alignment. In future versions of XHTML, the align attribute will not be available. The align attribute conforms to the XHTML1.0 Transitional document type.

Align Paragraphs on a Web Page

1   Open the text editor window that contains the paragraph.htm document.

The document becomes active in the text editor.

2   Add the `align="center"` name-value pair to the first <p> tag:

```
<p align="center"> White space is an important element of design, and one
that we often take for granted when working with word-processing or pa
layout programs. With those types of programs, if we want to add seve
blank lines to the page, we just do it and see the results immedia
Want to break a line of text? Just add a hard return to the text
```

The **align="center"** attribute instructs the browser to align the paragraph in the center of the page. Make sure there is a space between the "**p**" and the **align="center"** attribute. There is always a space after the tag command and the tag's attributes.

3 Add the **align="right"** attribute to the second paragraph:

```
<p align="right"> Things are not quite so simple in XHTML. White space in
our file is ignored by the browser, so if we want to see it in our final
document, we're going to have to add it specifically using tags. </p>
```

The **align="right"** name-value pair aligns the paragraph on the right of the Web page.

4 Save the changes to the document. Refresh the document in your browser.

The document reflects the alignment changes in the paragraphs.

FIGURE 1.12

5 Leave paragraph.htm open in your text editor.

To Extend Your Knowledge...

DEPRECATED TAGS

Deprecated tags are included in the current HTML 4.01 standard, but might become obsolete in the next approved standard or substandard. These tags have been deprecated because newer, easier ways of rendering the same Web page elements have been established. Many presentational tags and attributes have been deprecated in favor of style sheets because they allow HTML authors to design with more flexibility, without sacrificing accessibility. Even though deprecated features might become obsolete in future versions of HTML, browsers that support the features will likely continue to do so.

LESSON 5   Creating Line Breaks

The **<p></p>** tags separate sections of text into paragraphs; but what if you want to force a line of text onto the next line without creating a space? Rather than use the **<p></p>** tags, you can create a line break to achieve the same result.

You create a line break with the **
** tag. The **
** tag is different from the other tags you've examined so far — it's an empty tag. It's called an ***empty tag*** because there's no actual content within the tag.

To boldface someone's name, as we did to Bunny Hop in the following example, the name is placed between the opening and closing bold tags. Bunny Hop is the content for those tags. (You learn more about boldface tags and other formatting tags later in this book.) For example:

```
<b>Bunny Hop</b>
```

The **
** tag, however, works differently. It simply forces a line break; no content is associated with tag. In HTML, the tag reads **
** (without a slash). One of the requirements of XHTML is that you use complete pairs of tags; technically, the XHTML tag should read **
**.

Since there's no actual content in the **
** tag, using a closing tag might look rather awkward. In addition, if a browser understands only HTML (and not XHTML), it may display the result of the **
** tag incorrectly. The designers of XML (and XHTML) understood this browser problem and defined a "shorthand" for empty elements; this shorthand combines both the opening and closing tag in one tag. Unfortunately, older browsers don't understand the shorthand. To prevent errors in these browsers, you must add a space before the slash. The tag becomes:

```
<br />
```

Older browsers, as well as current browsers and programs designed to read XHTML, can interpret the **
** tag.

Create a Line Break

1   **Open paragraph.htm in the text editor.**

2   **Remove the all <p></p> tags (with the attributes) from the XHTML documents, so the text displays as follows:**

```
White space is an important element of design, and one that we often take
for granted when working with word-processing or page-layout programs. With
those types of programs, if we want to add several blank lines to the page,
we just do it and see the results immediately. Want to break a line of
text? Just add a hard return to the text.
```

Things are not quite so simple in XHTML. White space in our file is ignored by the browser, so if we want to see it in our final document, we're going to have to add it specifically using tags.

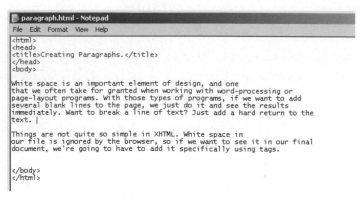

FIGURE 1.13

3   **Position your cursor after the first section of text and type "<br />". The body text displays as follows:**

White space is an important element of design, and one that we often take for granted when working with word-processing or page-layout programs. With those types of programs, if we want to add several blank lines to the page, we just do it and see the results immediately. Want to break a line of text? Just add a hard return to the text.

Things are not quite so simple in XHTML. White space in our file is ignored by the browser, so if we want to see it in our final document, we're going to have to add it specifically using tags.

This removes the space between the two sections of text and forces a line break.

4   **Save the changes to the document. Refresh your browser.**

The **
** tag forces a line break, but does not separate the sections into paragraphs.

FIGURE 1.14

5   **Close paragraph.htm in your text editor.**

To Extend Your Knowledge...

LINE BREAK TAG DEPRECATED IN 2.0

The line break tag (**
) has been deprecated in XHTML 2.0 in favor of the **<line></line> tags. The **<line>** tag encloses text that should display on its own line. For example:

> **<p>**HTML 4.0 is no longer the recommended standard for the Web.
>
> **<line>**XHTML 1.1 is the current working standard. **</line>**
>
> XHTML 2.0 is currently in draft form, and will soon be the standard for the Web.**</p>**

As of this writing, XHTML 2.0 is in draft form — it is not yet the recommended version. We mention it as a sneak peek of what's likely to come in the next version of XHTML.

MORE REASONS TO USE THE LINE BREAK

The **
** tag is useful in situations where the **<p>** tag would not be well suited, such as when you need to insert an address. If you add an address to a Web page, using the **<p>** tag creates a space between each line of the address. Using the **
** tag allows you to format an address more appropriately. For example:

> Jane Doe**
**
>
> 1000 Your Avenue**
**
>
> Your Town, ST 11111**
**

This creates an address that appears on a Web page, as follows:

> Jane Doe
>
> 1000 Your Avenue
>
> Your Town, ST 11111

LESSON 6   Creating Headings

At times, you may want to display topic headings within your documents. Browsers identify headings as important content, so they normally display headings in larger sizes and bolder typeface than the rest of the text in the document. Adding headings makes it easier to read a document, and the content appears more organized.

The different sizes (levels) of section headings in documents allow readers to understand the relative importance of the information presented in each section. For example, an article might include the title at the beginning and smaller subtitles throughout the document. XHTML headings come in six sizes, **<h1></h1>** through **<h6></h6>**, so you can present an extensive hierarchy of information when necessary.

It might seem logical that the h6 heading would be the largest and h1 the smallest — but the opposite is true. Heading levels indicate the importance of the text, not its size. An h1 heading is of highest importance, and an h6 heading is of least importance.

Add Headings to a Web Page

1 **In your text editor, choose File>Open. Navigate to the RF_XHTML_L1>Project_01 folder.**

2 **Double-click the headings.htm file**

The headings.htm file displays in the browser. Notice the existing XHTML code in the document. Remember, to see a file with an .html or .htm extension, change your Files of type from the default *.txt to All Files.

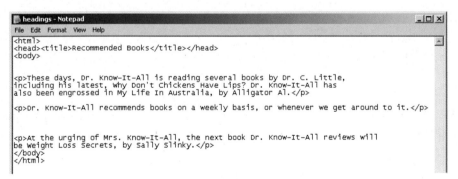

FIGURE 1.15

3   **Add the following headings to the headings.htm document.**

```
<html>

<head>

<title>Recommended Books</title>

</head>

<body>

<h1>Dr. Know-It-All Recommendations</h1>

<p>These days, Dr. Know-It-All is reading several books by Dr. C. Little,
including his Latest, Why Don't Chickens Have Lips? Dr. Know-It-All has
also been engrossed in My Life In Australia, by Alligator Al.</p>

<p>Dr. Know-It-All recommends books on a weekly basis, or whenever we get
around to it.</p>

<h2>Upcoming Books</h2>

<p>At the urging of Mrs. Know-It-All, the next book Dr. Know-It-All reviews
will be Weight Loss Secrets, by Sally Slinky.</p>

</body>

</html>
```

Adding a heading to each section of the Web page makes it easier to read.

4   **Choose File>Save As from the text editor. Save the document as "headings.htm" in your WIP_01 folder.**

This saves the new version of the file in your WIP_01 folder.

5   **Switch to the browser window. Navigate to the WIP_01>headings.htm file. Display the document in your browser.**

Notice the first heading is a Level 1 heading, and the second is a Level 2 heading.

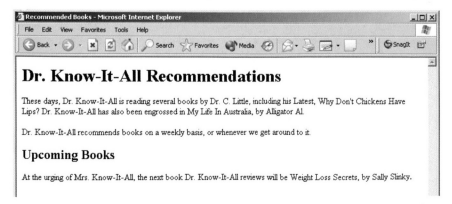

FIGURE 1.16

6 Switch back to the text document and add the `align="center"` name-value pair to the headings, as follows:

```
<html>

<head>

<title>Recommended Books</title>

</head>

<body>

<h1 align="center">Dr. Know-It-All Recommendations</h1>

<p>These days, Dr. Know-It-All is reading several books by Dr. C. Little,
including his Latest, Why Don't Chickens Have Lips? Dr. Know-It-All has
also been engrossed in My  Life In Australia, by Alligator Al.</p>

<p>Dr. Know-It-All recommends books on a weekly basis, or whenever we get
around to it.</p>

<h2 align="center">Upcoming Books</h2>

<p>At the urging of Mrs. Know-It-All, the next book Dr. Know-It-All reviews
will be Weight Loss Secrets, by Sally Slinky.</p>

</body>

</html>
```

In an earlier lesson, you learned how to use the align attribute to align paragraphs on a Web page. You can also use the align attribute with a heading tag to align a heading left, right, or center on the page.

7 **Save the changes in the text document. Refresh headings.htm in the browser.**

The headings are center-aligned on the page.

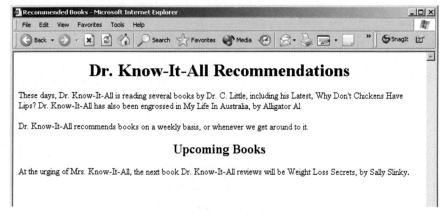

FIGURE 1.17

8 Leave headings.htm open in the text editor.

To Extend Your Knowledge...

XHTML 2.0 STRUCTURED HEADINGS

XHTML 1.1 includes six levels of numbered headings. XHTML 2.0 offers another method called "structured headings." Structured headings use the single **<h>** element in combination with the section element to indicate the structure of the document. The importance of a heading is determined by its nesting order. Headings are rendering according to their importance/nesting order. For example:

<h>This is a top-level heading because it is listed first**</h>**

<p>...**</p>**

<section>

   <p>...**</p>**

  <h>This is a second-level heading because it is nested below the top-level heading**</h>**

   <p>...**</p>**

  <section>

  <h>This is a third-level heading because it is nested within the second-level heading**</h>**

   <p>...**</p>**

  </section>

 </section>

LESSON 7 | Indenting Text

It is sometimes necessary to indent entire paragraphs of information on a Web page. You do this to emphasize the material and to make it stand out from the rest of the copy. Direct quotes are oftentimes set off in this manner.

You can create indented paragraphs with the **<blockquote>** tag, which is similar to pressing the Tab key on your keyboard. *Blockquotes* provide convenient and consistent indentation in a document. The container tags **<blockquote>** and **</blockquote>** enclose the section to be indented (usually paragraphs of text).

Indent Elements on a Web Page

1   **Continue working in the open headings.htm file in your text editor.**

2   **Choose File>Save As, and save the file as "indenting.htm" in your WIP_01 folder.**

Indenting.htm is the active file in your text editor window.

3   Change the text file by including the **<blockquote>** container tags as follows:

```
<html>

<head>

<title>Recommended Books</title>

</head>

<body>

<h1 align="center">Dr. Know-It-All Recommendations</h1>

<blockquote>

<p>These days, Dr. Know-It-All is reading several books by Dr. C. Little,
including his Latest, Why Don't Chickens Have Lips? Dr. Know-It-All has
also been engrossed in My  Life In Australia, by Alligator Al.</p>

<p>Dr. Know-It-All recommends books on a weekly basis, or whenever we get
around to it.</p>

</blockquote>

<h2 align="center">Upcoming Books</h2>

<p>At the urging of Mrs. Know-It-All, the next book Dr. Know-It-All reviews
will be Weight Loss Secrets, by Sally Slinky.</p>

</body>

</html>
```

This indents the first two paragraphs of text that follow the first heading.

4   **Save the changes in the text editor window. Open indenting.htm in your browser.**

The first two paragraphs are indented from the rest of the body text.

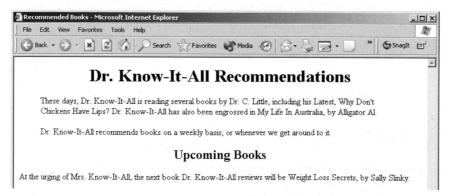

FIGURE 1.18

5 Place your cursor before the second paragraph in the blockquoted section. Nest (blockquote) an additional section of text, as follows:

```
<html>

<head>

<title>Recommended Books</title>

</head>

<body>

<h1 align="center">Dr. Know-It-All Recommendations</h1>

<blockquote>

<p>These days, Dr. Know-It-All is reading several books by Dr. C. Little,
including his Latest, Why Don't Chickens Have Lips? Dr. Know-It-All has
also been engrossed in My  Life In Australia, by Alligator Al.</p>

<blockquote>

<p>Dr. Know-It-All recommends books on a weekly basis, or whenever we get
around to it.</p>

</blockquote>

</blockquote>

<h2 align="center">Upcoming Books</h2>

<p>At the urging of Mrs. Know-It-All, the next book Dr. Know-It-All reviews
will be Weight Loss Secrets, by Sally Slinky.</p>

</body>

</html>
```

The second blockquote indents the section of text to a greater degree. This is nested blockquote.

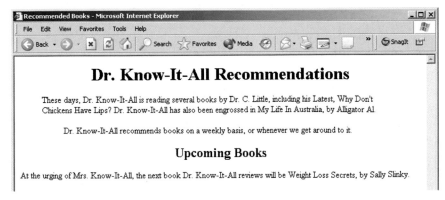

FIGURE 1.19

6   **Save the changes in the document. Refresh the page in the browser.**

The changes display in the Web browser.

7   **Leave indenting.htm open in both applications.**

Cite Text Using Blockquotes

The `cite=""` attribute allows you to indicate the source of a quote. The attribute's value should be a quote-enclosed URL that points to the online document and, if possible, the exact location of the quote within the document.

1   **In the text editor window of the open file, add a `cite=""` attribute in the second set of block-quote tags, as follows:**

```
<html>

<head>

<title>Recommended Books</title>

</head>

<body>

<h1 align="center">Dr. Know-It-All Recommendations</h1>

<blockquote>

<p>These days, Dr. Know-It-All is reading several books by Dr. C. Little,
including his Latest, Why Don't Chickens Have Lips? Dr. Know-It-All has
also been engrossed in My  Life In Australia, by Alligator Al.</p>

<blockquote cite="http://www.againsttheclock.com">

<p>Dr. Know-It-All recommends books on a weekly basis, or whenever we get
around to it.</p>

</blockquote>

</blockquote>

<h2 align="center">Upcoming Books</h2>

<p>At the urging of Mrs. Know-It-All, the next book Dr. Know-It-All reviews
will be Weight Loss Secrets, by Sally Slinky.</p>

</body>

</html>
```

This provides the source of the information that was quoted. In this case, we used Against The Clock's Web site as an example, even though it is not the source for the text. Most authors use the blockquote tags to indent content, but its intended purpose is for quoted text.

2   **Save the changes to indenting.htm. Refresh the file in your browser.**

You see no difference in the display of the document in the browser. The cite attribute provides the source of information in the code only.

3   **Close indenting.htm in both applications.**

To Extend Your Knowledge...

JUSTIFY HEADINGS AND TEXT

If you set the align value to `align="justify"`, all lines except the last are stretched to fill the entire width of the page. The justify option has been deprecated in XHTML. (The justify alignment option has no affect on one-line headings.)

SUMMARY

In Project 1, you began your study of XHTML by exploring the use of hypertext documents and the evolution of XHTML from HTML. You learned how to create hypertext documents in a text editor and view your work in a Web browser.

You learned how the XHTML scripting language is comprised of a series of tags, and how the use of tags is one of the key structural differences between XHTML and HTML. While learning some of the commonly used XHTML tags, you discovered that some tags offer attributes that further define how an element displays on a Web page.

KEY TERMS

Attributes	Empty tag	Syntax
Backward compatibility	HTML	Tag
Blockquotes	Hypertext document	Value
Browser	Meta data	Validation
Cascading style sheets (CSS)	Name-value pair	W3C
Characters	Nested tag	White space
Closing tag	Nested blockquote	XHTML
Container tag	Opening tag	XHTML Frameset
Deprecated	Parsed	XHTML Strict
Document tags	Scripting language	XHTML Transitional
Element	String	XML

CHECKING CONCEPTS AND TERMS

MULTIPLE CHOICE

Circle the letter of the correct answer for each of the following questions.

1. A container tag _____.
   a. is an opening and closing tag, such as <p></p>, where the closing tag is required in the XHTML standard
   b. is an opening and closing tag, such as <p></p>, where the closing tag is not required in the XHTML standard

2. To create a paragraph on a Web page, use the following tag/s:
   a. <h1></h1>
   b.
   c. <p></p>

3. When using an empty tag, you create a space between the command and the slash (/) to _____.
   a. make the command more readable
   b. ensure proper support with older browsers
   c. conform to the HTML standard

4. The align attribute for the <p> tag _____.
   a. has been deprecated in favor of style sheets
   b. was added to the XHTML standard as a new method of alignment
   c. only left- and right-aligns sections of text

5. Headings _____.
   a. are all at the same level of importance
   b. are only used to make text bold
   c. come in six different levels and make a Web page more readable
   d. indent sections of text

6. XHTML was designed to clean up sloppy HTML code and _____.
   a. conform to a standard to provide better support across applications
   b. become the cross-over to XML applications
   c. make it easier to extend the language
   d. All of the above.

7. Document tags are required to create a valid XHTML document.
   a. True
   b. False

8. The <head></head> tags _____.
   a. contain information about the document, including the title and meta information
   b. enclose the body content
   c. create a new paragraph in your Web page

9. Line breaks force a break to the next line without creating a blank line between the sections of text.
   a. True
   b. False

10. What is the purpose of the Title tag?
    a. To provide a description of the document in the source file.
    b. To provide the name of the person who wrote the document.
    c. To provide the title of the document in the browser's Title bar.

DISCUSSION

1. What are some of the key differences between XHTML and HTML?

2. Why is it important to create standards for creating Web pages?

3. How did the browser wars influence the way Web pages were/are designed?

SKILL DRILL

Skill Drill exercises reinforce project skills. Each skill reinforced is the same, or nearly the same, as a skill presented in the project. Detailed instructions are provided in a step-by-step format. You should work through these exercises in order.

1. Create an XHTML Template

You are about to create a rather large Web site that consists of several documents. To save time and effort, you decide it would be best to create a template with XHTML document tags.

1. Launch a text editor.

2. Type the following document tags in the text editor.

    ```
    <html>

    <head>

    <title>Template</title>

    </head>

    <body>

    </body>

    </html>
    ```

FIGURE 1.20

3. Choose File>Save from the main Menu bar and save the document as "template.htm" in your WIP_01 folder.

FIGURE 1.21

You can open this template and choose File>Save As each time you want to create a new XHTML document.

4. Keep the file open for the next Skill Drill.

2. Add Paragraphs

In this exercise, you create a new document from template.htm and add two paragraphs using the **<p>** tags.

1. With template.htm open in the text editor, choose File>Save As.

2. Rename the file "skilldrill1.htm". Save it in you WIP_01 folder.

FIGURE 1.22

3. Delete the word "Template" between the **<title></title>** tags, and replace it with "Hello World!" (without the quotation marks).

4. Place your cursor on the line below **\<body>** and type the following:

```
<p>

When you really come down to it, a Web page is just a text file that refers
to other files, such as images. The browser knows how to interpret this
file because it understands the system of tags that describes the content.
Each string of text is described by tags, whether it represents a headline,
an image, someone's name rendered in bold or the overall body of content.
Every page uses a standard structure.

</p>

<p>

Tags are the foundation of a Web page. They describe how items should look
and what they are. Tags tell the browser what to do with specific pieces of
information, and they define the structure of a page.

</p>
```

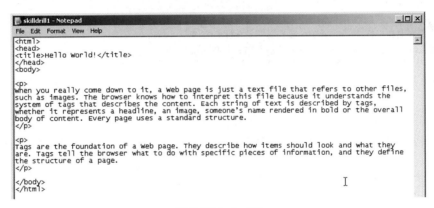

FIGURE 1.23

5. Save the changes to skilldrill1.htm.

6. Open skilldrill1.htm in a browser to view the results.

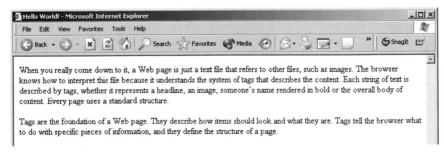

FIGURE 1.24

7. Keep the file open for the next exercise.

3. Align Paragraphs

Left-aligned text is the default alignment in a Web browser window. You can change the alignment to right or center. In this exercise, you center-align and left-align the paragraphs.

1. In the open file, center-align both paragraphs, as follows:

```
<p align="center">

When you really come down to it, a Web page is just a text file that refers
to other files, such as images. The browser knows how to interpret this
file because it understands the system of tags that describes the content.
Each string of text is described by tags, whether it represents a headline,
an image, someone's name rendered in bold or the overall body of content.
Every page uses a standard structure.

</p>

<p align="center">

Tags are the foundation of a Web page. They describe how items should look
and what they are. Tags tell the browser what to do with specific pieces of
information, and they define the structure of a page.

</p>
```

2. Save the changes to skilldrill1.htm and refresh the file in your browser.

3. Return to the text editor and change the alignment value to left in the bottom paragraph, as follows:

```
<p align="center">

When you really come down to it, a Web page is just a text file that refers
to other files, such as images. The browser knows how to interpret this
file because it understands the system of tags that describes the content.
Each string of text is described by tags, whether it represents a headline,
an image, someone's name rendered in bold or the overall body of content.
Every page uses a standard structure.

</p>

<p align="left">

Tags are the foundation of a Web page. They describe how items should look
and what they are. Tags tell the browser what to do with specific pieces of
information, and they define the structure of a page.

</p>
```

4. Save the changes to the file in the text editor. Refresh the file in your browser.

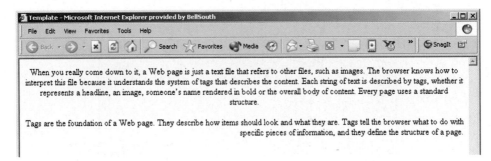

FIGURE 1.25

5. Leave the file open and continue to the next exercise.

4. Create Headings

Headings add visual structure to a document, allow for easier reading, and help to organize content. Headings are available in six levels, with h1 at the top of the hierarchy, and h6 at the bottom. In this exercise, you add a main (h1) heading and a subheading.

1. In the open skilldrill1.htm in the text editor, position your cursor on the line below the **<body>** tag.

2. Press Enter/Return and then type the following:

```
<h1>Working With Hypertext</h1>
```

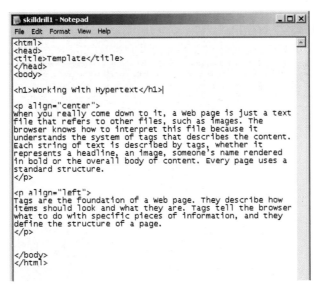

FIGURE 1.26

3. Position your cursor below the first closing **</p>** tag and press Enter/Return.

4. Type the following:

```
<h2>Tags</h2>
```

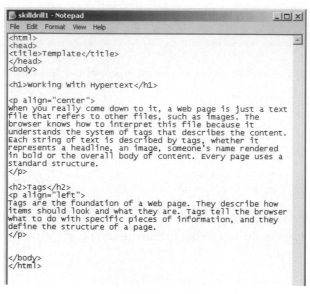

FIGURE 1.27

5. Save the changes to skilldrill1.htm. Refresh your browser to render the headings.

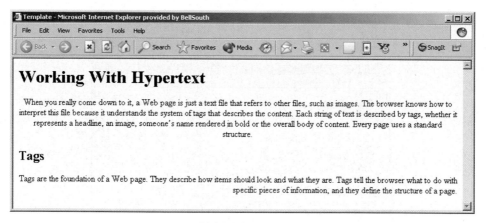

FIGURE 1.28

Adding headings makes it easier to read the document, and the content appears more organized.

6. Leave the file open for the next exercise.

5. Indent Paragraphs of Text

Indenting sections of text can make a document easier to read. In this exercise, you indent both of the paragraphs in skilldrill1.htm.

1. In the open skilldrill1.htm in the text editor, enclose both paragraph sections (exclude the headings) in blockquotes, as follows:

```
<blockquote>

<p align="center">

When you really come down to it, a Web page is just a text file that refers
to other files, such as images. The browser knows how to interpret this
file because it understands the system of tags that describes the content.
Each string of text is described by tags, whether it represents a headline,
an image, someone's name rendered in bold or the overall body of content.
Every page uses a standard structure.

</p>

</blockquote>

<h2>Tags</h2>

<blockquote>

<p align="left">

Tags are the foundation of a Web page. They describe how items should look
and what they are. Tags tell the browser what to do with specific pieces of
information, and they define the structure of a page.

</p>

</blockquote>
```

2. Save the changes to skilldrill1.htm. Refresh your browser and view the result.

FIGURE 1.29

3. Switch back to the text editor. Remove the alignment on the paragraphs so they return to the default alignment (left) and they are indented.

```
<blockquote>

<p>

When you really come down to it, a Web page is just a text file that refers
to other files, such as images. The browser knows how to interpret this
file because it understands the system of tags that describes the content.
Each string of text is described by tags, whether it represents a headline,
an image, someone's name rendered in bold or the overall body of content.
Every page uses a standard structure.

</p>

</blockquote>

<h2>Tags</h2>

<blockquote>

<p>

Tags are the foundation of a Web page. They describe how items should look
and what they are. Tags tell the browser what to do with specific pieces of
information, and they define the structure of a page.

</p>

</blockquote>
```

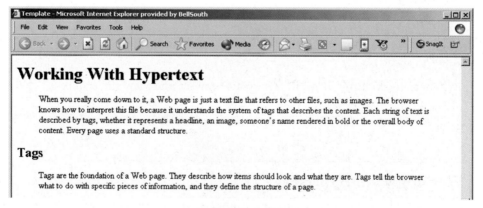

FIGURE 1.30

4. Save the changes in the text file and refresh the document in the browser.

5. Close the file in both applications.

CHALLENGE

Challenge exercises expand on, or are somewhat related to, skills presented in the lessons. Each exercise provides a brief introduction, followed by instructions presented in a numbered-step format that are not as detailed as those in the Skill Drill exercises. You should work through these exercises in order.

1. Format a Document and Correct Nested Tags

You offered to format your instructor's course outline so it's easier to read. You decide to format the heading alignment. You know that tags must be nested correctly, so you correct the nesting in the document, as well.

You might notice some unfamiliar tags in this exercise. You learn more about them later.

1. Navigate to your Work_In_Progress folder. Open courseoutline.htm in a Web browser.

2. Choose View>Source from the browser's main Menu bar.

3. Change the heading at the top of the page to a Level 2 heading (h2).

4. Scan through the document carefully. Note how the tags are nested. Correct the order of any nested tags that appear to be out of place.

5. Save your changes and display the document in the browser.

FIGURE 1.31

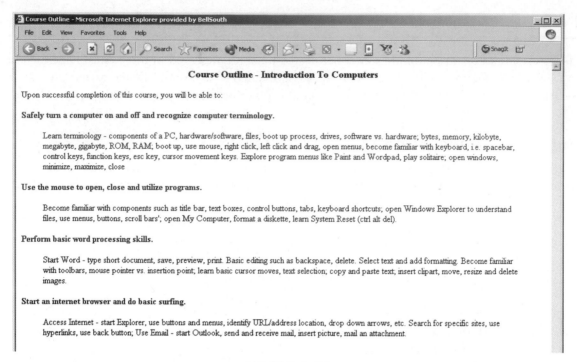

FIGURE 1.32

6. Keep the file open for the next exercise.

2. Use Line Breaks to Format an Outline

Now that the tags are nested correctly, and you applied a better heading size, you can use line breaks to group sections of text and apply additional formatting to enhance the outline.

1. In the open file, activate the text editor.

2. Blockquote the sections of text beneath each of the paragraphs (the sections of text enclosed by the **<p></p>** tags). Currently, no tags enclose these sections of text.

3. Cite each blockquoted section to the Against The Clock URL (http://www.AgainstTheClock.com).

4. Center-align the paragraphs above the blockquoted text.

5. Underline the centered paragraphs of text using the **<u></u>** tags.

6. Save the changes to the source file (text file). Refresh the document in the browser to view the formatting.

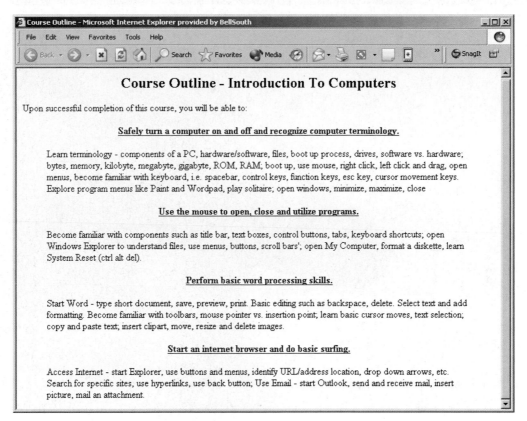

FIGURE 1.33

7. Close the document in both applications.

PORTFOLIO BUILDER

Create an Online Resume

A Resume For You, Inc. hired you to create online samples of their resumes styles. Although they do not publish resumes online, they want to show the different layout styles they offer to as wide an audience as possible.

Your assignment is to work on two of the most popular resume styles. Create two resume examples using standard formatting tags. To complete this exercise, you should use the following information:

- Create a sketch on paper that illustrates the layout styles you are going to design.

- Use your name and contact information as the owner of the document. You can include your work experience and history, or you can invent the resume content, perhaps choosing two different professions. Search the Web for samples of different types of resumes.

- The resumes must show formatting, including bolding, underlining, and italics. Include headings sizes, indentation, and text alignment. You can use your paper sketches to identify where to place the formatted elements before you begin the actual coding.

Formatting
Text and Lists

OBJECTIVES

In this project, you learn how to

- Create basic text effects
- Change text color
- Work with different text sizes
- Apply font styles
- Create ordered and unordered lists
- Create definition lists

WHY WOULD I DO THIS?

When Web designers reviewed the plans for XHTML, some were alarmed to discover that certain tags, such as underline (**<u>**) and strikethrough (**<s>**), were being eliminated. Many designers wondered how they were going to control the appearance of text on their Web pages without these and other related tags.

When HTML was first created, the intent was to define the nature of each section of text, such as a heading or a paragraph, and make that information computer-readable. The ability to control the appearance of the text (i.e., its presentation on the page) was an afterthought — one that has recently received significant attention. HTML did not have the necessary functionality to fulfill this requirement, so the W3C implemented new methods, namely XHTML and cascading style sheets.

Tags determine the structure of the document, defining such items as the headers, individual paragraphs, and tables. *Style*, on the other hand, such as font color and size, must be handled separately — and cascading style sheets were designed to do just that. Unfortunately, not all browsers currently support CSS, as we noted in Project 1. Until all commonly used browsers support CSS, it is best to use XHTML Transitional to ensure that your content appears as intended on your viewers' screens.

In this project, you learn how to format text with XHTML Transitional. Later in the book, you explore other methods of achieving the same effect.

VISUAL SUMMARY

 Formatting tags allow you to change the default appearance of the text that displays in a Web browser. A ***default*** is the assumed value when no other value is provided. Default text usually displays in a Web browser as 12-point black Times New Roman, unless the default settings have been changed in the browser.

Web designers can use a variety of formatting tags to change the appearance of default text. As mentioned earlier, some of these formatting tags have been deprecated in favor of CSS. Consider the following examples. Figure 2.1 shows how text displays in a browser without any formatting. Figure 2.2 shows the same Web page after formatting tags were applied.

FIGURE 2.1

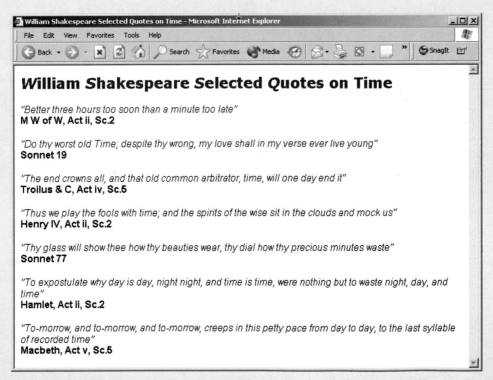

FIGURE 2.2

The above illustration demonstrates how text renders when formatting tags are applied. Some tags emphasize the text (bold and italics), while others change the appearance of text (color and size). We discuss several formatting tags in this project.

LESSON 1 Basic Text Effects

The XHTML 1.0 standard includes several methods to change the typographic settings of the text on Web pages. You can change the typeface, color, text effects, and size. *Typeface* is the name of the font, such as Arial, Times, or Helvetica.

You can choose from three basic text effects when using XHTML Transitional, much the same as you would in a word processor. The three basic effects are:

- **<b></b>** applies boldface type

- **<i></i>** applies italic type

- **<u></u>** underlines the type

The following illustration demonstrates how the **<b>**, **<u>**, and **<i>** tags render text in a Web browser.

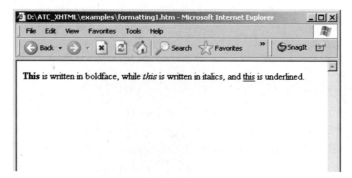

FIGURE 2.3

The underline (**<u></u>**) tags were not well supported by many browsers when they were introduced in the HTML 3.2 standard. They have since been deprecated in the HTML 4.0 reference. The deprecated **<u></u>** tags are accepted in XHTML Transitional, but not in XHTML Strict. Keep in mind that underlined text could be mistaken for a hyperlink, as viewers have grown accustomed to associating underlined text with hyperlinks.

At times, you may want to draw attention to important points within your text. Boldfaced text allows you to do so. Italics are often used for single-word emphasis. There are more advanced text effects you can create using CSS; however, some of the CSS text effects are still not widely supported across Web browser applications.

To Extend Your Knowledge...

In Project 1, the example code was very simple. In Projects 2–8, however, the example code is longer and more complex. Rather than include every line of code in the exercises in Projects 2–8, we use ellipses (...) to show you where we truncated the code. We show you three or more lines of code before and after each section of code that you should modify in the step. This ensures that you place the new code in the correct location within the script.

Apply Basic Formatting to a Web Page

1   **Launch your text editor.**

2   **Navigate to the RF_XHTML_L1>Project_02 folder. Double-click basic_formatting.htm.**

The basic_formatting.htm file displays in the text editor window. Notice the existing content and tags. You work with this document in the next several exercises.

For the remainder of the book, rather than include the complete path of RF_XHTML_L1>Project_0x folder, we simply refer to the Project_02 folder, Project_03 folder, and so forth.

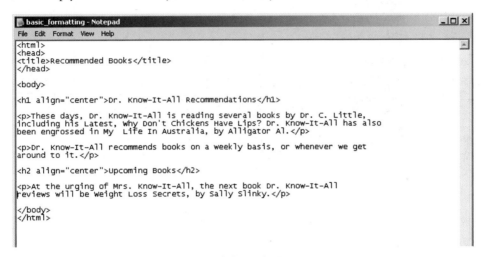

FIGURE 2.4

3   **Change the text in basic_formatting.htm by underlining, bolding, and italicizing parts of the content as follows:**

```
...

<h1 align="center">Dr. Know-It-All Recommendations</h1>

<p>These days, <b>Dr. Know-It-All</b> is reading several books by <b>
Dr. C. Little</b>, including his Latest, <i>Why Don't Chickens Have
Lips?</i> <b>Dr. Know-It-All</b> has also been engrossed in <i>My Life
In Australia</i>, by <b>Alligator Al</b>.</p>

<p><b>Dr. Know-It-All </b>recommends books on a <u>weekly basis</u>, or
whenever we get around to it.</p>

<h2 align="center">Upcoming Books</h2>

<p>At the urging of <b>Mrs. Know-It-All</b>, the next book <b>Dr. Know-It-
All</b> reviews will be <i>Weight Loss Secrets</i>, by <b>Sally
Slinky</b>.</p>

...
```

This applies the effects to selected text. It enhances the display of the document when viewed in a browser.

4 Choose File>Save As from your text editor. Save the document in your WIP_02 folder as "basic_formatting.htm".

This creates a new version of the file in your WIP_02 folder.

FIGURE 2.5

5 Launch your Web browser. Navigate to the WIP_02 folder. Double-click basic_formatting.htm.

Basic_formatting.htm displays in your browser with the new text effects you applied. You can begin to see how you can subtly (or dramatically) change the appearance of your Web pages by adding text effects.

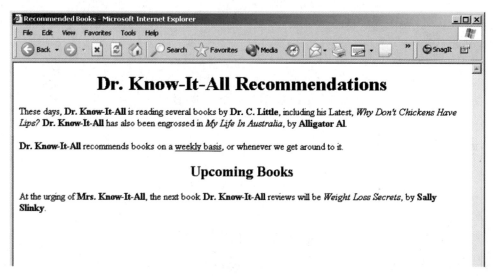

FIGURE 2.6

6 Leave the file open in your text editor and browser.

To Extend Your Knowledge...

ELIMINATION OF THE <B>, <U>, AND <I> TAGS

Users who are familiar with HTML 4.1 might realize that there is a relatively small transition from HTML 4.x to XHTML 1.1. This is not the case with XHTML 2.0, however, which represents a significant divergence from HTML 4.x.

The **<b>**, **<u>**, and **<i>** tags have been completely dropped in XHTML 2.0. The **<strong>** tag is expected to replace the **<b>** tag; style sheets are another possible replacement for the **<b>** tag. The **<u>** tag currently has no replacement tag. The **<em>** tag will replace the **<i>** tag.

The **<strong>** and **<em>** tags are considered structural tags rather than presentational tags, and were included in the original HTML standard.

LESSON 2 | Changing Font Color

You can change text color with the **<font></font>** container tags and the **color=""** attribute (adding a value between the quotes). Please note that the **<font>** container tag is not a stand-alone tag. It requires one or more attributes to change the appearance of text.

Let's explore the **color=""** attribute. You can choose from two options when changing the color of text with the **<font color=""></font>** tags. The first option is to define one of the 16 color names that are universal across Web browsers. Four of those color names are listed below:

- **<font color="red">Red Text.</font>**
- **<font color="green">Green Text.</font>**
- **<font color="purple">Purple Text.</font>**
- **<font color="blue">Blue Text.</font>**

Figure 2.7 illustrates how the above code changes text color in a Web browser.

FIGURE 2.7

The 16 color names are defined in Figure 2.8.

Color Name:	Hex Number:
Black	#000000
Silver	#C0C0C0
Gray	#808080
White	#FFFFFF
Maroon	#800000
Red	#FF0000
Purple	#800080
Fuschia	#FF00FF

Color Name:	Hex Number:
Green	#008000
Lime	#00FF00
Olive	#808000
Yellow	#FFFF00
Navy	#000080
Blue	#0000FF
Teal	#008080
Aqua	#00FFFF

FIGURE 2.8

In the right column in the above chart, notice the hexadecimal number assigned to each color name. A **hexadecimal number** is a six-character figure, such as RRGGBB. It is an alternate value for a color name. For example, `<font color="#008000">` produces the color Green on a Web page. The advantage of this method is that in addition to using the 16 color names, you have access to many more color choices — 156, to be precise.

In the Project_02 folder is a file named color.htm. It lists all the hexadecimal codes and their respective colors, as shown in Figure 2.9.

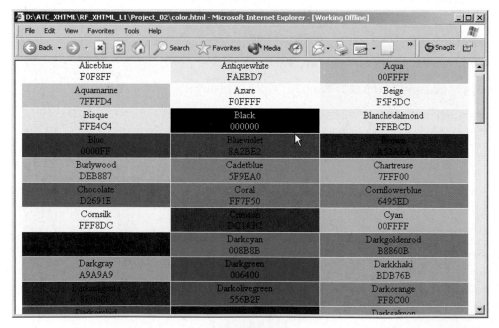

FIGURE 2.9

Change Font Color

1   **Continue working in the open basic_formatting.htm in your text editor.**

2   **Change the color of the text in the document by adding the `<font color="">` tags to the sections of text as follows:**

```
...

<h1 align="center"><font color="maroon">Dr. Know-It-All
Recommendations</font></h1>

<p><font color="#808080">These days, <b>Dr. Know-It-All</b> is reading
several books by<b> Dr. C. Little</b>, including his Latest, <i>Why Don't
Chickens Have Lips?</i> <b>Dr. Know-It-All </b>has also been engrossed in
<i>My Life In Australia</i>, by <b>Alligator Al</b></font></p>

<p><font color="#808080"><b>Dr. Know-It-All </b>recommends books on a
<u>weekly basis</u>, or whenever we get around to it.</font></p>

<h2 align="center"><font color="maroon">Upcoming Books</font></h2>

<p><font color="#808080">At the urging of <b>Mrs. Know-It-All</b>, the next
book <b>Dr. Know-It-All</b> reviews will be <i>Weight Loss Secrets</1>, by
<b>Sally Slinky</b>.</font></p>

...
```

Notice that you used the color name value for the headings and the hexadecimal value for the paragraphs. You can use either method interchangeably. The "#" is required in the XHTML Transitional standard, but it is not required in HTML. Remember to always include the quotes around the value.

3   **Save the changes to basic_formatting.htm. Refresh the document in your browser.**

The document reflects the color changes you applied to the text. Use the colors in the color.htm chart in the Project_02 folder to ensure that the color displays as intended across browsers. Avoid using custom colors, because they might not render as desired on other machines/platforms.

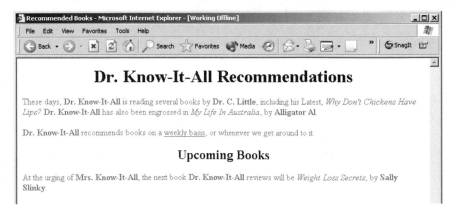

FIGURE 2.10

4   **Leave the file open in your text editor and browser.**

To Extend Your Knowledge...

FONT ISSUES

A lot of controversy surrounds the use of the `<font>` tag when creating Web pages. Some browsers provide poor support for the `<font>` tag. In addition to restrictions on using the `<font>` tag, remember that it has been deprecated since HTML 4.0. Nonetheless, if you choose to use the `<font>` tag, most browsers still support it, providing you follow the rules outlined in this book. If you want to comply with the XHTML standards, however, you should create your pages using XHTML Transitional.

LESSON 3 Changing Font Size

You can use the `size=""` attribute to change the size of your font. The `size=""` attribute can range from `size="1"` to `size="7"`, with "1" being the smallest and "7" being the largest. The default setting for text size in most browsers is "3". The size system for using the font tag is based on the assumption that the user's browser has not been changed from the default setting. If the user changes the setting on his browser, a Web page might not display as intended.

Using absolute values of the `size=""` attribute (`<font size="1">`) can be risky. Assigning relative values is often a better choice if you decide to use XHTML to change the size of text on your Web page. For instance, assigning the relative value of `<font size="+1">` or `<font size="-1">` produces more predicable results than assigning the absolute value of `<font size="1">` or `<font size="7">`. The "+" indicates how many values of size you want to increase the default font size (which in most cases is 3). For instance, `<font size="+2">` increases the font size to 5, whereas `<font size="-2">` decreases the font size to 1.

As you gain experience, you will begin to use CSS for formatting and XHTML for content display. CSS provides excellent control over the display of your documents, and produces predictable results across platforms.

Change the Font Size

1 **Continue working in the open basic_formatting.htm in your text editor.**

2 **Change the font size in the paragraphs to "4", as follows:**

```
...

<p><font color="#808080" size="4">These days, <b>Dr. Know-It-All</b> is
reading several books by<b> Dr. C. Little</b>, including his Latest, <i>Why
Don't Chickens Have Lips?</i> <b>Dr. Know-It-All </b>has also been
engrossed in <i>My Life In Australia</i>, by <b>Alligator
Al</b>.</font></p>
```

```
<p><font color="#808080" size="4"><b>Dr. Know-It-All </b>recommends books
on a <u>weekly basis</u>, or whenever we get around to it.</font></p>

<h2 align="center"><font color="maroon">Upcoming Books</font></h2>

<p><font color="#808080" size="4">At the urging of <b>Mrs. Know-It-All</b>,
the next book <b>Dr. Know-It-All</b> reviews will be <i>Weight Loss
Secrets</i>, by <b>Sally Slinky</b>.</font></p>

...
```

Additional attributes can be included in the same tag. Notice that you simply added a space and the attribute **size="4"** to the existing **<font color="">** opening tag. This increases the text size to 4 in the browser window.

? If you have problems...

When using a word processor, text size usually changes in increments of 2, starting at 8, then 10, 12, 14, and so on. In XHTML, standard text size starts at 1, which is typically the same as 8 in a word processor, and increases in increments of 1.

---

3 Save the changes to basic_formatting.htm. Refresh the document in your browser and view the result.

The paragraph text displays one size larger in the browser.

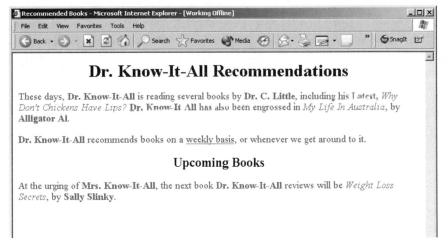

FIGURE 2.11

4 Leave the file open for the next exercise.

LESSON 4   Changing the Font Style

You can use the **face=""** attribute to change the typeface from the default, which is Times New Roman on Windows-based systems, and Times on a Macintosh. You can set the typeface to any valid font style that is installed on your computer. In practical use, however, only three styles are more-or-less guaranteed be display on every computer: Courier, Times, and Helvetica.

When choosing a typeface for your text, keep in mind that while you have this typeface on your machine, your viewers may not have it on their computers. Make sure the appearance of your text is acceptable in Times, as well as any other font you choose. If a viewer does not have the specified font installed on her machine, the page displays in a different font — and that could significantly alter the appearance of your Web page on the viewer's screen.

You can specify alternate font faces by adding commas between font names. For example, **<font face="Helvetica, Verdana, Arial">** tells the computer that when Helvetica is not available, it should display Verdana. When both Helvetica and Verdana are not supported, it should display Arial. The browser displays the default font when no matching font can be found.

Change the Font Face

1   **Continue working in basic_formatting.htm in your text editor.**

2   **Add the attribute face="arial" to the <font> tag containing the headings, as follows:**

```
...

<p><font color="#808080" size="4">These days, <b>Dr. Know-It-All</b>
is reading several books by<b> Dr. C. Little</b>, including his Latest,
<i>Why Don't Chickens Have Lips?</i> <b>Dr. Know-It-All </b>has also been
engrossed in <i>My Life In Australia</i>, by <b>Alligator
Al</b>.</font></p>

<p><font color="#808080" size="4"><b>Dr. Know-It-All </b>recommends books
on a <u>weekly basis</u>, or whenever we get around to it.</font></p>

<h2 align="center"><font color="maroon" face="arial">Upcoming
Books</font></h2>

<p><font color="#808080" size="4">At the urging of <b>Mrs. Know-It-All</b>,
the next book <b>Dr. Know-It-All</b> reviews will be <i>Weight Loss
Secrets</i>, by <b>Sally Slinky</b>.</font></p>

...
```

This instructs the browser to change the font from the default Times (or Times New Roman) to the Arial typeface.

3 Save the changes in the text file and refresh the document in the browser.

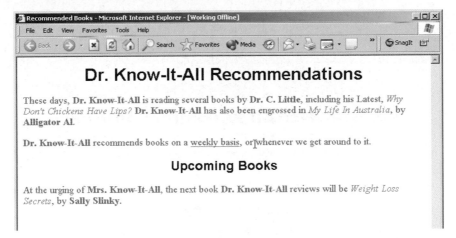

FIGURE 2.12

4 Switch back to the file in the text editor. Add comma-separated typeface styles to the heading, as follows:

```
. . .

<p><font color="#808080" size="4">These days, <b>Dr. Know-It-All</b>
is reading several books by<b> Dr. C. Little</b>, including his Latest,
<i>Why Don't Chickens Have Lips?</i> <b>Dr. Know-It-All </b>has also been
engrossed in <i>My Life In Australia</i>, by <b>Alligator
Al</b>.</font></p>


<p><font color="#808080" size="4"><b>Dr. Know-It-All </b>recommends books
on a <u>weekly basis</u>, or whenever we get around to it.</font></p>

<h2 align="center"><font color="maroon" face="verdana, arial, helvetica">
Upcoming Books</font></h2>

<p><font color="#808080" size="4">At the urging of <b>Mrs. Know-It-All</b>,
the next book <b>Dr. Know-It-All</b> reviews will be <i>Weight Loss
Secrets</i>, by <b>Sally Slinky</b>.</font></p>

. . .
```

This provides three options for font support. You can use any typeface you prefer, but remember that the more rare the typeface, the less likely the end user has it installed on his machine.

5   **Save the changes. Refresh the document in your Web browser and view the result.**

In this case, the text displays in Verdana (which is similar to Arial) since the font is installed on the computer.

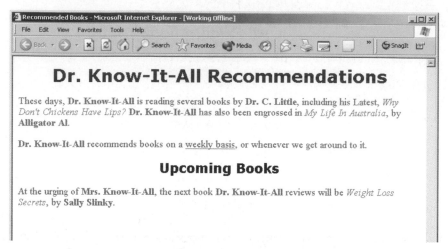

FIGURE 2.13

6   **Leave the file open for the next exercise.**

To Extend Your Knowledge...

WHY NOT XHTML 2.0 NOW?

Even though XHTML 2.0 is not currently supported by any of the major browsers, it is important to understand how the new standard will affect the Web. XHTML 2.0 offers many advantages to developers, but until browser-makers release browsers that support the new standard — and a critical mass of viewers use those browsers — XHTML 1.0 will remain in effect. Learning about XHTML 2.0 now, however, will ease the transition from the old standard to the new.

LESSON 5   Formatting the Body

You can add attributes to the **<body>** tag to format the body text. Body attributes are used to assign colors to the *foreground* (text), the *background* (the canvas of your Web page), as well as to unvisited, active, and visited links. You can use the **text=""** attribute to change the default text color, and you can use the **bgcolor=""** attribute to change the background color.

For instance, to change the text color throughout the Web page, you would apply the following tags:

```
<body text="blue"> or <body text="#3399cc">
```

To change the solid background color on the page, you would apply:

```
<body bgcolor="blue"> or <body bgcolor="#3399cc">
```

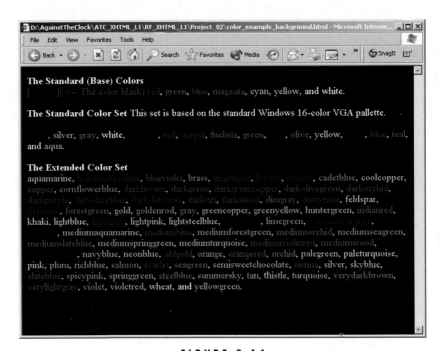

FIGURE 2.14

Figure 2.14 illustrates a black background with text of various colors in the foreground. You can find this Web page (color_example_background.htm) in the Project_02 folder.

Format the Body of a Web Page

1   Continue working in the open basic_formatting.htm in your text editor.

2   Remove the color attributes from the `<font>` tags that contain the paragraphs of text so the only attribute remaining is `<font size="4">`.

    . . .

```
<h1 align="center"><font color="maroon" face="Arial">Dr. Know-It-All
Recommendations</font></h1>

<p><font size="4">These days, <b>Dr. Know-It-All</b> is reading several
books by<b> Dr. C. Little</b>, including his Latest, <i>Why Don't Chickens
Have Lips?</i> <b>Dr. Know-It-All </b>has also been engrossed in <i>My Life
In Australia</i>, by <b>Alligator Al</b>.</font></p>

<p><font size="4"><b>Dr. Know-It-All </b>recommends books on a <u>weekly
basis</u>, or whenever we get around to it.</font></p>

<h2 align="center"><font color="maroon" face="Arial">Upcoming
Books</font></h2>

<p><font size="4">At the urging of <b>Mrs. Know-It-All</b>, the next book
<b>Dr. Know-It-All</b> reviews will be <i>Weight Loss Secrets</i>, by
<b>Sally Slinky</b>.</font></p>
```

    . . .

The `<font>` tag is applied *locally* to a specific element, so it takes precedence over formatting instructions applied *globally* within the `<body>` tags. In order to render the color instructions from the `<body>` tag, you first must remove any local instructions, such as from a `<font>` tag.

3   Save the changes. Refresh the document in the browser and view the result.

The text displays in the default color (black).

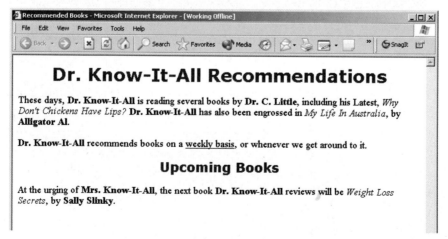

FIGURE 2.15

4 | Switch back to the text editor window and add `text="#006699"` to the `<body>` tag, as follows:

`<body text="#006699">`

This globally changes the color of text that does not have local instructions applied through a `<font>` tag.

5 | Save the changes to the file. Refresh the document in the browser and view the result.

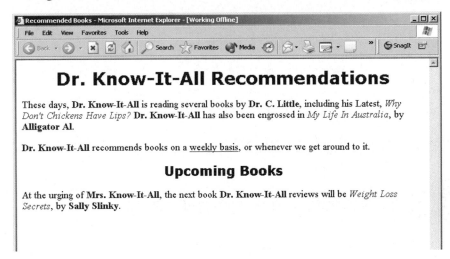

FIGURE 2.16

6 | Switch back to the text editor window and apply the attribute `bgcolor="#ffffcc"` to the `<body>` tag.

`<body text="#006699" bgcolor="#ffffcc">`

The Web page background color changes to light yellow. Even if you decide to leave the Web page background color white, you should still define the `bgcolor="#ffffff"` (hexadecimal code for white) in the body tag. Some browsers display a default gray background unless you specify the `bgcolor=""` attribute.

To Extend Your Knowledge...

MORE FONT ISSUES

Even though they are still widely supported, body attributes have been deprecated in favor of style sheets. As long as you conform to the XHTML Transitional standard, however, you can still use the body attributes. In fact, when you become more familiar with cascading style sheets, we suggest you use both CSS and XHTML Transitional to ensure you comply with both older and newer Web browsers.

In the XHTML 2.0 draft, the font tag is replaced with CSS.

7   Save the changes to the file. Refresh the document in the browser and view the result.

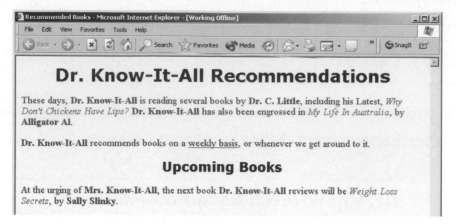

FIGURE 2.17

8   Close basic_formatting.htm in the text editor.

LESSON 6 Creating Unordered Lists

A *list* is a collection of items. Those items can be either ordered or unordered. You can apply attributes to the list tags to control how the list items are presented on the Web page. An ***unordered list*** is not numbered; it contains items preceded by bullets in the shape of small filled circles (the default shape), solid squares, or open circles. You can use the **<ul></ul>** container tags to create an unordered list, as follows:

```
<ul>

<li> List Item 1</li>

<li> List Item 2</li>

<li> List Item 3</li>

<li> List Item 4</li>

<li> List Item 5</li>

</ul>
```

The above code creates the following list in a browser:

FIGURE 2.18

You can change the default bullet type of an unordered list (`<ul type="circle">`) by adding the `type=""` attribute to the `<ul>` tag. You can choose from the following values:

- ***Disc*** creates a bullet in the shape of a disc.

- ***Square*** creates a bullet in the shape of a square.

- ***Circle*** creates a bullet in the shape of a circle.

FIGURE 2.19

The `<li></li>` tags designate ***list items***. You must use the `<li>` tags in conjunction with the `<ul>` tags to create an unordered list. By default, each list item appears on a separate line, so there is no need to insert line breaks as you advance from one list item to the next.

Create an Unordered List

1   **In the text editor, open casserole.htm from your Project_02 folder.**

The file displays with existing content and tags. Notice that the `<br />` tag is used in two of the paragraphs in the file.

```
<title>Tuna Noodle Casserole</title>
</head>

<body>

<h2 align="center">
<font face="Arial" color="#008000">Recipe of the Day: Tuna Noodle Casserole</font>
</h2>

<h3>
Ingredients:
</h3>

<p>
2 cans cream of mushroom soup<br />
2 cans tuna (drained)<br />
1 can chopped mushrooms (drained)<br />
1 small pkg. frozen peas<br />
1 large pkg. wide noodles <br />
1 tsp. lemon dill seasoning
</p>

<h3>
Cooking Instructions:
</h3>

<p>
Preheat oven to 325 degrees.<br />
Prepare noodles as package directs, drain and set aside.<br />
Add all other ingredients in large casserole dish and mix together.<br />
Add noodles to the mixture and stir until blended.<br />
Cook in oven for 20 minutes or until mixture is golden brown on top.
</p>

</body>
</html>
```

FIGURE 2.20

2   **Open casserole.htm in your Web browser and view the document.**

The document displays with limited formatting. Even though the items on the page are relatively easy to read, XHTML lists would provide better organization and presentation.

FIGURE 2.21

3   **Switch back to casserole.htm in the text editor. In the first paragraph section, remove the <p> tags and <br /> tags and replace them, as follows:**

```
...

<h3>Ingredients:</h3>

<ul>

<li>2 cans cream of mushroom soup</li>

<li>2 cans tuna (drained)</li>

<li>1 can chopped mushrooms (drained)</li>

<li>1 small pkg. frozen peas</li>

<li>1 large pkg. wide noodles</li>

<li>1 tsp. lemon dill seasoning</li>

</ul>

...
```

This creates a bulleted (unordered) list of the items. You can change the default bullet format by using the **type**="" attribute.

4   **Save your changes. Refresh the document in your Web browser and view the result.**

An unordered bulleted list is designed to list items in random order. This list of ingredients requires no step-by-step instruction, so a bulleted list serves the purpose well.

FIGURE 2.22

5   **Leave the file open for the next exercise.**

LESSON 7   Creating Ordered Lists

Ordered lists (numbered lists) contain items that must be listed in a particular order. You create an ordered list with the `<ol></ol>` container tags. You must use the `<li>` tags in conjunction with the `<ol>` tags to create an ordered list. You can use traditional Arabic numerals, Roman numerals, or letters to identify each item.

Figure 2.23 illustrates the default Arabic numeral display of an ordered list. Figure 2.24 demonstrates the Uppercase letter style.

FIGURE 2.23

FIGURE 2.24

Available types for ordered lists include:

     1 Arabic Numerals (default)

     A Uppercase letters   **a** Lowercase letters

     I Uppercase Roman numerals   **i** Lowercase Roman numerals

Create an Ordered List

1   **In the open casserole.htm, switch to the text editor. Remove the <p> tags and <br /> tags from the last paragraph. Replace the tags, as follows:**

```
...

<h3>Cooking Instructions:</h3>

<ol>

<li>Preheat oven to 325 degrees.</li>

<li>Prepare noodles as package directs, drain and set aside.</li>

<li>Add all other ingredients in large casserole dish and mix
together.</li>

<li>Add noodles to the mixture and stir until blended.</li>

<li>Cook in oven for 20 minutes or until mixture is golden brown on
top. </li>

</ol>

...
```

This creates a numbered list of the items. You can change the default number style by using the **type=""** attribute. For example, the **type="I"** attribute changes the default number list to uppercase Roman numerals.

2   **Save your changes. Refresh the document in your Web browser and view the result.**

The Cooking Instructions section displays as a numbered list. This type of list is appropriate because the reader is following step-by-step instructions.

FIGURE 2.25

3   **Close the file in both applications.**

LESSON 8 Creating Definition Lists

Definition lists are slightly different than other lists because they contain a term and its definition. This type of list is most useful for FAQs or defining terms on a Web page. Definition lists are comprised of the following elements: **<dl>** (begin definition list), **<dt>** (definition term), **<dd>** (definition), and **</dl>** (end definition list). Below is an example of a definition list:

```
<dl>

  <dt>Geek</dt>

  <dd> A person who is single-minded or accomplished in scientific or
technical pursuits but is felt to be socially inept. </dd>

  <dt>Hacker</dt>

  <dd>a clever programmer.</dd>

</dl>
```

The above code displays in a browser, as follows:

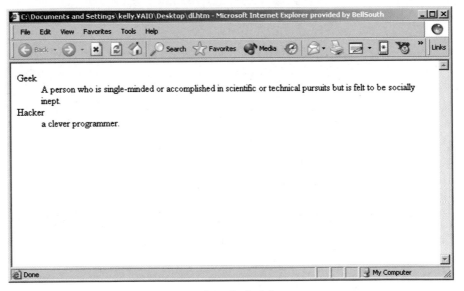

FIGURE 2.26

Create a Definition List

1   **Create a new document in your text editor.**

You can use the template.htm file that you created in Project 1.

2   **Create a definition list, as follows:**

```
<html>

<head>

<title>My Definition Page</title>

</head>

<body>

<h3>Hypertext Definitions</h3>

<dl>

<dt>XHTML</dt>

<dd>eXtensible Hypertext Markup Language. A scripting language used to
create hypertext documents for the Web.</dd>

<dt>URL</dt>

<dd>Universal Resource Locator. A Web address, or file path to a file on
the World Wide Web.</dd>

</dl>

</body>

</html>
```

This creates a new document containing a definition list.

3   **Save the document as "definitions.htm". Open the document in a Web browser.**

The definition list displays in the browser window. The term displays above the definition, which is indented slightly to allow for easy reading.

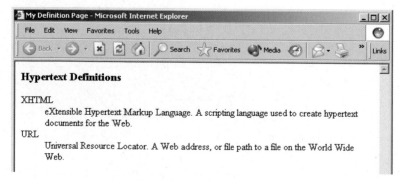

FIGURE 2.27

4   **Switch to the text editor. Apply bold formatting to the terms.**

You can format any part of the definition list, but the most popular element to format is the term itself. This creates contrast between the term and its definition.

```
<html>

<head>

<title>My Definition Page</title>

</head>

<body>

<h3>Hypertext Definitions</h3>

<dl>

<dt><b>XHTML</b></dt>

<dd>eXtensible Hypertext Markup Language. A scripting language used to
create hypertext documents for the Web.</dd>

<dt><b>URL</b></dt>

<dd>Universal Resource Locator. A Web address, or file path to a file on
the World Wide Web.</dd>

</dl>

</body>

</html>
```

5   **Save the changes and refresh the document in the browser.**

The terms display in boldface type.

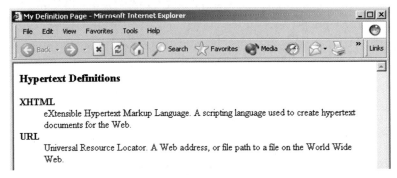

FIGURE 2.28

6   **Close the file in both applications.**

To Extend Your Knowledge...

XHTML 2.0 NAVIGATION LISTS

To date, Web designers have built navigation lists from virtually any element or script. XHTML 2.0 includes a new kind of list, represented by the **<nl>** element. The XHTML 2.0 draft states that navigation lists are "intended to define collections of selectable items for presentation."

In an XHTML 2.0 document, a navigation list would resemble the following:

```
<nl>

    <name>Title Number 1</name>

    <li href="#link">List Item</li>

    <li>

        <nl>

            <name> Title Number 2</name>

            <li href="#link">List Item</li>

            <li href="#link">List Item</li>

        </nl>

    </li>

</nl>
```

SUMMARY

In this project, you learned that in addition to structural tags, HTML offers presentational tags. Even though the presentational tags have been deprecated in the HTML 4.1 standard in favor of cascading style sheets, you can still use them in XHTML Transitional. Using the basic text effect tags, you can apply bolding, underling, and italics to Web page content. This allows you to draw the viewer's attention to key points in your text.

You also learned how to make aesthetic changes to your text, such as how to change the text color, size, and typeface. You discovered that some of the formatting features, such as color values, include multiple options.

You discovered that lists provide an excellent way to display key points of information. You learned how to create ordered lists to present information in a step-by-step manner, unordered lists to present information in a random order, and definition lists to present a term and its associated definition.

CAREERS IN DESIGN

BASICS FOR WEB PAGE DESIGNERS

You can choose from a number of exciting job categories within the Web-publishing industry. Depending on the diversity of your skill set, you may be able to apply your talents in many different areas. When considering a career in Web publishing, you need to be familiar with the following general skills.

Programming. If you are going to enter a career in Web site design/development, you must know how to program in XHTML. It might be useful to learn an advanced programming language, such as Perl, PHP, ColdFusion, and/or ASP. Knowing how to use JavaScript is an excellent skill, as well.

You should also be able to use a graphics program, such as Photoshop or Fireworks, even if you only use the program for basic techniques, such as cropping an image or saving it as a particular format for the Web.

Design and Layout. In order to create professional-looking Web pages, it is essential that you understand the basic design principles and methodologies for Web design. These methodologies include design considerations for a variety of platforms, how to apply color effectively, how to develop effective copy, and other valuable visual techniques.

Webmaster. It is useful to possess a general understanding of how a Web server operates, even if you have no desire to become a full-blown Webmaster. To enhance your effectiveness as a Web site designer/developer, you should know what happens to a file when you upload it to the server, how to manage files, and be familiar with some of the technology behind the Web server — at the very least.

KEY TERMS

Background	Global settings	Ordered list
Default	Hexadecimal number	Style
Definition list	List	Typeface
Font	List item	Unordered list
Foreground	Local settings	

CHECKING CONCEPTS AND TERMS

MULTIPLE CHOICE

Circle the letter of the correct answer for each of the following questions.

1. Which of the following tags is not widely supported?

   a. <b> tag

   b. <i> tag

   c. <u> tag

   d. None of the above.

2. The <font> tag is not a stand-alone tag. In order for the tag to affect text, you must use an attribute with it.

   a. True

   b. False

3. The **<font>** tag offers three formatting attributes. They are _____.

   a. align, type, and color

   b. color, face, and size

   c. color, size, and height

4. You can use hexadecimal numbers (codes) and color names when selecting a color for text.

   a. True

   b. False

5. The **<font>** tag has been deprecated in favor of _____.

   a. XML

   b. CSS

   c. JavaScript

   d. None of the above.

6. Using the Times, Helvetica, or Courier typeface ensures that the font style displays as intended on most machines.

   a. True

   b. False

7. Ordered lists _____.

   a. provide a step-by-step numbered list of items

   b. provide three options of bullet styles

   c. are not part of XHTML

8. Unordered lists _____.

   a. are bulleted lists that use a standard black dot next to each list item

   b. allow you to change the bullet list style with the type="" attribute

   c. present a term and its definition

9. Definition lists consist of two parts: a term and its description.

   a. True

   b. False

10. XHTML 2.0 suggests that the presentational tags, including <b>, <u> and <i>, should be eliminated.

    a. True

    b. False

DISCUSSION

1. Why were most of the formatting tags deprecated in XHTML 2.0?

2. When would it be beneficial to use the <font> tag, and why?

3. Why would it be wise to apply both cascading style sheets and the <font> tag to text on your Web pages?

SKILL DRILL

Skill Drill exercises reinforce project skills. Each skill reinforced is the same, or nearly the same, as a skill presented in the project. Detailed instructions are provided in a step-by-step format. You should work through these exercises in order.

1. Add Basic Text Effects to an Existing Web Page

Your task is to create a Web page for a community program that offers free courses to the citizens of Pembroke, Florida.

1. Copy course.htm from your Project_02 folder to your WIP_02 folder.

2. Open course.htm in a text editor and a browser.

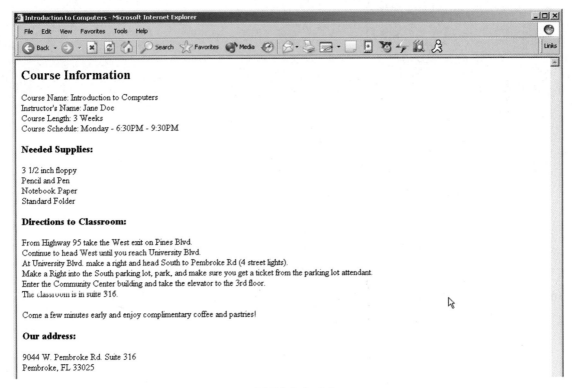

FIGURE 2.29

3. Add basic text effects to course.htm in the text editor, as follows:

```
...

<h2>Course Information</h2>

<p>

<b>Course Name:</b> Introduction to Computers<br />

<b>Instructor's Name: </b>Jane Doe<br />

<b>Course Length: </b>3 Weeks<br />

<b>Course Schedule:</b> Monday - 6:30PM - 9:30PM

</p>

<h3>Needed Supplies:</h3>

<p>

3 1/2 inch floppy<br />

Pencil and Pen<br />

Notebook Paper<br />

Standard Folder

</p>

<h3>Directions to Classroom:</h3>

<p>

From Highway 95 take the West exit on Pines Blvd. <br />

Continue to head West until you reach University Blvd.<br />

At University Blvd. make a right and head South to Pembroke Rd (4 street
lights).<br />

Make a Right into the South parking lot, park, and make sure you get a
ticket from the parking lot attendant. <br />

Enter the Community Center building and take the elevator to the 3rd floor.
<br />

The classroom is in suite 316.</p>

<p>

Come a few minutes early and enjoy <b>complimentary</b> coffee and pas-
tries!

</p>

<h3>Our address:</h3>

...
```

4.   Save course.htm in your text editor. Refresh the document in the browser and view the result.

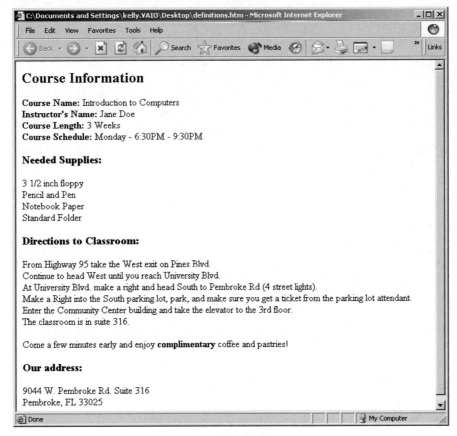

FIGURE 2.30

5.   Keep the file open for the next exercise.

2. Add Font Formatting

You decide the typeface in your community program Web page requires enhancements. You need to change the color, size, and typeface of the text to make it more interesting.

1. In the open file, switch to course.htm in the text editor.

2. Apply the following font changes:

```
...
<h2><font color="#800000" face="Arial">Course Information</font></h2>

<p>

<b>Course Name:</b> Introduction to Computers<br />

<b>Instructor's Name: </b>Jane Doe<br />

<b>Course Length: </b>3 Weeks<br />

<b>Course Schedule:</b> Monday - 6:30PM - 9:30PM

</p>

<h3><font color="#008080" face="Arial">Needed Supplies: </font></h3>

<p>

3 1/2 inch floppy<br />

Pencil and Pen<br />

Notebook Paper<br />

Standard Folder

</p>

<h3><font color="#008080" face="Arial">Directions to Classroom: </font>
</h3>

<p>

From Highway 95 take the West exit on Pines Blvd. <br />

Continue to head West until you reach University Blvd.<br />

At University Blvd. make a right and head South to Pembroke Rd (4 street
lights).<br />

Make a Right into the South parking lot, park, and make sure you get a
ticket

from the parking lot attendant. <br />

Enter the Community Center building and take the elevator to the 3rd floor.
<br /> </p>

<p>The classroom is in suite 316.</p>
```

```
<p>

<font size="4" color="#800000">Come a few minutes early and enjoy <b>com-
plimentary</b> coffee and pastries! </font> </p>

<h3> <font color="#008080" face="Arial"> Our address: </font> </h3>

<p>9044 W. Pembroke Rd. Suite 316<br />

Pembroke, FL 33025</p>

...
```

3. Save the file in the text editor. Refresh your browser and view the result of your changes.

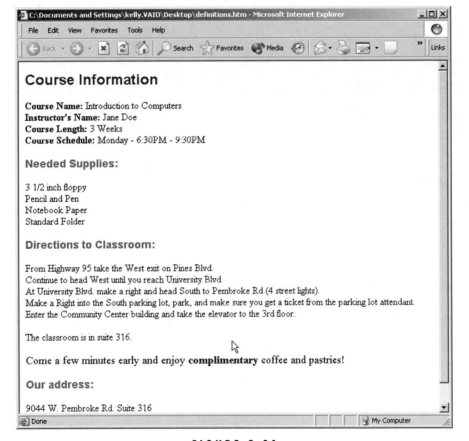

FIGURE 2.31

4. Keep the file open for the next exercise.

3. Create Ordered and Unordered Lists

The information on your community project Web page lacks organization. Turning some of the content into lists would make the information easier to read. You decide to make the class supplies section an unordered list, and make the driving instructions section an ordered list.

1. In the open document, switch to course.htm in the text editor.

2. Create an ordered and unordered list, as follows:

```
...
<h3><font color="#008080" face="Arial">Needed Supplies:</font></h3>
<ul>
<li>3 1/2 inch floppy</li>
<li>Pencil and Pen</li>
<li>Notebook Paper</li>
<li>Standard Folder </li>
</ul>
<h3><font color="#008080" face="Arial">Directions to Classroom:</font></h3>

<ol>
<li>From Highway 95 take the West exit on Pines Blvd.</li>
<li>Continue to head West until you reach University Blvd.</li>
<li>At University Blvd. make a right and head South to Pembroke Rd (4
street lights).</li>
<li>Make a Right into the South parking lot, park, and make sure you get a
ticket from the parking lot attendant.</li>
<li>Enter the Community Center building and take the elevator to the 3rd
floor.  </li>
</ol>
<p>The classroom is in suite 316.</p>
...
```

3. Save the changes to the file. Refresh the document in your browser and view the result.

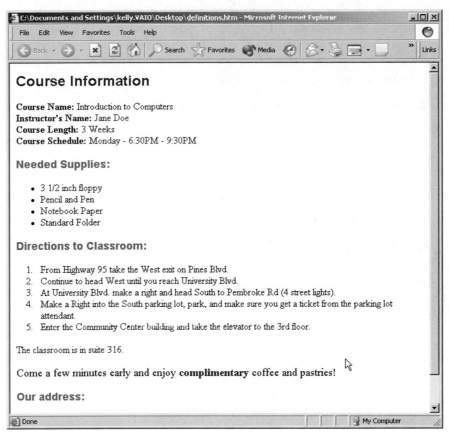

FIGURE 2.32

4. Keep the file open for the next exercise.

4. Create a Definition List

A definition list is an excellent choice when creating an FAQ. You can apply formatting for questions and answers quickly and easily, whereas using other elements might require more coding. In this exercise, you provide answers to frequently asked questions about the course.

1. In the open document, switch to the text editor.

2. Add a definition list that outlines two popular questions that are asked about the course.

   ```
   ...
     <li>3 1/2 inch floppy</li>
     <li>Pencil and Pen</li>
     <li>Notebook Paper</li>
     <li>Standard Folder </li>
   </ul>
   <h3><font color="#008080" face="Arial">FAQs:</font></h3>
   <dl>
   <dt>Can the course be counted toward college credits?</dt>
   <dd>No. The course is not a college credited course.</dd>
   <dt>Are there any prerequisites?</dt>
   <dd>No. The course is an introductory course and therefore no knowledge of
   computers is required.</dd>
   </dl>
   ...
   ```

3. Bold the definition terms.

   ```
   ...
   <h3><font color="#008080" face="Arial">FAQs:</font></h3>
   <dl>
   <dt> <b> Can the course be counted toward college credits?</b></dt>
   <dd>No. The course is not a college credited course.</dd>
   <dt><b>Are there any prerequisites?</b></dt>
   <dd>No. The course is an introductory course and therefore no knowledge of
   computers is required.</dd>
   </dl>
   ...
   ```

4.   Save the changes to the file. Refresh the document in your browser and view the result.

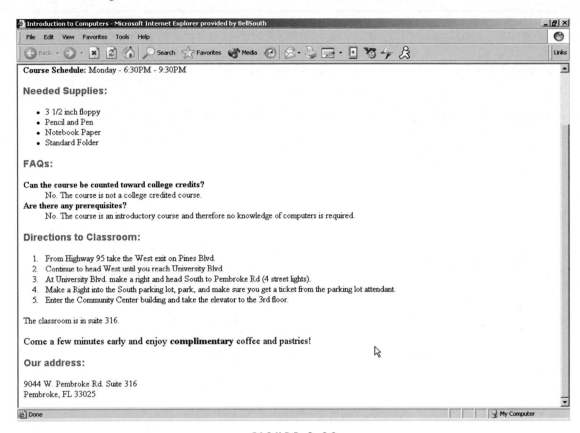

FIGURE 2.33

5.   Close the file in both applications.

CHALLENGE

Challenge exercises expand on, or are somewhat related to, skills presented in the lessons. Each exercise provides a brief introduction, followed by instructions presented in a numbered-step format that are not as detailed as those in the Skill Drill exercises. You should work through the exercises in order.

1. Replace Text Enhancement Tags with Structural Tags

Your instructor asked you to enhance the formatting of a course outline. You decide to convert some of the formatting tags to structural tags, as well as change the size of some sections of text.

1. Navigate to numoutline.htm in your WIP_02 folder. Open the file in a Web browser.

2. Choose View>Source from the browser's main Menu bar.

3. Change the bolded text's formatting tags to a structural option that is supported in XHTML 2.0 (**<strong>** and **<em>**). If necessary, reference the To Extend Your Knowledge at the end of Lesson 1.

4. Add the Level 2 heading "Hypertext Today" to the top of document.

5. Increase the bolded text (**<strong>**) to a relative size using the **<font>** tag.

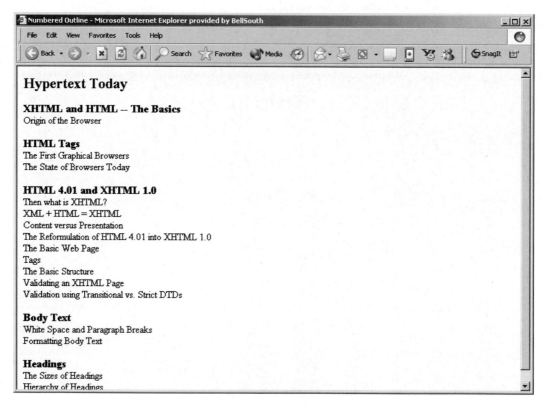

FIGURE 2.34

6. Save the changes and keep the file open for the next exercise.

2. Create an Ordered Outline

You were asked to place the content of the short outline in sequential order. Some of the items in the outline need to be nested.

1. In the open document, add an opening ordered list tag directly beneath `<h2>Hypertext Today</h2>` in the source document.

2. Add a closing ordered list tag directly before the closing body tag in the source document.

3. In each paragraph section, the first sentence is bold. Remove the opening paragraph tag before each bold sentence and replace it with an opening list item tag.

4. A line break is at the end of each bold sentence. Remove the line break tag and replace it with a closing ordered list tag.

5. Save the changes to the text file and view the document in your Web browser.

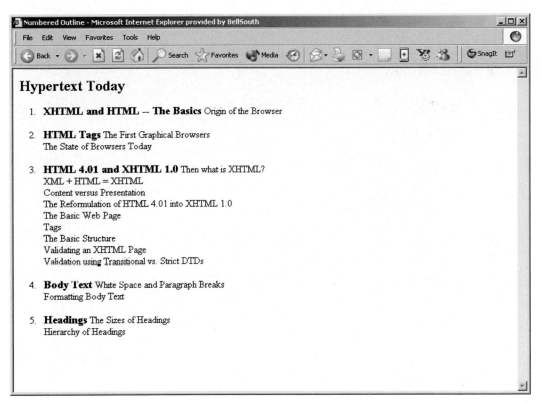

FIGURE 2.35

6. Keep the file open for the next exercise.

3. Create a Nested List

You created the main portion of an ordered list, but it's not very readable, nor is it structured properly. To resolve these problems, create nested ordered lists.

1. In the open file, remove all of the line breaks in the text file. The line breaks are forcing the text to the next line; you achieve the same effect using a nested list, only in an ordered format.

2. Place an opening ordered list tag directly below each bold sentence that is enclosed in list item tags. You use these items to begin creating a list. The bolded text, such as XHTML, HTML, and HTML Tags, act as the list headings.

3. Add list item tags to each sentence (such as "The Origin of the Browser") that follows the ordered list tag you just inserted.

4. Place a closing ordered list tag after the last list item of each section, and before the bolded sentence of the next section.

5. Save the changes to the text file and view the document in your browser.

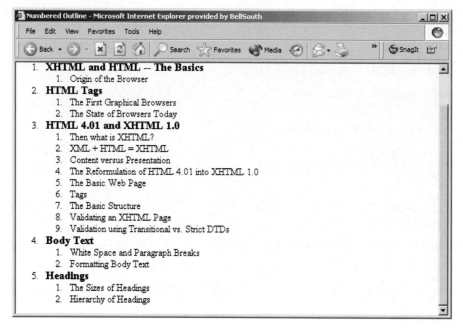

FIGURE 2.36

6. Keep the file open for the next exercise.

4. Change List Values and Apply Formatting

The structure of your instructor's outline is much improved, and the subheadings are nested below the main headings. The next challenge is to change the subheading values to lowercase letters.

1. In the open file, add the type attribute with the lowercase letter value to the remainder of the nested opening <ol> tags, except the first <ol> tag.

2. Change the color of the nested ordered lists (beneath the bolded sections) to Gray.

3. Change the main ordered lists value to uppercase Roman numerals.

4. Change the color of the main ordered list's items to Green.

5. Save your changes and view the result in a browser.

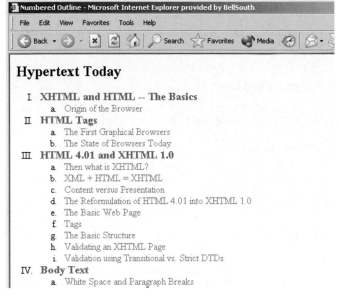

FIGURE 2.37

6. Close the file in both applications.

Create a Play Bill

A local theater hired you to create a one-page Web site that offers information about an upcoming play, *To Kill a Mockingbird*, by Harper Lee. Part of your job is to research the play, and then provide a short synopsis of the story, as well as other relevant information, on the Web page. To complete this exercise, you should use the following information:

- Research the Web and other locations about the timeless play, *To Kill a Mockingbird*.

- Create a Web page with the title:

  To Kill a Mockingbird

  The Mulberry Theatre

- Provide the following address:

  The Mulberry Theatre

  101 N. Preserve Way

  Fort Lauderdale, FL 33025

- Provide a listing of the cast:

  James Wardrop as Atticus   Vicki Penny as Scout

  Howard Day as Jem   Lynn Walker as Calpurnia

  Javier Manner as Boo Radley   Renzo Lyoll as Dill

  Billy Nelson as Tom Robinson

- Provide a description of the play and information about the author.

- List the following dates:

  August 24, 2005   August 28, 2005   September 4, 2005

- Format the page by changing the font colors. Format the cast members and the dates into a list. Provide headings for each section and assign different alignments.

Adding Graphical Elements

OBJECTIVES

In this project, you learn how to

- Embed images into Web pages

- Provide alternate text for images

- Control the positioning of an image

- Specify height and width attributes

- Apply image spacing

- Insert a low-source image

- Create horizontal lines

WHY WOULD I DO THIS?

Text formatting is an important element in creating the overall look and feel of a Web site; but let's not overlook another critical Web page design element — graphical images. Virtually every site on the Web includes images of one sort or another, including corporate logos, pictorial site directories, navigation buttons, illustrated page content, and banners.

Designers sometimes take the use of images to the extreme, which leads to excessively large Web pages with long download times. Remember that every image on a page adds to its size; and the bigger the page, the longer viewers must wait for it to download. For every additional second a viewer must wait to see an image, the greater the chance he will become frustrated and move to another site.

In Project 3, you discover how to work with images to enhance text-based Web pages. There is no need to worry if your graphical abilities are limited — a plethora of image resources is available on the Web.

VISUAL SUMMARY

Several types of images can be added to a Web page, and each has its own strengths and weaknesses. Figure 3.1 highlights a few commonly used image types.

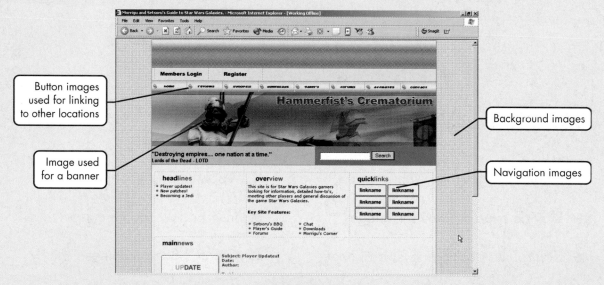

FIGURE 3.1

Graphics Interchange Format, better known as *GIF*, is the original Web graphics format. It uses *indexed color*, meaning that each *pixel* (picture element; small dots that comprise an image) in the image is assigned a number from 0 to 255. This number represents the pixel's color on a color look-up table. Indexed color is limited to a maximum of 256 colors. This format works best with images that have large areas of a single color, such as *line art*. GIF images can be compressed (made smaller) to allow for quicker download. GIF images have two other advantages:

- GIF images can be transparent. When a color is *transparent*, you can see through it. In a GIF file, one color is designated as the transparent color, and any pixels of that color allow the background to show through. This is useful for several reasons, not the least of which is that it allows you to create a single image that can be used on different backgrounds.

- GIFs can be animated. The result is similar to a flipbook: multiple still images are viewed in rapid succession to create the appearance of movement. GIF animations can *loop* (repeat). Be aware that while animated GIFs can enliven a page when used properly, they can also be distracting when overused. Animated GIFs annoy many users.

Figure 3.2 is an example of a Web page that uses a transparent GIF.

The "Home" banner image is transparent so the background shows through.

FIGURE 3.2

The *JPEG* (also *JPG*) format was created by the Joint Photographic Experts Group. This group realized that they needed an alternative to GIFs because the GIF file format could not successful render the subtle color changes and complex gradients found in photographs. The JPEG format was created specifically for photographic images. Any image with gradual color changes looks better and renders at smaller file sizes in the JPEG format.

Photographs should be saved as JPEGs.

FIGURE 3.3

The *PNG* (Portable Network Graphics) format generates files that are similar to GIFs. PNG was created in response to a legal issue. Most GIF images are based on *LZW compression*, a specific type of file compression that is covered by a patent issued to Unisys Corporation. This patent states that any graphics program that reads or creates images with LZW compression must be licensed. The major software companies, such as Adobe and Macromedia, obtained licenses for their programs and can freely use the LZW compression technique. Small developers and independent Web site operators, however, could not afford the high price of the LZW license. They needed a low-cost alternative. The PNG image format was the fulfillment of this need. PNG was standardized in 1996.

LESSON 1 Inserting an Image in a Web Page

You can add images to a Web page with the `<img />` tag. Please note that the `<img />` tag is an empty tag. In the code `<img src="logo.gif" />`, *src* refers to the *source attribute*; it specifies which file appears on the page. When we "add" an image to a Web page, we don't actually add it — we reference it.

For instance, when you insert an image into a Microsoft Word file, you can insert the image into the file, or you can link the image to the file. If you insert the image and send the Word document to an associate, the recipient will be able to see the image in the document, even though he doesn't have the original image on his system. The Word file contains everything the recipient needs to view the text and image.

If you link the image to the Word file, all you add is a reference to where Word can find the image on your hard drive. If you then send the file to a friend, she will see a large red "X" where the image should be located. Word can't locate the image because the reference points to your hard drive — not the recipient's hard drive.

Adding an image to a Web page is similar to linking an image to a Word document. What you actually add is a reference to the location of the image that tells the browser where to find it. The image can be located on your hard drive or on any server you choose. As long as the *path* (specific directory location) to the file is correct, the browser can find the image and load it correctly.

When your image and its associated Web page are located in the same directory, you do not need to include a complete path when you reference the image. If your image is located in a *remote directory* (a directory other than the directory where the Web page resides), you must define the path within the `src=""` attribute.

The following is a reference to an image file in a remote directory:

```
<img src="images/picture.gif" />
```

This is an example of an image file on a Web server:

```
<img src="http://www.againsttheclock.com/images/picture.gif" />
```

As you can see from the second example above, an image can be located on a different server than the Web page. For the examples in this book, however, let's assume they are on the same server.

In the following exercises, you add an image to a Web page, add a border to the image, and view the result in your browser.

Add an Image

1   Copy all the files from your Project_03 folder into your WIP_03 folder.

2   From the WIP_03 folder, open images.htm in both the text editor and the browser.

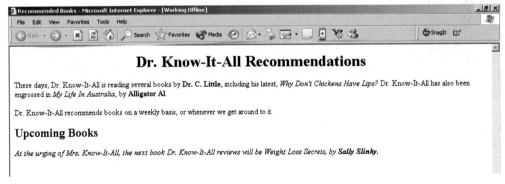

FIGURE 3.4

The page loads in the browser. It displays some formatted text.

3   **Apply the `<img />` tag to add the images, as follows:**

```
...

<h1 align="center">Dr. Know-It-All Recommendations</h1>

<p> <img src="book1.jpg" />These days, Dr. Know-It-All is reading several
books by <b>Dr. C. Little</b>, including his latest, <i>Why Don't Chickens
Have Lips?</i> Dr. Know-It-All has also been engrossed in <i>My Life In
Australia</i>, by <b>Alligator Al</b>.</p>

<p>Dr. Know-It-All recommends books on a weekly basis, or whenever we get
around to it.</p>

<h2>Upcoming Books</h2>

<p><img src="book2.jpg" /><i>At the urging of Mrs. Know-It-All, the next
book Dr. Know-It-All reviews will be <i>Weight Loss Secrets</i>, by
<b>Sally Slinky</b>.</i></p>

...
```

Remember that you do not need to add a file path to the image directory because the images are in the same directory as the Web page.

4   **Save the file in the text editor. Refresh the document in your browser and view the result.**

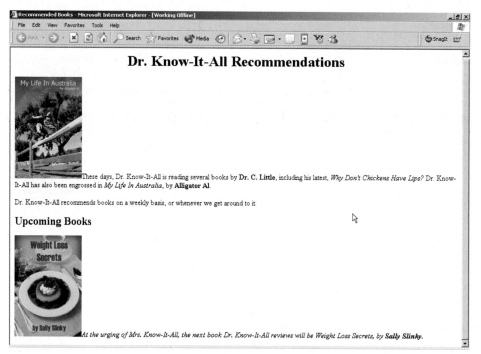

FIGURE 3.5

The images display in the predefined location. Notice how the text is positioned. You learn how to control the positioning of the image later in this project.

5   **Leave the file open for the next exercise.**

Add a Border to an Image

Unless an image is used as a link, the image displays by default without a border on a Web page. You can use the **border=""** attribute to add a border to an image. Doing so creates a black border around the image. You can specify the width of the border, depending on the size of the image and how it is used. Image border widths are measured in pixels.

1   **In the open document, switch to the text editor. Add a border width of 1 pixel to the first image, as follows:**

```
...

<h1 align="center">Dr. Know-It-All Recommendations</h1>

<p><img src="book1.jpg" border="1"  />These days, Dr. Know-It-All is read-
ing several books by <b>Dr. C. Little</b>, including his latest, <i>Why
Don't Chickens Have Lips?</i> Dr. Know-It-All has also been engrossed in
<i>My Life In Australia</i>, by <b>Alligator Al</b>.</p>

<p>Dr. Know-It-All recommends books on a weekly basis, or whenever we get
around to it.</p>

<h2>Upcoming Books</h2>

<p><img src="book2.jpg" /><i>At the urging of Mrs. Know-It-All, the next
book Dr. Know-It-All reviews will be <i>Weight Loss Secrets</i>, by
<b>Sally Slinky</b>.</i></p>

...
```

This instructs the browser to display a border size of 1 pixel around the image.

2   **Add a border width of 8 pixels to the second image, as follows:**

```
...

<h1 align="center">Dr. Know-It-All Recommendations</h1>

<p><img src="book1.jpg" border="1"  />These days, Dr. Know-It-All is read-
ing several books by <b>Dr. C. Little</b>, including his latest, <i>Why
Don't Chickens Have Lips?</i> Dr. Know-It-All has also been engrossed in
<i>My Life In Australia</i>, by <b>Alligator Al</b>.</p>

<p>Dr. Know-It-All recommends books on a weekly basis, or whenever we get
around to it.</p>

<h2>Upcoming Books</h2>

<p><img src="book2.jpg" border="8" /><i>At the urging of Mrs. Know-It-All,
the next book Dr. Know-It-All reviews will be <i>Weight Loss Secrets</i>,
by <b>Sally Slinky</b>.</i></p>

...
```

This instructs the browser to display a border size of 8 pixels around the image.

3   **Save the changes to the text file and refresh the document in the browser.**

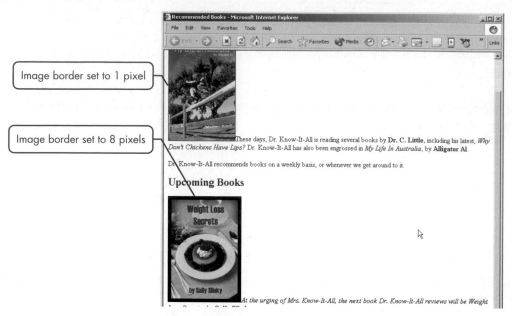

Image border set to 1 pixel

Image border set to 8 pixels

FIGURE 3.6

The first image displays on the page with a 1-pixel black border. The second image displays with an 8-pixel black border.

4   **Switch to the text editor. Change the image borders to zero, as follows:**

```
...

<h1 align="center">Dr. Know-It-All Recommendations</h1>

<p><img src="book1.jpg" border="0" />These days, Dr. Know-It-All is reading
several books by <b>Dr. C. Little</b>, including his latest, <i>Why Don't
Chickens Have Lips?</i> Dr. Know-It-All has also been engrossed in <i>My
Life In Australia</i>, by <b>Alligator Al</b>.</p>

<p>Dr. Know-It-All recommends books on a weekly basis, or whenever we get
around to it.</p>

<h2>Upcoming Books</h2>

<p><img src="book2.jpg" border="0" /><i>At the urging of Mrs. Know-It-All,
the next book Dr. Know-It-All reviews will be <i>Weight Loss Secrets</i>,
by <b>Sally Slinky</b>.</i></p>

...
```

The images display without borders. If you don't want borders to appear around your images, you can exclude the **border="0"** attribute altogether. Web authors set the border attribute to "0" to eliminate the border around a linked image in most browsers. The border attribute has been deprecated since HTML 4.0.

5   **Save the changes to the document. Leave the file open in both applications.**

To Extend Your Knowledge...

FILE ORGANIZATION

When you plan a Web project, you must determine how to organize your files. Organizing your Web site files makes it easier to reference specific items, including your images. Some designers create a top-level folder for the hypertext documents, and a subfolder for the images. Organize your files according to your personal workflow.

LESSON 2 Adding Alternate Text

Even though *bandwidth* (the speed of a user's connection to the Internet) is getting faster every year, many users still turn off images in their Web browsers. This is particularly true with users outside the United States, many of whom do not enjoy the benefits of high-speed connections. Other viewers use text-only browsers. To provide a positive experience for those viewers who have limited bandwidth, Web developers add alternate text to the image tag.

Alternate text (usually abbreviated *alt text*) is intended as a textual alternative to the image. Alt text describes the *purpose* of the image, rather than the *appearance* of the image, if the graphic fails to download. More importantly, alt text allows visually impaired visitors to "hear" the site instead of see it; a screen reader reads the alt text to the user. Alt text is specified with the `alt=""` attribute.

With the advent of XHTML, alt text is a requirement. You must include the `alt=""` attribute for every `<img />` tag you place on a Web page. The browser displays alt text under five circumstances:

- The user turned off images.

- The image is not yet downloaded.

- The image is not available.

- The browser is not capable of displaying images.

- The browser is part of specialized hardware used by persons with disabilities.

Add Alternate Text

1 In the open file, switch to the text editor.

2 Add alt text to the image tag as follows:

```
...
<h1 align="center">Dr. Know-It-All Recommendations</h1>
```

```
<p><img src="book1.jpg" alt="My Life In Australia" />These days, Dr. Know-
It-All is reading several books by <b>Dr. C. Little</b>, including his lat-
est, <i>Why Don't Chickens Have Lips?</i> Dr. Know-It-All has also been
engrossed in <i>My Life In Australia</i>, by <b>Alligator Al</b>.</p>

<p>Dr. Know-It-All recommends books on a weekly basis, or whenever we get
around to it.</p>

<h2>Upcoming Books</h2>

<p><img src="book2.jpg" alt="Weight Loss Secrets" /><i>At the urging of
Mrs. Know-It-All, the next book Dr. Know-It-All reviews will be <i>Weight
Loss Secrets</i>, by <b>Sally Slinky</b>.</i></p>

...
```

Alt text is now in place, in case the image does not display in the browser window or the user turns off images.

3   **Save the changes to the file. Refresh the document in the browser.**

4   **Position your cursor over the image.**

This activates a tool tip that displays the text in the **alt=""** attribute. If the image is unavailable, the text displays on the page instead of the image. The rollover text does not display for Macintosh users.

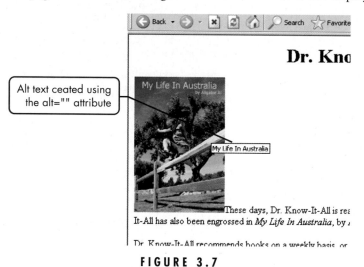

Alt text ceated using the alt="" attribute

FIGURE 3.7

5   **Leave the file open in both applications.**

To Extend Your Knowledge...

NO IMAGE TAG IN XHTML 2.0

XHTML 2.0 doesn't have an **<img>** element; the tag is obsolete in this draft of the specification. The replacement is the **<object></object>** tags. The object element allows you to supply more information about the image, and actually format the display of the alternate text.

For example:

```
<object> id="baby"
  type="image/jpeg"
  data="baby.jpg"
  width="152"
  height="160">
<p>A baby in a cradle.</p>
</object>
```

LESSON 3 Controlling the Image

You added images to your Web page in Lesson 1, but you didn't arrange the images in an attractive manner. Similar to body copy and headings, images can carry a number of attributes that affect the image's appearance. These attributes allow you to control alignment, how text wraps around the image, the size of the image, and the appearance of a small temporary image that appears on screen while the final image loads. In this lesson, you focus on image alignment and text wrapping.

In the graphic in the previous exercise, notice that the bottom of the image and the first line of text are located on the same line. Until recently, this was the only way to display text and images on the same line. Today, there is an alternative: you can control the relationship of text and images using the **align=""** attribute.

The **align=""** attribute has five possible values:

- Top
- Bottom
- Middle
- Left
- Right

If you don't indicate a preference, the browser applies the default value of bottom. Bottom alignment was applied to the image in the previous exercise. While you may assume that "bottom" means the image is placed at the bottom of the page, it actually means that the text is aligned along the bottom of the image.

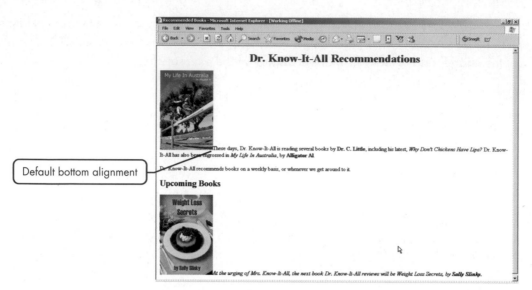

FIGURE 3.8

As you see above, the text aligns along the bottom of the image by default.

If you apply top, bottom, or middle alignment, only a single line of text appears next to the image, no matter how much available space is on the page. If you want to wrap text around an image, the image must be aligned to the left or right.

When you apply left or right alignment, situations will arise when you must move your content below an image. To do that, you can add a special attribute to the **
** tag called the **clear=""** attribute. For instance, if you apply **<br clear="left" />** next to the image, the text moves down the page until there are no more images on the left.

By default, text or other images display next to an embedded image, even if that image is contained in a **<p>** tag (unless the image is placed in a table; you'll learn more about tables later). The **clear=""** attribute is designed to separate text from images, allowing the reader to focus first on the image, and then on the accompanying text.

Align the Images

1   **In the open file, switch to the text editor. Set the first image to middle alignment, and set the second image to top alignment, as follows:**

```
...

<h1 align="center">Dr. Know-It-All Recommendations</h1>

<p><img src="book1.jpg" align="middle" alt="My Life In Australia" />These
days, Dr. Know-It-All is reading several books by <b>Dr. C. Little</b>,
including his latest, <i>Why Don't Chickens Have Lips?</i> Dr. Know-It-All
has also been engrossed in <i>My Life In Australia</i>, by <b>Alligator
Al</b>.</p>

<p>Dr. Know-It-All recommends books on a weekly basis, or whenever we get
around to it.</p>

<h2>Upcoming Books</h2>

<p><img src="book2.jpg" align="top" alt="Weight Loss Secrets" /><i>At the
urging of Mrs. Know-It-All, the next book Dr. Know-It-All reviews will be
<i>Weight Loss Secrets</i>, by <b>Sally Slinky</b>.</i></p>

...
```

The first image has one line of text aligned at the middle of the image. The second image has one line of text aligned at the top of the image.

2   **Save the file in the text editor. Refresh the browser and view the result.**

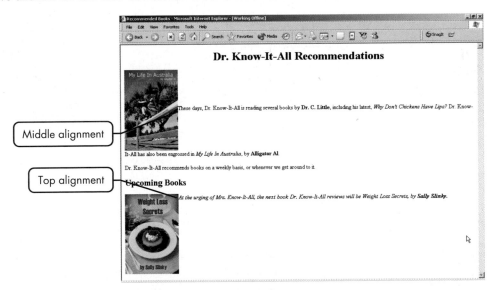

FIGURE 3.9

Even though you moved the text up and there's plenty of space next to the image, only one line of text displays next to the image. It would look much better with wrapped text. To wrap the text, you must apply left and right alignment.

3   **Set right alignment on "My Life In Australia" and left alignment on "Weight Loss Secrets," as follows:**

```
...

<h1 align="center">Dr. Know-It-All Recommendations</h1>

<p><img src="book1.jpg" align="right" alt="My Life In Australia" />These
days, Dr. Know-It-All is reading several books by <b>Dr. C. Little</b>,
including his latest, <i>Why Don't Chickens Have Lips?</i> Dr. Know-It-All
has also been engrossed in <i>My Life In Australia</i>, by <b>Alligator
Al</b>.</p>

<p>Dr. Know-It-All recommends books on a weekly basis, or whenever we get
around to it.</p>

<h2>Upcoming Books</h2>

<p><img src="book2.jpg" align="left" alt="Weight Loss Secrets" /><i>At the
urging of Mrs. Know-It-All, the next book Dr. Know-It-All reviews will be
<i>Weight Loss Secrets</i>, by <b>Sally Slinky</b>.</i></p>

...
```

4   **Save the file in the text editor. Refresh the document in the browser and view the result.**

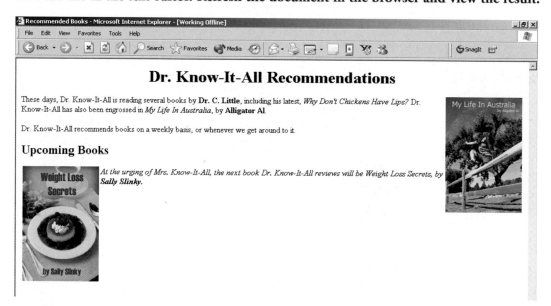

FIGURE 3.10

Once you align an image to the left or right, the remaining content (including other images) wraps around the image. If this is not your intended result, you can use the **<br clear="" />** attribute to instruct the browser to move down to the next clear area after the image.

5   **Leave the file open for the next exercise.**

Clear a Break After an Image

1 In the open file, insert the **
** tag before the Upcoming Books heading, as shown below:

```
...

<h1 align="center">Dr. Know-It-All Recommendations</h1>

<p><img src="book1.jpg" align="right" alt="My Life In Australia" />These
days, Dr. Know-It-All is reading several books by <b>Dr. C. Little</b>,
including his latest, <i>Why Don't Chickens Have Lips?</i> Dr. Know-It-All
has also been engrossed in <i>My Life In Australia</i>, by <b>Alligator
Al</b>.</p>

<p>Dr. Know-It-All recommends books on a weekly basis, or whenever we get
around to it.</p>

<br clear="right" />

<h2>Upcoming Books</h2>

<p><img src="book2.jpg" align="left" alt="Weight Loss Secrets" /><i>At the
urging of Mrs. Know-It-All, the next book Dr. Know-It-All reviews will be
<i>Weight Loss Secrets</i>, by <b>Sally Slinky</b>.</i></p>

...
```

2 Save the file in the text editor. Refresh the browser and view the result.

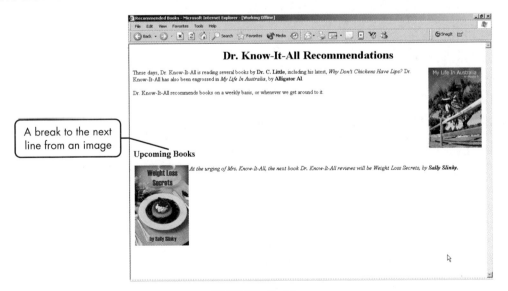

FIGURE 3.11

Notice that the clear attribute forces the browser to move the next section of content down, clearing the space next to the image above it. You could have used the **<br clear="all">** name-value pair to render the same effect. The **clear="all"** attribute clears all sides of an element.

3 Leave the file open in both applications.

LESSON 4 Specifying Image Height and Width

Two of the most important image attributes are height and width. The XHTML standard requires that these attributes be applied to every image. Without a specified height and width in the `<img>` tag, the browser must download the entire image before it can begin to display the image on the screen. Providing the width and height allows the image to download faster.

The dimensions you provide represent the size of the image as it appears on the Web page; these dimensions do not necessarily reflect the actual size of the original image. Please note that *scaling* (reducing or enlarging) the height and width attributes does not affect the size of the file. You might expect an image that has been scaled to 50% of its original dimensions would be 50% smaller in every way. This, however, is not the case. A 300 kb file is a 300 kb file, no matter how small or large it appears on your Web page.

You should only use this scaling technique during the initial planning of the site, while you are trying to identify proper image placement and size on the page. Remember that when you scale up an image, you sacrifice image quality because the image becomes *pixelated* (you can see the individual pixels in the image). Pixelation results in lower quality and *resolution* (clarity and definition of the file). When you scale down an image, it becomes distorted because you are forcing all of the pixels to occupy too small a space. When a Web site is ready to *post* (place the final version on the Web for public viewing), all images should be at their final sizes.

Resize an Image's Display

1   **In the open file, switch to the text editor.**

2   **In your text editor, set the images' widths to 180 px, and set the heights to 269 px, which is 120% of the images' original sizes.**

```
...

<h1 align="center">Dr. Know-It-All Recommendations</h1>

<p><img src="book1.jpg" align="right" alt="My Life In Australia"
width="180" height="269" />These days, Dr. Know-It-All is reading several
books by <b>Dr. C. Little</b>, including his latest, <i>Why Don't Chickens
Have Lips?</i> Dr. Know-It-All has also been engrossed in <i>My Life In
Australia</i>, by <b>Alligator Al</b>.</p>

<p>Dr. Know-It-All recommends books on a weekly basis, or whenever we get
around to it.</p>

<br clear="right" />

<h2>Upcoming Books</h2>

<p><img src="book2.jpg" align="left" alt="Weight Loss Secrets" width="180"
height="269" /><i>At the urging of Mrs. Know-It-All, the next book Dr.
Know-It-All reviews will be <i>Weight Loss Secrets</i>, by <b>Sally
Slinky</b>.</i></p>

...
```

3 Save the file in your text editor. Refresh the browser and view the result.

The instructions you gave the browser force the images to display at the larger dimensions.

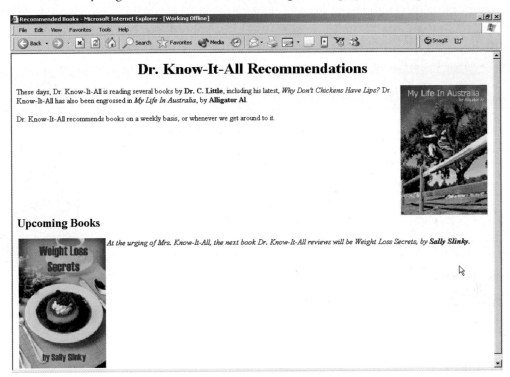

FIGURE 3.12

4 Change the width and height values to the actual size of the images, as follows:

```
...

<p>

<img src="book1.jpg" align="right" alt="My Life In Australia" width="150"
height="224" />These days, Dr. Know-It-All is reading several books by
<b>Dr. C. Little</b>, including his latest, <i>Why Don't Chickens Have
Lips?</i> Dr. Know-It-All has also been engrossed in <i>My Life In
Australia</i>, by <b>Alligator Al</b>.</p>

<p>Dr. Know-It-All recommends books on a weekly basis, or whenever we get
around to it.</p>

<br clear="right" />

<h2>Upcoming Books</h2>

<p>

<img src="book2.jpg" align="left" alt="Weight Loss Secrets" width="150"
height="223" /><i>At the urging of Mrs. Know-It-All, the next book Dr.
Know-It-All reviews will be <i>Weight Loss Secrets</i>, by <b>Sally
Slinky</b>.</i></p>

...
```

5 | Save the file in your text editor. Refresh the browser and view the result.

The images display at their original sizes. Adding the height and width values decreased the download time from the server to the user's browser because the attributes tell the browser how many pixels to reserve. When using the **height=""** and **width=""** attributes, the browser does not have to calculate the space needed for the image, which saves time.

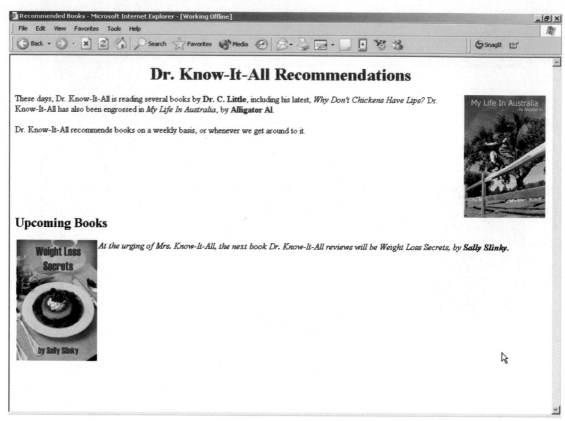

FIGURE 3.13

6 | Leave the file open in both applications.

To Extend Your Knowledge...

DETERMINING IMAGE SIZE

You can determine the size of an image in several ways, including opening the image in a graphics-editing program such as Adobe Photoshop, Adobe Illustrator, or Macromedia FreeHand. In certain situations, you can determine this information from the browser.

In the Netscape Navigator for Macintosh, you can place your mouse over the image and hold down the mouse button. When the menu pops up, you can choose View Image In New Window. The height and width of the image appear in the Title bar. You can gather the same information in Navigator for Windows by right-clicking the image and choosing View Image from the context-sensitive pop-up menu.

On Internet Explorer for Windows, you can right-click the image and choose Properties. The height and width are listed under Dimensions. Unfortunately, this does not work with IE for Macintosh.

LESSON 5   Working with Space Around an Image

You can add space between an image and other elements, such as text, using the **hspace=""** and **vspace=""** attributes. The **hspace=""** attribute allows you to change the horizontal space between an image and other objects on a Web page. The **vspace=""** attribute allows you to change the vertical space between an image and other objects on a Web page.

Non-Breaking Space

Even though these attributes provide control over the display of an image relative to other objects on a Web page, we recommend that you do not use **hspace=""** or **vspace=""** attributes; both have been deprecated. Instead, you can use the non-breaking space character entity to add space between elements.

A ***character entity*** is a code in HTML/XHTML that produces a symbol, such as the copyright symbol. In this case, however, an empty space the size of one character is created when you add a ***non-breaking space***. (You learn more about character entities later in this book.) By default, XHTML allows for only one character space between elements, no matter how many spaces you provide in your source code. When you use the non-breaking space, however, you can add as many additional character spaces as necessary.

The format of the non-breaking space is a bit different than what you've worked with so far. It does not use the open and close carats (< and >) to contain the command. Rather, the ampersand (&) character is used to start the character entity command, followed by the command name, and then the semicolon is used to end the command. For example:

```
 
```

The non-breaking space character entity acts exactly as a normal text space, except that the browser addresses each one individually. If you place four non-breaking spaces in your code, the browser puts four spaces between objects. This type of space can be applied to any object, not just an image.

Add Vertical Space to an Image

1   In the open file, switch to the text editor.

2   Add 20 pixels of vertical space to the bottom image, as follows:

```
...

<img src="book1.jpg" align="right" alt="My Life In Australia" width="150"
height="224" />These days, Dr. Know-It-All is reading several books by
<b>Dr. C. Little</b>, including his latest, <i>Why Don't Chickens Have
Lips?</i> Dr. Know-It-All has also been engrossed in <i>My Life In
Australia</i>, by <b>Alligator Al</b>.</p>

<p>Dr. Know-It-All recommends books on a weekly basis, or whenever we get
around to it.</p>

<br clear="right" />

<h2>Upcoming Books</h2>

<p>

<img src="book2.jpg" align="left" alt="Weight Loss Secrets" width="150"
height="223" vspace="20" /><i>At the urging of Mrs. Know-It-All, the next
book Dr. Know-It-All reviews will be <i>Weight Loss Secrets</i>, by
<b>Sally Slinky</b>.</i></p>

...
```

This instructs the browser to place 20 pixels of vertical space above and below the image.

3   Save the changes to the text file and refresh the document in the browser.

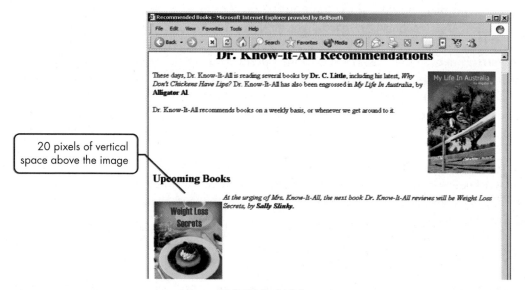

FIGURE 3.14

4   Leave the file open in both applications.

Add Horizontal Space to an Image

1 In the open file, switch to the text editor.

2 Add 50 pixels of horizontal space to the bottom image, as follows:

```
...

<img src="book1.jpg" align="right" alt="My Life In Australia" width="150"
height="224" />These days, Dr. Know-It-All is reading several books by
<b>Dr. C. Little</b>, including his latest, <i>Why Don't Chickens Have
Lips?</i> Dr. Know-It-All has also been engrossed in <i>My Life In
Australia</i>, by <b>Alligator Al</b>.</p>

<p>Dr. Know-It-All recommends books on a weekly basis, or whenever we get
around to it.</p>

<br clear="right" />

<h2>Upcoming Books</h2>

<p>

<img src="book2.jpg" align="left" alt="Weight Loss Secrets" width="150"
height="223" vspace="20" hspace="50" /><i>At the urging of Mrs. Know-It-
All, the next book Dr. Know-It-All reviews will be <i>Weight Loss
Secrets</i>, by <b>Sally Slinky</b>.</i></p>

...
```

This instructs the browser to place 50 pixels of horizontal space between the image and other elements.

3 Save the changes to the text file and refresh the document in the browser.

There are 50 pixels of space to the left and right of the bottom image. Notice that there is a space between the image and the edge of the Web page (on the left).

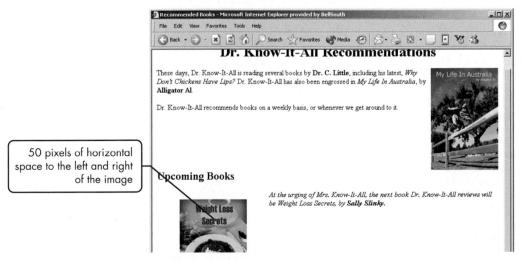

FIGURE 3.15

4 Leave the file open in both applications.

Add Non-Breaking Space

1   In the open file, switch to the text editor.

2   Add 10 non-breaking spaces between the words "Upcoming" and "Books", as follows:

```
...

<p>

<img src="book1.jpg" align="right" alt="My Life In Australia" width="150"
height="224" />These days, Dr. Know-It-All is reading several books by
<b>Dr. C. Little</b>, including his latest, <i>Why Don't Chickens Have
Lips?</i> Dr. Know-It-All has also been engrossed in <i>My Life In
Australia</i>, by <b>Alligator Al</b>.</p>

<p>Dr. Know-It-All recommends books on a weekly basis, or whenever we get
around to it.</p>

<br clear="right" />

<h2>Upcoming                 
   Books</h2>

<p>

<img src="book2.jpg" align="left" alt="Weight Loss Secrets" width="150"
height="223" vspace="20" hspace="50" /><i>At the urging of Mrs. Know-It-
All, the next book Dr. Know-It-All reviews will be <i>Weight Loss
Secrets</i>, by <b>Sally Slinky</b>.</i></p>

...
```

Although the use of the non-breaking space is not practical in this example, it illustrates how you can create empty spaces between elements on a Web page. As you work more with Web pages, you will discover other (more appropriate) uses for the non-breaking space.

Note that the non-breaking space code is in all lowercase letters. In XHTML, this is required. If capital letters were used (such as), not only would the tag fail to work, it would display as text in the browser window.

3   **Save the changes to the text file and refresh the document in the browser.**

There are 10 spaces between the words Upcoming and Books. You can use as many non-breaking spaces as you need to separate elements. If you use the non-breaking space to render a specific page layout, keep in mind that your page might display differently on other machines (depending on the screen resolution settings).

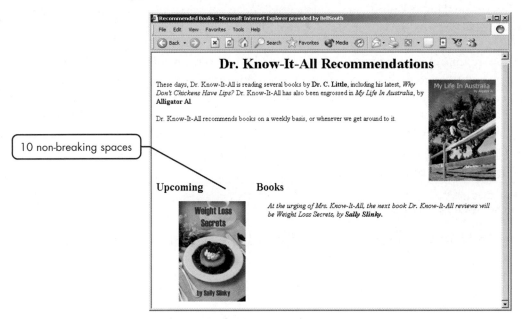

FIGURE 3.16

4   **Remove the 10 non-breaking spaces from the code in the text editor.**

5   **Save the changes to the text file and refresh the document in the browser.**

The additional space is removed.

6   **Leave the file open in both applications.**

LESSON 6 Lowsrc (Low Source) Images

Another image attribute you should be familiar with is lowsrc. A *lowsrc* image is a smaller version of the final image. The smaller image is downloaded and displayed while the full image continues to download. A temporary lowsrc image gives the viewer something to look at while he waits for the final image to download and appear on his screen. This attribute it not widely used due to ever-increasing amounts of bandwidth; but even when bandwidth was scarce, developers did not take full advantage of this feature.

Originally, lowsrc images were low-quality or black-and-white versions of the actual images. Today, however, designers apply creativity to their lowsrc images, and develop interesting line-art wire frames or skeletal versions of the final images. JPEG images load from the top down, so the effect of filling a wire frame can be quite striking. Adding a compelling lowsrc image might make the difference between a viewer leaving your site during a long boring download, and staying on your site to watch the lowsrc image metamorphose into the final image.

Specify a Lowsrc Image

1   **In the open file, switch to the text editor.**

2   **Specify the lowsrc image you want to display for each image on the Web page. as follows:**

```
...

<h1 align="center">Dr. Know-It-All Recommendations</h1>

<p><img src="book1.jpg" align="right" alt="My Life In Australia"
width="150" height="224" lowsrc="book1_low.jpg" />These days, Dr. Know-It-
All is reading several books by <b>Dr. C. Little</b>, including his latest,
<i>Why Don't Chickens Have Lips?</i> Dr. Know-It-All has also been
engrossed in <i>My Life In Australia</i>, by <b>Alligator Al</b>.</p>

<p>Dr. Know-It-All recommends books on a weekly basis, or whenever we get
around to it.</p>

<br clear="right" />

<h2>Upcoming Books</h2>

<p><img src="book2.jpg" align="left" alt="Weight Loss Secrets" width="150"
height="223" lowsrc="book2_low.jpg" /><i>At the urging of Mrs. Know-It-All,
the next book Dr. Know-It-All reviews will be <i>Weight Loss Secrets</i>,
by <b>Sally Slinky</b>.</i></p>

...
```

3   **Save the changes to the file. Refresh the document in the browser and view the result.**

A lowsrc image only appears if the full image isn't available, usually because the full image hasn't yet loaded. Since your files are local and load rapidly, you may have difficulty seeing the lowsrc image before the final image displays. If you had to download the page from a Web server, you would see the lowsrc image.

4   **Leave the file open in both applications.**

LESSON 7 | Horizontal Rules

Horizontal rules (lines) are often used to create visual dividers on a Web page. The ***horizontal rule*** is a straight line that goes from the left side of the screen to the right side. To divide sections with horizontal rules, you can apply the **<hr />** empty tag.

You can apply several different attributes to change the default appearance of horizontal rules. You can change the width, thickness, alignment, and style of a horizontal rule. The **size=""** attribute sets the thickness, and the **width=""** attribute sets the width. The width can be specified as pixels, or as a percentage of the screen size.

The **align=""** attribute aligns horizontal rules to the left, right, or center. By default, horizontal rules posses a three-dimensional "cutout" appearance. If you prefer your rules to appear without the default shading, you can apply the **noshade=""** attribute. If the default color of the horizontal rules interferes with the colors on your Web page, you can use the **color=""** attribute to assign a predefined color (color name) or hexadecimal color to the rules.

The **align=""**, **size=""**, and **width=""** attributes were deprecated in the HTML 4 standard in favor of style sheets. You can use the attributes in XHTML Transitional, but we recommend that you avoid them whenever possible.

Add a Horizontal Line

1   **In the open file, switch to the text editor.**

2   **Position your cursor below the first heading. Insert a horizontal rule, as follows:**

```
...

<h1 align="center">Dr. Know-It-All Recommendations</h1>

<hr />

...
```

A gray bar displays across the Web page. It separates the heading from the page content. Notice that the **<hr />** tag is empty.

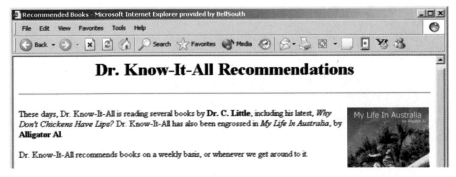

FIGURE 3.17

3   **Leave the file open in both applications.**

Modify a Horizontal Line

1 In the open file, switch the text editor.

2 Modify the horizontal rule by adding the following attributes:

```
...

<h1 align="center">Dr. Know-It-All Recommendations</h1>

<hr width="50%" noshade="noshade" color="blue" />

...
```

A blue horizontal line that is 50% of the screen width displays on the Web page. The horizontal line has no shading. Keep in mind that these attributes were deprecated in favor of style sheets, but they work if you are using XHTML Transitional.

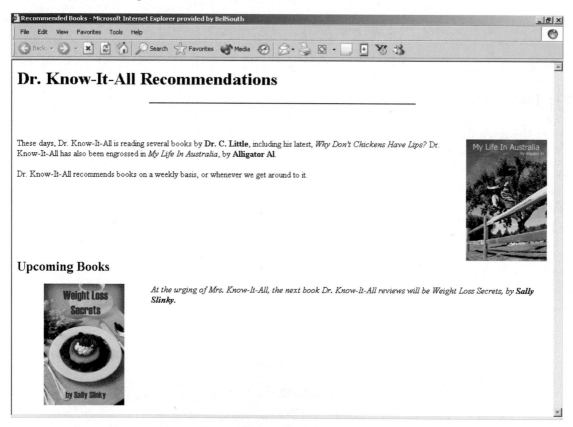

FIGURE 3.18

3 Close the file in both applications.

SUMMARY

In Project 3, you learned about the types of images you can use within your Web pages. You learned to use the `src=""` attribute to reference images. You also learned about the other attributes the XHTML standards require you to use when referencing images on a Web page.

You discovered that some viewers browse the Web with the graphics feature turned off in their browsers; other users are unable to display graphics on their systems due to slow Internet connections. You learned how to apply alt text to your images to resolve both of these issues for your viewers.

You explored how to control image alignment relative to text and other content to create a visually pleasing Web page layout. With these basic design elements, you should feel confident in your abilities to modify text and images on a Web page.

KEY TERMS

Alt text	Line art	PNG
Bandwidth	Loop	Post
Character entity	Lowsrc	Remote directory
GIF	LZW compression	Resolution
Horizontal rule	Non-breaking space	Scaling
Horizontal spacing	Path	Src/Source attribute
Indexed color	Pixel	Transparency
JPEG/JPG	Pixelated	Vertical Spacing

CHECKING CONCEPTS AND TERMS

MULTIPLE CHOICE

Circle the letter of the correct answer for each of the following questions.

1. Which image format supports 256 colors?

   a. GIF

   b. JPG

   c. PNG

   d. None of the above.

2. Why is the alt="" attribute so important?

   a. It provides information to the viewer in the event an image does not display. It is required in XHTML 1.1.

   b. The alt="" attribute provides helpful tool tips.

   c. It allows you to include an alternate image on the page.

3. What additional tag can you use to control how an image aligns with text?

   a. <h2>

   b. <font>

   c. <br clear="all">

4. The <img> tag offers five possible values for alignment.

   a. True

   b. False

5. To avoid a gap of white space when aligning text with an image, use the following value/s:

   a. Bottom

   b. Top

   c. Left

   d. Right

   e. c and d

6. The height and width attributes are required when using the <img /> tag.

   a. True

   b. False

7. Horizontal rules _____.

   a. separate content on a Web page

   b. are still part of the standard, but some attributes are deprecated

   c. display as gray lines across a Web page

8. You can add space between any types of elements on a Web page by _____.

   a. inserting the clear="" attribute with the paragraph tag

   b. inserting non-breaking space/s

   c. adding empty spaces in the source code

9. The image tag is eliminated in the XHTML 2.0 draft in favor of the <object> element.

   a. True

   b. False

10. A lowsrc image is a larger image file than the src="" image.

    a. True

    b. False

DISCUSSION

1. How can you prevent slow download times when you include images on your Web pages?

2. Why do you think the height, width, and alt tags are required in the XHTML standard?

3. Besides the obvious aesthetic reasons, why is it important to display images on a Web page?

SKILL DRILL

Skill Drill exercises reinforce project skills. Each skill reinforced is the same, or nearly the same, as a skill presented in the project. Detailed instructions are provided in a step-by-step format. You should work through these exercises in the order provided.

1. Add Images to a Web Page

A community service organization hired you to create an online newsletter. They want you to develop a simple text page with a few images to highlight each story.

1. From your WIP_03 folder, open news.htm in a text editor and browser.

    This document displays two headings and two paragraphs of text that have been indented (block-quoted) multiple times.

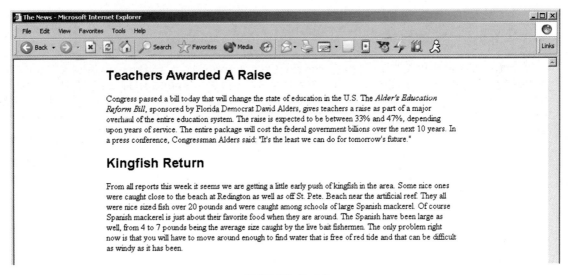

FIGURE 3.19

2. Insert the images and required attributes, as follows:

```
...

<p align="center">

<img src="header.gif" width="590" height="68" alt="Newsletter" />

</p>

<blockquote>

<blockquote>

<blockquote>

<blockquote>

<h2><font face="Arial">Teachers Awarded A Raise</font></h2>

<p>

<img src="teachers.jpg"  />

Congress passed a bill today that will change the state of education in the
U.S. The <i>Alder's Education Reform Bill</i>, sponsored by Florida
Democrat David Alders, gives teachers a raise as part of a major overhaul
of the entire education system. The raise is expected to be between 33%
and 47%, depending upon years of service. The entire package will cost the
federal government billions over the next 10 years. In a press conference,
Congressman Alders said: "It's the least we can do for tomorrow's future."

</p>

</blockquote>

</blockquote>

</blockquote>

</blockquote>

<blockquote>

<blockquote>

<blockquote>

<blockquote>

<h2><font face="Arial">Kingfish Return </font></h2>

<p>

<img src="boat.jpg" />

From all reports this week it seems we are getting a little early push of
kingfish in the area. Some nice ones were caught close to the beach at
Redington as well as off St. Pete. Beach near the artificial reef. They all
...
```

3. Provide the height and width information to decrease the time it takes for the images to download to the viewer's browser.

```
...

<p>

<img src="teachers.jpg" width="165" height="125" />

Congress passed a bill today that will change the state of education in the
U.S. The <i>Alder's Education Reform Bill</i>, sponsored by Florida
Democrat David Alders, gives teachers a raise as part of a major overhaul
of the entire education system. The raise is expected to be between 33%
and 47%, depending upon years of service. The entire package will cost the
federal government billions over the next 10 years. In a press conference,
Congressman Alders said: "It's the least we can do for tomorrow's future."

</p>

</blockquote>

</blockquote>

</blockquote>

</blockquote>

<blockquote>

<blockquote>

<blockquote>

<blockquote>

<h2><font face="Arial">Kingfish Return </font></h2>

<p>

<img src="boat.jpg" width="125" height="187" />

From all reports this week it seems we are getting a little early push of
kingfish in the area. Some nice ones were caught close to the beach at
Redington as well as off St. Pete. Beach near the artificial reef. They all
...
```

4. Provide alternate text in case the images do not display properly.

```
...

<p>

<img src="teachers.jpg" width="165" height="125" alt="Teachers Awarded A
Raise">

Congress passed a bill today that will change the state of education in the
U.S. The <i>Alder's Education Reform Bill</i>, sponsored by Florida
Democrat David Alders, gives teachers a raise as part of a major overhaul
of the entire education system. The raise is expected to be between 33%
and 47%, depending upon years of service. The entire package will cost the
federal government billions over the next 10 years. In a press conference,
Congressman Alders said: "It's the least we can do for tomorrow's future."

</p>

</blockquote>

</blockquote>

</blockquote>

</blockquote>

<blockquote>

<blockquote>

<blockquote>

<blockquote>

<h2><font face="Arial">Kingfish Return </font></h2>

<p>

<img src="boat.jpg" width="125" height="187" alt="Kingfish Return" />

From all reports this week it seems we are getting a little early push of
kingfish in the area. Some nice ones were caught close to the beach at
Redington as well as off St. Pete. Beach near the artificial reef. They all
...
```

5. Save news.htm in your text editor. Refresh the document in the browser to view the changes.

Notice that the code in the **<blockquote>** tag is nested. You can nest **<blockquote>** tags to add multiple indentations. Be sure there is an ending **</blockquote>** tag for every opening **<blockquote>** tag.

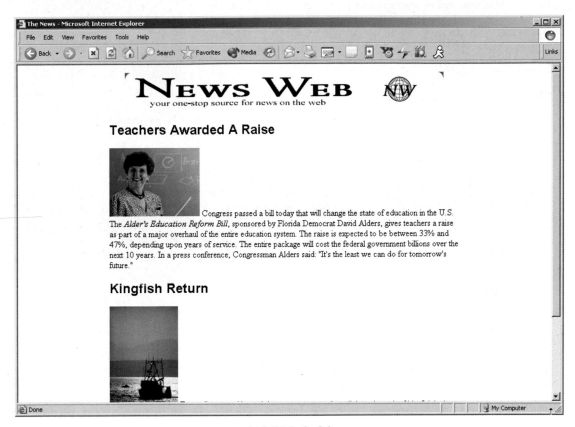

FIGURE 3.20

6. Leave the file open for the next exercise.

2. Align Images

The images display on the community service Web page, but the layout is less than ideal. To enhance the aesthetic appeal of the page, align the images with the appropriate section of text.

1. In the open document, switch to the text editor.

2. Apply the following image attribute changes.

```
...

<p>

<img src="teachers.jpg" align="right" width="165" height="125"
alt="Teachers Awarded A Raise" />

Congress passed a bill today that will change the state of education in the
U.S. The <i>Alder's Education Reform Bill</i>, sponsored by Florida
Democrat David Alders, gives teachers a raise as part of a major overhaul
of the entire education system. The raise is expected to be between 33%
and 47%, depending upon years of service. The entire package will cost the
federal government billions over the next 10 years. In a press conference,
Congressman Alders said: "It's the least we can do for tomorrow's future."

</p>

</blockquote>

</blockquote>

</blockquote>

</blockquote>

<blockquote>

<blockquote>

<blockquote>

<blockquote>

<h2><font face="Arial">Kingfish Return </font></h2>

<p>

<img src="boat.jpg" align="left" width="125" height="187" alt="Kingfish
Return" />

From all reports this week it seems we are getting a little early push of
kingfish in the area. Some nice ones were caught close to the beach at
Redington as well as off St. Pete. Beach near the artificial reef. They all
...
```

3.   Save the file in the text editor. Refresh the document in your browser and view the result.

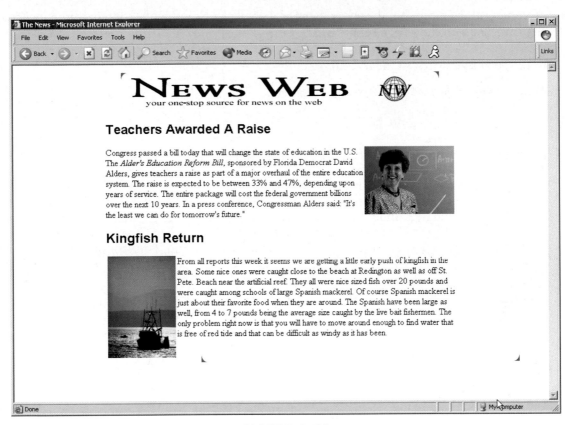

FIGURE 3.21

4.   Leave the file open for the next exercise.

3. Clear a Break Between Aligned Images

The page is coming along nicely, but the text and image alignment are causing the content to run together. You must fix this problem with the **`<br clear="all" />`** tag.

1. In the open file, switch to the text editor.

2. Add two **`<br clear="all" />`** tags as follows:

```
...

Congress passed a bill today that will change the state of education in the
U.S. The <i>Alder's Education Reform Bill</i>, sponsored by Florida
Democrat David Alders, gives teachers a raise as part of a major overhaul
of the entire education system. The raise is expected to be between 33%
and 47%, depending upon years of service. The entire package will cost the
federal government billions over the next 10 years. In a press conference,
Congressman Alders said: "It's the least we can do for tomorrow's future."

</p>

</blockquote>

</blockquote>

</blockquote>

</blockquote>

<br clear="all" />

<blockquote>

<blockquote>

<blockquote>

<blockquote>

<h2><font face="Arial">Kingfish Return </font></h2>

<p>

<img src="boat.jpg" align="left" width="125" height="187" alt="Kingfish
Return" />

From all reports this week it seems we are getting a little early push of
kingfish in the area. Some nice ones were caught close to the beach at
Redington as well as off St. Pete. Beach near the artificial reef. They all
were nice sized fish over 20 pounds and were caught among schools of large
Spanish mackerel. Of course Spanish mackerel is just about their favorite
food when they are around. The Spanish have been large as well, from 4 to 7
pounds being the average size caught by the live bait fishermen. The only
problem right now is that you will have to move around enough to find water
that is free of red tide and that can be difficult as windy as it has been.

</p>
```

```
</blockquote>

</blockquote>

</blockquote>

</blockquote>

<br clear="all" />

<p align="center">

<img src="footer.gif" width="590" height="25" alt="Newsletter" />

</p>

...
```

3. Save the changes to news.htm. Refresh the document in your browser and view the result.

FIGURE 3.22

4. Save the changes and keep the file open.

4. Add Horizontal and Vertical Space

The text is too close to the bottom image. You need to add some space between the text and the image.

1. In the open file, switch to text editor.

2. Add horizontal spacing to the bottom image, as follows:

```
...

<h2><font face="Arial">Kingfish Return </font></h2>

<p>

<img src="boat.jpg" align="left" width="125" height="187" alt="Kingfish
Return" hspace="10" / >

From all reports this week it seems we are getting a little early push of
kingfish in the area. Some nice ones were caught close to the beach at
Redington as well as off St. Pete. Beach near the artificial reef. They all
...
```

3. Add vertical spacing to the bottom image, as follows:

```
...

<h2><font face="Arial">Kingfish Return </font></h2>

<p>

<img src="boat.jpg" align="left" width="125" height="187" alt="Kingfish
Return" hspace="10" vspace="10" />

From all reports this week it seems we are getting a little early push of
kingfish in the area. Some nice ones were caught close to the beach at
Redington as well as off St. Pete. Beach near the artificial reef. They all
...
```

4. Save the changes to news.htm. Refresh the document in your browser and view the result.

5. Save the changes and keep the file open.

5. Add a Horizontal Line

The newsletter is almost complete, but you decide to add several horizontal rules to provide a more organized appearance on the page.

1. In the open file, switch to the text editor.

2. Add a basic horizontal rule at the top of the page that is 50 percent of the screen width. This rule separates the heading from the content.

```
...

<p align="center">

<img src="header.gif" width="590" height="68" alt="Newsletter" />

</p>

<hr width="50%" />

<blockquote>

<blockquote>

<blockquote>

<blockquote>

<h2><font face="Arial">Teachers Awarded A Raise</font></h2>

<p>

<img src="teachers.jpg" align="right" width="165" height="125"
alt="Teachers Awarded A Raise" />

Congress passed a bill today that will change the state of education in the
U.S. The <i>Alder's Education Reform Bill</i>, sponsored by Florida
Democrat David Alders, gives teachers a raise as part of a major overhaul
...
```

3. Add another horizontal line between the two sections of content. It should be 50 percent of the screen width.

```
   . . .

   Congress passed a bill today that will change the state of education in the
   U.S. The <i>Alder's Education Reform Bill</i>, sponsored by Florida
   Democrat David Alders, gives teachers a raise as part of a major overhaul
   of the entire education system. The raise is expected to be between 33%
   and 47%, depending upon years of service. The entire package will cost the
   federal government billions over the next 10 years. In a press conference,
   Congressman Alders said: "It's the least we can do for tomorrow's future."

   </p>

   </blockquote>

   </blockquote>

   </blockquote>

   </blockquote>

   <br clear="all" />

   <hr width="50%" />

   <blockquote>

   <blockquote>

   <blockquote>

   <blockquote>

   <h2><font face="Arial">Kingfish Return </font></h2>

   <p>

   <img src="boat.jpg" align="left" width="125" height="187" alt="Kingfish
   Return" hspace="10" vspace="10" />

   From all reports this week it seems we are getting a little early push of
   kingfish in the area. Some nice ones were caught close to the beach at
   Redington as well as off St. Pete. Beach near the artificial reef. They all
   . . .
```

4. Save the changes to news.htm. Refresh the document in your browser and view the result.

5. Close the file in both applications.

CHALLENGE

Challenge exercises expand on, or are somewhat related to, skills presented in the lessons. Each exercise provides a brief introduction, followed by instructions presented in a numbered-step format that are not as detailed as those in the Skill Drill exercises. You should work through these exercises in the order provided.

1. Add a Background Image

The newsletter you volunteered to create was very successful. Your next assignment is to spice up the document with some graphic elements. The first step is to add a background image.

1. From your WIP_03 folder, open news.htm in a Web browser and a text editor.

2. If you can log on to the Web, launch your Web browser and go to www.google.com. Conduct a search on background images that would complement the news.htm Web page.

   If you are unable to access the Web, you can use the image called back.gif in the WIP_03 folder.

3. Download the background image to your WIP_03 folder.

4. Add the **background="back.gif"** attribute-value pair to the **<body>** tag. If you selected your own background image, use that image instead.

5. Save the changes to the text file and refresh the document in the browser.

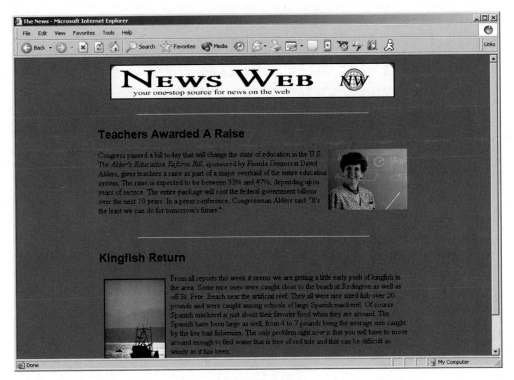

FIGURE 3.23

6. Leave the file open in both applications.

2. Add Borders and Find Dimensions

The newsletter looks better with a background image. You decide, however, that the existing images on the page are incompatible with the background. These are photographic images, so it would be unwise to convert them to transparent GIFs. Instead, you decide to add a border around the images to separate them from the new background image.

1. In the open document, add the **border="2"** attribute-value pair to both **<img>** tags on the Web page.

2. Remove the top horizontal line.

3. From your WIP_03 folder, insert topstory.gif above the text and image content (beneath the banner).

4. Right-click the image.

   You can see the image's dimensions in the Properties dialog box.

5. Insert the image's dimensions in the **<img />** tag.

6. Provide alternate text for the new image. Center-align the image on the Web page.

7. Apply an image border to the image.

8. Save the changes to the text file. Refresh the document in the browser and view the result.

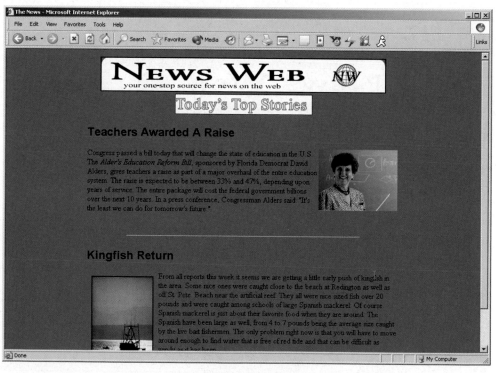

FIGURE 3.24

9. Keep the file open in both applications.

3. Add Navigation

You can use images to create hyperlink navigation so your viewers can access other pages on your site. Even though you have not yet learned how to create hyperlinks, you can build the layout of your navigation and add the links later.

1. In the open file, position your cursor beneath topstory.gif. Insert bullet.gif.

   Bullet.gif should be in your WIP_03 folder.

2. Type "About Us" next to the first bullet image.

3. Insert a space after About Us. Insert bullet.gif. Type "Archives" next to the second bullet image.

4. Insert a space after Archives. Insert bullet.gif. Type "Contact Us" next to the third bullet image.

5. Align each text link in the middle of bullet.gif.

6. Find and insert bullet.gif's dimensions in each **`<img />`** tag.

7. Provide alternate text for each bullet.

   Ideally, this would be the name of the actual link. For now, you can simply add the descriptive text of your choice.

8. Apply the bold style to each text link.

9. Save the changes to the text file. Refresh the document in the browser and view the result.

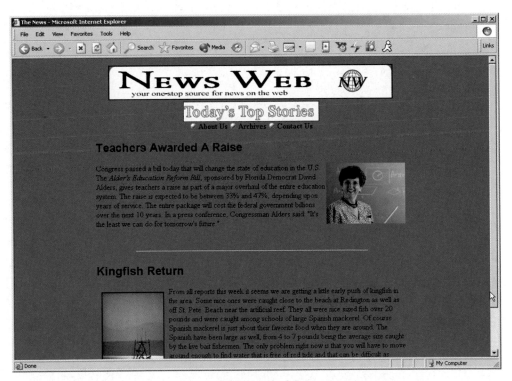

FIGURE 3.25

10. Leave the file open in both applications.

4. Create Different Page Layouts

The Web page is complete. You decide it would be best to offer your client several design choices to promote ideas and discussion. You create several versions of the Web page to show your client.

1. Save the open document as "news02.htm" in your WIP_03 folder.

2. Download another background image to change the color scheme of the page.

3. Move the images in the text areas to the opposite side of the layout.

4. Change the font to a different color, style, and size.

5. Create at lease three versions of the page, each with a different background, layout, color, and font.

6. Close all of the files when you are done.

P O R T F O L I O   B U I L D E R

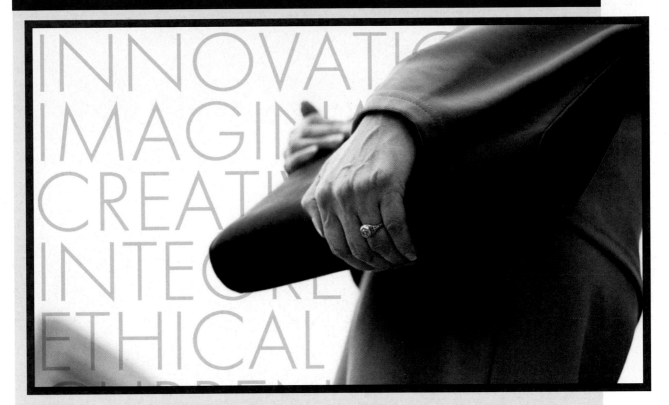

Add Graphics to an Existing Document

The local theater that hired you to create a Web page about the play *To Kill a Mockingbird* wants you to add a few images. Use the Web page you created in the Portfolio Builder from Project 2 as your base, and then add appropriate images to support the theme of the play. If you did not complete the Portfolio Builder in Project 2, do so now. Then, complete this Portfolio Builder.

To complete this exercise, you should do the following:

- Open the document you created in the Portfolio Builder in Project 2. Save it under a new file name. This gives you two versions of the Web page for your portfolio.

- Part of becoming a Web page author is finding appropriate images for your pages; you can create images yourself, purchase images from a graphic artist, or use royalty-free art you find on the Web that you have permission to use. Conduct a Web search to locate images that support your theme.

- Insert the image/s on the Web page. Align them with the text. Make sure you provide the proper size information and alternative text.

- You can also provide other graphical features, such as horizontal rules (graphic horizontal rules are sometimes called dividers). Place the dividers between the sections of text on your page.

PROJECT **4**

Creating Hyperlinks

OBJECTIVES

In this project, you learn how to

- Work with text hyperlinks

- Add links to a page

- Create image hyperlinks

- Add titles to hyperlinks

- Remove borders from images

- Apply absolute and relative links

- Create a base link

- Include email links on Web pages

WHY WOULD I DO THIS?

Every Web surfer has experienced *hyperlinks*, which are the clickable areas on a Web page that take the viewer to another page or display additional information. In Project 3, you learned that when you add an image to a Web page, you actually add a reference to the image; you do not add the image itself. To make image references work correctly, the browser must know exactly where that image is located. So far, that's been an easy task to accomplish because the image has been in the same folder as the Web page itself. When it comes to linking to other pages, however, references become a bit more complicated.

Organizing information in a Web page is one thing; providing an easy way to access that information is another. Hyperlinks are designed to provide viewers with an easy method of accessing unlimited content. So far, we have considered Web pages as individual documents. The beauty of a Web page, however, is its ability to link pages together with hyperlinks, allowing users to navigate through the online information you provide.

As a Web page designer, you need to provide links to additional information that is located on remote sites. Links to other documents, images, downloads, and email addresses are essential elements of most Web sites. In this project, you learn how to create hyperlinks to provide access to a wide range of online resources.

V I S U A L   S U M M A R Y

An image or a section of text can be used to hyperlink one Web page to another. It doesn't matter if the linked pages are located on the same or different sites. Clicking the link takes the user to another Web page or to another location on the same page. Words or phrases that serve as links are underlined, appear in a different color, or both. Images that serve as links usually display a border; this differentiates linked images from non-linked images.

A *URL* (*Uniform Resource Locator*) is the Web address of a particular resource, such as an image or a Web page. The hyperlinks in your Web pages link to *relative URLs* (local files or addresses) or *absolute URLs* (addresses or files in different locations, such as other Web servers). For example, the following is an absolute URL to Against The Clock's home page: http://www.AgainstTheClock.com, as shown below.

FIGURE 4.1

Let's take a moment to analyze the parts of a sample URL:

$$\text{http://www.AgainstTheClock.com/XHTML/contents.htm.}$$

There are four parts to this URL:

- http:// is the *hypertext protocol,* which is used to transfer hypertext documents (Web pages) across the Internet.

- www.AgainstTheClock.com is the name of the computer on which the file is located. For a Web site, the computer is also known as the *Web server*.

- XHTML is the name of a folder.

- contents.htm is the file in the XHTML folder.

To construct a complete URL, you combine all of these parts, each of which is separated with a forward slash (/). When you apply a URL to a link or image, the browser interprets (reads) the URL and knows exactly where to search for the particular file that is listed in the Address field.

LESSON 1   Adding Hyperlinks to Text

The concept of hypertext and links originated in the 1940s. They were only ideas back then, however, and were not put into practical use until the dawn of the Internet and the World Wide Web. On the Web, the most common form of link is the text link. A user can click a ***text link***, which is a series of words or a URL, to access additional information on a topic. This type of link is called an ***anchor tag***, coded with **\<a>\</a>** tags.

The most common anchor tag sends the user to a different page. The new page can be within the same site, or it can be on an entirely different site. The destination page is called the ***target***; it is listed in the ***hypertext reference attribute*** (abbreviated ***href***). For instance, if you want to add a link to a page that takes a user to home.htm, you should insert the following code:

```
<a href="home.htm" title="Home Page Link">Click here to go to our home
page!</a>
```

Anything between the opening and closing tags is formatted as a link. If the browser supports it, the ***title attribute*** causes tool-tip-style information to appear when the user points to a link. In the above code example, the tool-tip-style information is "Home Page Link," as shown below:

FIGURE 4.2

The URL contained in the link can point to anything — a page on the same server, a page halfway across the world, or even another application. In the following exercise, let's put your knowledge of hyperlinks into action and add a text link to a document.

Create a Text Hyperlink

1   **Copy the content of your Project_04 folder to your WIP_04 folder.**

2   **Locate recs.htm in your WIP_04 folder. Open the file in your text editor and browser. View the document in the browser.**

At the top of the file, we added a reference to our question-and-answer page (faq.htm), and a horizontal rule (**\<hr />** tag).

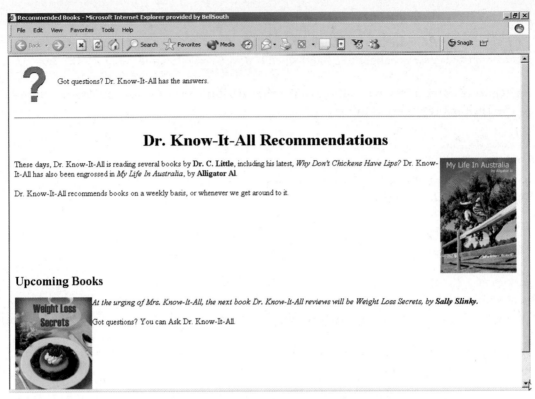

FIGURE 4.3

3   Use the <a></a> tags to create a hyperlink to faq.htm, as follows:

```
<html>

<head><title>Recommended Books</title></head>

<body>

<p><img src="q.gif" align="middle" alt="?" />Got questions? Dr. Know-It-All
has the

<a href="faq.htm">answers</a></p>

<hr />

<h1 align="center">Dr. Know-It-All Recommendations</h1>

...
```

When the user clicks the text link "answers," he advances to faq.htm.

4 **Save the file in the text editor. Refresh the browser and view the result.**

The text "answers," which is contained within the **<a></a>** tags, appears blue with an underline. Notice that the cursor changes to a hand when it hovers over the link.

5 **Switch to rec.htm in the text editor. Add a title attribute for "Frequently Asked Questions" to the anchor (<a>) tag, as follows:**

```
...

<p><img src="q.gif" align="middle" alt="?" />Got questions?
Dr. Know-It-All has the <a href="faq.htm" title="Frequently Asked
Questions" >answers</a>.</p>

<hr />

<h1 align="center">Dr. Know-It-All Recommendations</h1>

...
```

When the user hovers the mouse over the link, additional information about the hyperlink displays.

6 **Save the file in the text editor. Refresh the browser. Roll your mouse over the new link, but don't click it.**

When the mouse is placed over the image, a small tool tip displays the text contained in the **title=""** attribute. Not all browsers support this functionality.

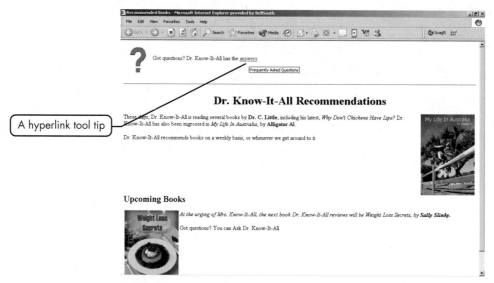

FIGURE 4.4

7 | **Click the link.**

We specified faq.htm as the href, so faq.htm displays in the browser window.

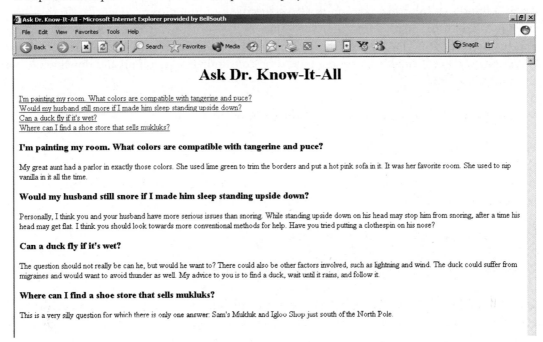

FIGURE 4.5

8 | **Save the changes and close the file in both applications.**

To Extend Your Knowledge...

MANY TYPES OF URLS

At last count, there were nearly 100 different types of URLs. You can specify a unique type of URL for every type of content available on the Internet. The following are the most commonly used URLs that you will incorporate in your Web pages:

http: ftp: mailto:

LESSON 2 Targets within a Page

In addition to linking to a full page, you can link to a specific location within a page. To do this, you use the *name attribute* to create an anchor as the target of a link. Targets provide convenient links to specific locations on a page so the user can jump to the desired location quickly and easily. Name attributes are commonly used on longer Web pages, since it can be distracting (and time-consuming) to scroll up and down while you search for a section of information.

The following code is used to create a target using the name attribute:

```
<a name="specific choice">link text</a>
```

In the above example, "specific choice" is the name of the target and becomes the destination on the Web page. The user advances to the named destination when she clicks the link.

You also need to create the link to point to this target:

```
<a href="name of the page#specific choice">link text</a>
```

In this instance, "name of the page" is the HTML page on which the target appears. The word that follows the pound sign (#) is the name we chose for the target. In an instance where both the link and the target refer to the same page, the target would omit the page name and begin with the pound sign and the name of the target.

Add an Anchor within a Page

1 **Open WIP_04>faq.htm in your text editor and browser. View the page in your browser.**

Notice the list of links at the top of the page. The list allows viewers to click a link and quickly move to the section of the document they want to read.

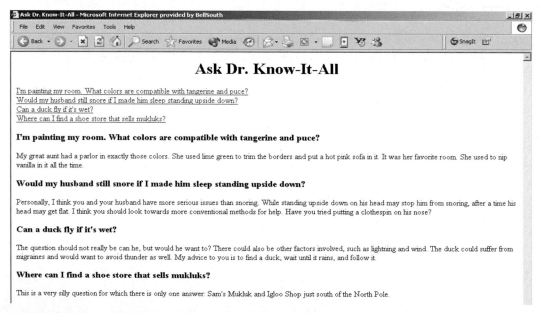

FIGURE 4.6

2   **Add a "Back to Top" link to each of the questions, as follows:**

```
...

<h3><a name="room">I'm painting my room. What colors are compatible with
tangerine and puce?</a></h3>

<p>My great aunt had a parlor in exactly those colors. She used lime green
to trim the borders and put a hot pink sofa in it. It was her favorite
room. She used to nip vanilla in it all the time.</p>

<p><a href="#top">Back To Top</a></p>

<h3><a name="snore">Would my husband still snore if I made him sleep
standing upside down?</a></h3>

<p>Personally, I think you and your husband have more serious issues than
snoring. While standing upside down on his head may stop him from snoring,
after a time his head may get flat. I think you should look towards more
conventional methods for help. Have you tried putting a clothespin on his
nose?</p>

<p><a href="#top">Back To Top</a></p>

<h3><a name="duck">Can a duck fly if it's wet?</a></h3>

<p>The question should not really be can he, but would he want to? There
could also be other factors involved, such as lightning and wind. The duck
could suffer from migraines and would want to avoid thunder as well. My
advice to you is to find a duck, wait until it rains, and follow it.</p>

<p><a href="#top">Back To Top</a></p>

<h3><a name="mukluk">Where can I find a shoe store that sells
mukluks?</a></h3>

<p>This is a very silly question for which there is only one answer: Sam's
Mukluk and Igloo Shop just south of the North Pole.</p>

<p><a href="#top">Back To Top</a></p>

</body>

</html>
```

This creates links to the targets within the document.

3   **At the top of the page, add the targets for these links.**

```
...

<body>

<h1 align="center">Ask Dr. Know-It-All</h1>

<a name="top"></a>

<a href="#room">I'm painting my room. What colors are compatible with
tangerine and puce?</a><br />

...
```

4   **Save the file in the text editor. Refresh the browser and view the result.**

At the bottom of each section of text, note the line of text that reads "Back To Top." Clicking this link allows the user to quickly return to the top of the page without scrolling.

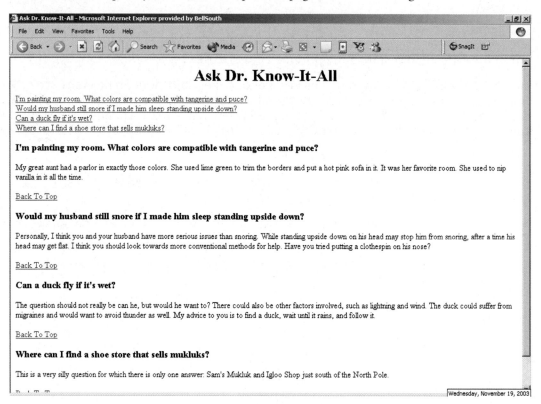

FIGURE 4.7

5   **Click the third question.**

The browser immediately jumps to the third question on the page.

6   **Click one of the Back To Top links.**

Even though the link says it will jump to the top of the page, notice that you don't arrive at that location. When you created the Back To Top link, you specified a particular target location that lies below the heading. To fix this, the target at the top of the page could be placed directly below the **\<body\>** tag.

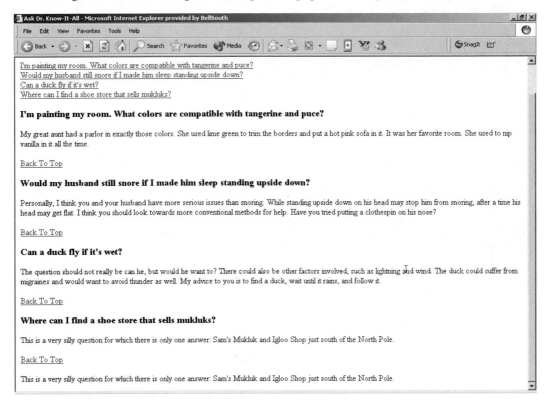

FIGURE 4.8

7   **Save your changes. Close the file in both applications.**

To Extend Your Knowledge...

LINKING CONVENIENCE

One important design concept: if you enable users to jump down the page, you should also enable them to jump back up. Don't forget to add links at the bottom of the page to return the visitor to the top of the page.

The browser moves to whatever location the target anchor specifies. Make certain that you place your anchors correctly.

LESSON 3 Adding Hyperlinks to Images

When you add a hyperlink to text, you enclose the text in the `<a></a>` tags. Doing so tells the browser that whatever is between the opening and closing tags is clickable, and it will transport the user to the destination specified by the href attribute.

Today, it is common practice to use images and icons instead of words for links. For instance, instead of using the word "Next," you might insert an icon with an arrow. Many times, the link to a home page is an image of a house. Some Web authors create a set of buttons or a graphical navigation menu to serve as their links.

Adding a link to an image works in the same manner as when you add a link to text. The process is the same, except that you enclose the `<img />` tag within the `<a></a>` tags to make the image clickable. For example:

```
<a href="location"><img src="name.gif" /></a>
```

Image links are often used to provide a graphical navigation layout, which many times is more aesthetically pleasing than using a text-based navigation system. Be mindful, however, of the type of images you use for the buttons. Simplicity is often the key to an easy-to-navigate, well-designed Web page.

Create an Image Link

1   **From your WIP_04 folder, open recs.htm in your text editor and browser. View the document in the browser.**

Recs.htm displays in the browser window, showing text and images on the Web page.

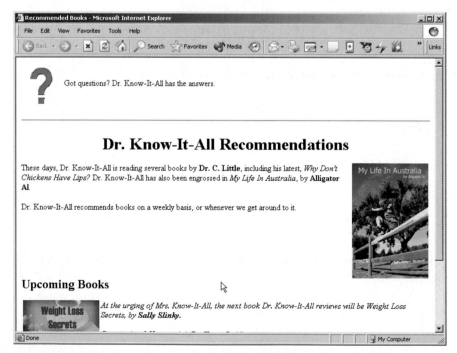

FIGURE 4.9

2   **Add a link to the image, as follows:**

```
<html>

<head><title>Recommended Books</title></head>

<body>

<p>

<a href="faq.htm"><img src="q.gif" align="middle" alt="?" /></a>

Got questions? Dr. Know-It-All has the <a href="faq.htm">answers</a>.</p>

<hr />

...
```

This creates a link to faq.htm that displays when the user clicks the image.

3   **Save the file in the text editor. Refresh the browser and view the result.**

The image is now a link and displays a blue (or purple) border. Click the image to verify that you jump to faq.htm.

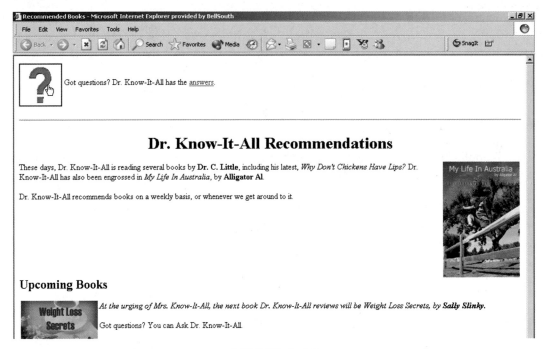

FIGURE 4.10

4   **Click the browser's Back button to return to recs.htm.**

Recs.htm displays in the browser window.

5   **Leave the file open in both applications.**

To Extend Your Knowledge...

ORGANIZING YOUR FILES

When you're planning a site, you should include plans for the file structure, including folder and file locations. *Assets* (files), such as images and sounds, should always be stored in their own folders. Each content section should have its own folder. It is important that you (and everyone else involved in the site's development) know where the files and folders are located. When you use a standard location for all of your URLs, you always have a consistent reference point for them.

LESSON 4 Removing Borders

As you noticed in the previous exercise, a linked image displays a blue (or purple) border. In the early days of the Web, designers used this border to indicate that when an image was clicked, it would advance the user to another page, replace a small image with a larger image, or provide additional details about the image. These days, however, designers typically prefer to use an image as a supplemental link, or to create a clickable image that doesn't require such an obvious cue as a blue border.

Today's sophisticated users do not need the visual cue of an image border, so designers usually remove them. They do so with the *border attribute,* which controls the border's width. The default border width is 2 pixels. To remove the border on a linked image, you can set the border width to 0 pixels, as follows:

```
<a href="home.htm"><img sre="home.gif" border="0" alt="Home" /></a>
```

The border attribute is specified as part of the image tag, but a blue border only appears if there is a link. As you know, once you click a link, it changes color on your screen — one color is applied to an unclicked link, and a different color is applied to a link after it has been clicked. In essence, the image border is a visual clue that tells the user whether he has clicked the link or not.

You can add attributes to the body tag to change the default color of links. For example, **<body link="green" vlink="yellow" alink="red">**, where:

- **link=""** changes the color of the link, which is blue by default.
- **vlink=""** changes the color of the visited link, which usually defaults to purple.
- **alink=""** is the color of the link at the moment the user clicks it.

You can set the values of the attributes to one of the 16 predetermined colors or a hexadecimal color. These attributes have been deprecated in HTML 4, however, and we recommend that you use CSS to change the default colors of your links.

You can control the presence (or absence) of borders, even if you don't yet know if an image will be linked. This can prevent an unintended border from appearing later.

Remove the Image Border

1 In the open recs.htm file in your text editor, set the width to "0":

```
<html>

<head><title>Recommended Books</title></head>

<body>

<p><a href="faq.htm"><img src="q.gif" align="middle" alt="?"
border="0" /></a>Got questions? Dr. Know-It-All has the
<a href="faq.htm">answers</a>.</p>

<hr />

...
```

This removes the blue (or purple) border around the image. If the image was not created as an image link, the border displays in black by default. The size of the border can vary, depending on what you require for a particular layout (**border="1"** or **border="5"**, for example).

2 Save the file in the text editor. Refresh the browser and view the result.

The blue border is gone, but the link is still available.

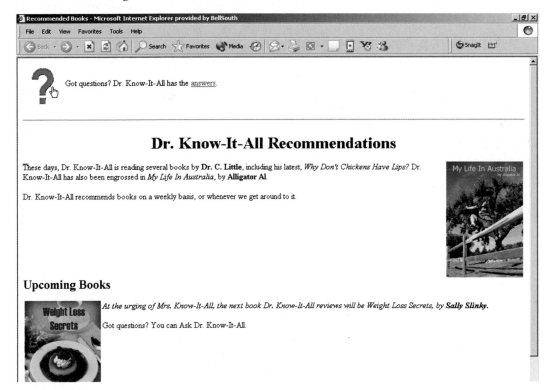

FIGURE 4.11

3 Leave the file open in both applications.

LESSON 5   Relative vs. Absolute URLs

As we discussed earlier, a browser interprets a URL as absolute or relative. An absolute URL, such as http://www.yahoo.com/index.htm, includes everything from the protocol to the file name. An absolute URL tells the browser everything it needs to know to locate a file. A relative URL includes less information about the location of the file because the file and the Web page are located on the same Web server; they are under the same domain name (the name of a computer on the Internet). When a file and its associated Web page are in the same domain, the browser does not require as much information to locate the file; it assumes that any information missing from the URL is supplied from the current Web page's URL.

Let's consider http://www.againsttheclock.com. It is an absolute URL, even though it does not include a file name. URLs such as this include default files, usually named "index.htm." When a user enters http://www.againsttheclock.com in the browser Address field, by default the browser jumps to http://www.againsttheclock.com/index.htm. In this case, http://www.againsttheclock.com and http://www.againsttheclock.com/index.htm are the same. You learn more about default files later in this book.

Link to an Absolute URL

1   In the open recs.htm, switch to the text editor.

2   Create a link to an absolute URL, as follows:

```
...
<p>Got questions? You can Ask Dr. Know-It-All.</p>

<br clear="all" />

<p align="center"><a href="http://www.againsttheclock.com">
Visit Our Sponsor</a></p>

</body>

</html>
```

This creates a text link on the Web page to an absolute URL (a remote location on the Web).

3   Save the changes to the file. Refresh the document in the browser and view the result.

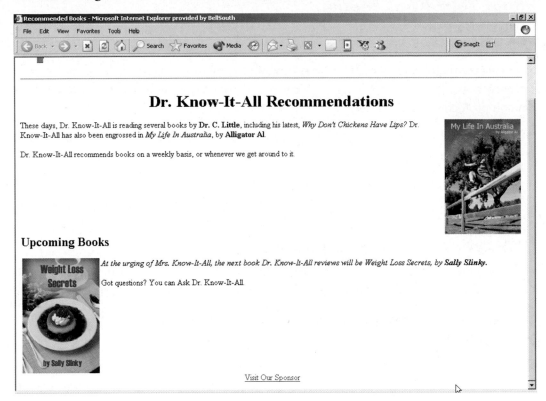

FIGURE 4.12

The link displays in the bottom-center of the page. Scroll down if you can't see the link.

4   Click the Visit Our Sponsor link.

The link takes you to the Against The Clock Web site. You must be online to see the www.againsttheclock.com home page.

FIGURE 4.13

5   Leave the file open in both applications.

To Extend Your Knowledge...

TYPES OF URLS

A **protocol** is a means of communication; it is a type of common vocabulary used between different computer programs. One protocol is http, which you see at the beginning of many URLs. Five of the most common protocols are listed below:

http: HTTP stands for HyperText Transfer Protocol. Web servers and browsers use this protocol to communicate. For example, http://www.yahoo.com.

https: HTTPS stands for Secure HyperText Transfer Protocol. It is similar to http, except that the messages are **encrypted** (scrambled) so they can't be intercepted and read by anyone other than the intended recipient. When you submit your credit card number over the Web, you are (hopefully) using a secure https page. For example, https://www.melitta.com/melittadirect/default.html.

file: A Web browser uses this protocol to access a page on the local hard drive. These URLs start with file:/// — note the extra slash. For example, file:///HardDrive/desktop/WIP/articles/recs.htm.

mailto: This protocol enables the user to send email to a particular person, such as the Webmaster. For example, mailto:webmaster@mysite.com.

ftp: FTP stands for File Transfer Protocol. It is primarily used for downloading large files because it is faster than http. Developers and designers use this protocol to upload files to a Web (FTP) site. For example, ftp://ftp10.netscape.com/pub/Netscape6/English/6.01/Mac/MACOS8.5/MacNetscape6Installer. sea.bin.

LESSON 6   Using the \<base\> Tag

In most cases, you enjoy better results when you use relative URLs rather than absolute URLs. Relative URLs allow you to move an entire site to a new location, such as a different server. The files do not require renaming, and the site continues to work as it did before the move.

In some situations, however, using relative URLs does not work well. For instance, if a user were to save a Web page to her local hard drive, and that page contained relative URLs, the images and links wouldn't work when she tried to view the page on her computer. The URLs would point to their original location, not the new location on the user's local hard drive.

Fortunately for Web developers, there is an answer to this dilemma. It's called the **\<base /\>** tag, which acts as a global reference point for a Web page. The browser automatically adds the **\<base /\>** tag to the beginning of each URL it encounters on a page. If you add **\<base href="http://www.nicholaschase.com/" /\>** to a page, the browser adds that **\<base /\>** tag to every URL on that page. For example, if the browser encounters **\<a href="index.htm"\>Home\</a\>**, it would automatically look for http://www.nicholaschase.com/ index.htm.

Provide a <base> URL

1   With recs.htm active in the text editor, add a **<base** /> tag to the page, as follows:

```
<html>

<head><title>Recommended Books</title></head>

<body>

<base href="http://www.xhtmlclass.com" />

<p>

<a href="faq.htm"><img src="/images/q.gif" align="middle" alt="?"
border="0" /></a>

Got questions? Dr. Know-It-All has the <a href="/faq.htm">answers</a>.</p>

<hr />

...
```

This provides a **<base>** URL for all the links within the document. (If you are working on a Web server, use its URL).

2   Save the file in the text editor. Refresh the browser and view the result.

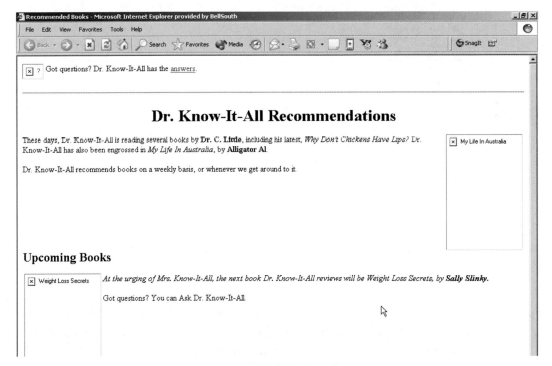

FIGURE 4.14

3 **Close the text editor, but leave the browser open.**

If you are using a Web server, you may see different images than before. If you are not using a Web server, the image disappears because the browser is looking for http://www.xhtmlclass.com/images/q.gif.

4 **Click the image or the text link.**

The Address field should display http://www.xhtmlclass.com/faq.htm. Again, if you are not working on a server, the page does not display, because the browser reads the URL as http://www.xhtmlclass.com/faq.htm. The base URL displays with the faq.htm file attached.

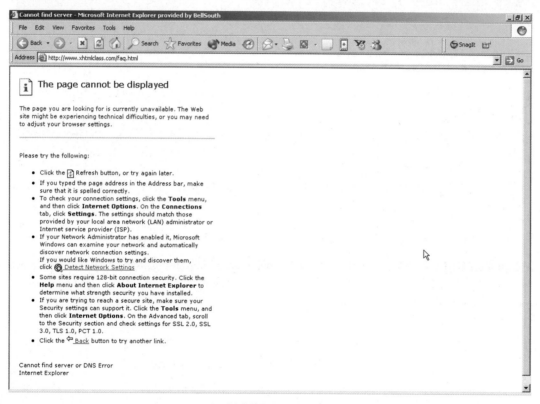

FIGURE 4.15

5 **Leave the file open in both applications.**

To Extend Your Knowledge...

MORE ON THE <BASE> TAG

The **<base />** tag offers the advantages of both relative and absolute links. The page continues to work when downloaded to a local machine. When an entire site is moved from one server to another, it continues to work when the new server's URL is added to the **<base />** tag.

LESSON 7 Linking to an Email Address

You already know how to link to files and Web addresses. The next task is to learn how to link to an email address from a Web page. Providing such a link offers site visitors a convenient point of contact to the Webmaster, sales representative, or another individual who is ready and willing to answer visitors' questions.

You use the same tags to create an email link as you would to create text and image links — with one small difference. The mailto source attribute contains a value command that launches the user's email client when the user clicks an email link. To create a link on your Web site that opens an email window, use a mailto: link, as follows:

```
<a href="mailto:AccountName@DomainName.com ">
send email to the Webmaster</a>
```

Most browsers open a new (blank) email message window when a visitor clicks the email link on a Web page. The recipient's address is automatically placed in the email client's "To:" field. The visitor can then add an appropriate subject line and the content of his choice. It's always best to provide the actual email address as the linked text, such as:

```
<a href="mailto:AccountName@DomainName.com ">
myaccount@mydomainname.com</a>
```

rather than a descriptive sentence or word.

Problems can occur with this method, however, if the visitor does not have an active email account on the machine he is using to surf the Web. Without an active email account, a message window cannot display, and the message cannot be sent.

Create an Email Link

1 **View the open faq.htm document in the browser.**

The document includes the most recent changes you made in the previous exercise.

2 **In the text editor, create a hyperlink beneath the "Where can I find a shoe store that sells mukluks?" hyperlink at the top of the page.**

```
...

<body>

<h1 align="center">Ask Dr. Know-It-All</h1>

<a name="top"> </a>

<a href="#room">I'm painting my room. What colors are compatible with
tangerine and puce?</a><br />

<a href="#snore">Would my husband still snore if I made him sleep standing
upside down?</a><br />
```

```
<a href="#duck">Can a duck fly if it's wet?</a><br />

<a href="#mukluks">Where can I find a shoe store that sells mukluks?</a>
<br />

<a href="mailto:name@youremail.com">E-mail the Webmaster</a><br />

...
```

Be sure to replace name@youremail.com with a valid email address. This creates a link to an email address and launches the email client installed on the machine.

? If you have problems...

If you are in a classroom environment, your computer might not have an installed email client. If an email client is not installed on your machine, the email link will not work properly. Consult with your instructor if this is an issue, or test your Web page on a machine that has an installed email client.

---

3   Save the changes to the text file. Refresh the document in your browser and view the result.

FIGURE 4.16

4   Close the file in both applications.

To Extend Your Knowledge...

ANYTHING AS A LINK

One of the more interesting aspects of XHTML 2.0 is the idea that virtually anything can act as a link. Rather than write:

```
<a href="http://webdesign.about.com/"><h2>Web Design at About</h2></a>
```

the heading (<h2>) element can act as a link:

```
<h2 href="http://webdesign.about.com/">Web Design at About</h2>
```

C A R E E R S   I N   D E S I G N

USING ROYALTY-FREE IMAGES

Being a Web designer does not necessarily mean that you have to be a graphic designer, as well. If you are working in a team environment, it's likely there is a graphic designer on board, and you can utilize his talents to complete the artistic components of your Web site.

If, however, you are a one-person show who has no interest in graphic design, yet you need images for your sites, you can find virtually any graphic as royalty-free clip art, digital art, or stock images. Many online template sources offer royalty-free pre-made Web interfaces, as well.

Before you include any of these resources, make sure that you get the proper permission — if permission is necessary. Some sites include a disclaimer stating that free use of their resources is limited to personal sites.

SUMMARY

In Project 4, you learned that a fundamental feature of hypertext is that you can link your documents to many other resources on the Web. You learned how to link to another location in the current document, to other documents on the local Web server, and to remote files on the Internet. You discovered that the target document is related to, and provides more information about, the source document.

You also learned how to use text and images to create links. You learned how to link to a specific point on a page and to an email address. You discovered the distinctions between relative URLs, absolute URLs, and the **<base />** tag, and discovered when to use each of them. You explored file organization, which makes it easier for you and other members of your team to locate files in a timely fashion.

KEY TERMS

Absolute URL

Anchor tag

Assets

Base tag

Border attributes

Destination

Email link

Encryption

File Transfer Protocol (FTP)

HyperText Transfer Protocol (HTTP)

HyperText Reference Attribute (HREF)

Hyperlink

Mailto protocol

Name attributes

Protocol

Relative URL

Secure HyperText Transfer Protocol (HTTPS)

Target

Text link

Title attribute

Uniform resource locator (URL)

Web server

CHECKING CONCEPTS AND TERMS

MULTIPLE CHOICE

Circle the letter of the correct answer for each of the following questions.

1. A URL is a _____.
   a. Web site address
   b. hyperlink
   c. protocol used to download emails
   d. None of the above.

2. What is the default display for a text link?
   a. Black text that is bold.
   b. Blue text that is underlined.
   c. A blue border is displayed around the text.

3. You use the _____ tags to create a hyperlink.
   a. <link></link>
   b. <a></a>
   c.

4. Linking within a Web page is _____.
   a. convenient for navigation in a long document
   b. not beneficial and should be avoided
   c. isn't available in XHTML

5. You can use images as hyperlinks if you place a link attribute within the <img /> tag.
   a. True
   b. False

6. Why would you use the title attribute in a hyperlink?
   a. To use as default text if the browser does not display the link.
   b. To provide the user with more information when he hovers his mouse over a hyperlink.
   c. There is no title attribute for the hyperlink.

7. What is the difference between absolute and relative URLs?
   a. Absolute URLs exist locally and relative URLs are remote.
   b. Relative URLs exist locally and absolute URLs are remote.
   c. There is no difference between them.

8. Why would you use the <base> tag?
   a. It is required in XHTML.
   b. It provides a base URL for all the links to reference.
   c. It provides a base image for all your links.

9. How is an email link different than any other link?
   a. An email link uses the href attribute.
   b. An email link uses the mailto: command.
   c. To create an email link, use the <email></email> tags instead of the <a></a> tags.

10. Why does an image link display with a blue border by default?
    a. To tell the user that the image is a hyperlink.
    b. To let users know they can edit the link if they want to.
    c. To add color to the image.

DISCUSSION

1. What is the benefit of using hyperlinks? Discuss a possible result of using too many hyperlinks within a document.

2. What are some of the issues regarding publishing Web pages (with hyperlinks) that should be considered during the production phase of the Web site?

3. What are some of the benefits of providing text links in addition to graphical links?

SKILL DRILL

Skill Drill exercises reinforce project skills. Each skill reinforced is the same, or nearly the same, as a skill presented in the project. Detailed instructions are provided in a step-by-step format. You should complete these exercises in the order provided.

1. Create Text Hyperlinks

You are developing a Web site for a golf supply company. Another designer completed the home page, but she forgot to add the navigation buttons that will eventually link to the other pages on the site. In this exercise, you create text links to the other pages and an email link from the main page.

1. From your WIP_04 folder, open golf.htm in a text editor and browser.

    The document displays an image and text that represent the navigation menu you will create.

FIGURE 4.17

2. Create text links to the other pages, as follows:

```
...

<body>

<p align="center">

<img src="golflogo.gif" alt="Golfbusiness Logo" alt="Logo" width="253"
height="84" />

</p>

<h4 align="center" ><font color="#008000">Welcome to golfbusiness.com.
Click the links below to navigate our Web site.</font></h4>

<p align="center" ><a href="golf.htm">golf carts</a> -
<a href="parts.htm">parts</a> -  <a href="maint.htm">golf
maintenance</a> - contact us</p>

</body>

...
```

3. Save golf.htm in your text editor. Refresh the document in the browser and view the changes.
   The links are active in the browser.

FIGURE 4.18

4. Keep the file open in both applications.

2. Create Image Hyperlinks

It is common for logos on a Web site to be linked to the main (home) page. Since the logo image is on the home page, you are going to link to an absolute URL instead.

1. Switch to the open golf.htm in the text editor.

   In the next step, you need an example of a remote URL to use as a link. Use Against The Clock's Web site, even though it is not a golfing site. It is for illustration purposes only.

2. Link golflogo.gif to http://www.againsttheclock.com, and remove the image border, as follows:

```
...

<body>

<p align="center">

<a href="http://www.againsttheclock.com">

<img src="golflogo.gif" alt="Golfbusiness Logo" alt="Logo" width="253"
height="84" border="0"  />

</a>

</p>

<h4 align="center" ><font color="#008000">Welcome to golfbusiness.com.
Click the links below to navigate our Web site.</font></h4>

<p align="center" ><a href="golf.htm">golf carts</a> -
<a href="parts.htm">parts</a> -  <a href="maint.htm">golf
maintenance</a> - contact us</p>

</body>

...
```

FIGURE 4.19

3. Hover your mouse over the image to test the link.

   The cursor changes to a hand.

4. Leave the file open in both applications.

3. Create a Base URL and Provide Link Titles

In this exercise, you provide a base URL for all the links in the Web page. You then add titles to your links so tool tips display when the user hovers his mouse over the links.

1. In the open document, add the base URL for the Web page in the head portion of the document.

```
<html>

<head>

<title>Golfbusiness.com</title>

<base href="http://www.againsttheclock.com" />

</head>

<body>

...
```

2. Add descriptive title attributes to the hyperlinks.

```
<html>

<head>

<title>Golfbusiness.com</title>

<base href="http://www.againsttheclock.com" />

</head>

<body>

<p align="center">

<a href="http://www.againsttheclock.com"  title="Goldbusiness.com" >

<img src="golflogo.gif" alt="Golfbusiness Logo" alt="Logo" width="253"
height="84" border="0"  />

</a>

</p>

<h4 align="center" ><font color="#008000">Welcome to golfbusiness.com.
Click the links below to navigate our Web site.</font></h4>

<p align="center" ><a href="golf.htm" title="Golf Carts" >
golf carts</a> - <a href="parts.htm" title="Golf Parts" >
parts</a> -  <a href="maint.htm" title="Golf Maintenance" >
golf maintenance</a> - contact us</p>

</body>

...
```

3. Save golf.htm in your text editor. Refresh the document in the browser and view the changes.

    The logo does not display because of the base URL that you added. Remember, you are working off your hard disk and not the Web sever www.againsttheclock.com/.

    The browser shows the base URL, and a descriptive tool tip displays when the mouse hovers over a link.

4. Leave the file open in both applications.

4. Link to an Email Address

In this exercise, you add a link to an email address to provide a point of contact for the user.

1. Create an email link, as follows:

    ```
    . . .

    <p align="center" ><a href="golf.htm">golf carts</a> - <a
    href="parts.htm">parts</a> - <a href="maint.htm">golf maintenance</a> -
    <a href="mailto:info@golfbusiness.com">contact us</a></p>

    . . .
    ```

2. Save the changes to golf.htm in your text editor. Refresh the document in your browser.

    The hyperlink "contact us" is active.

FIGURE 4.20

3. Close the file in both applications.

CHALLENGE

Challenge exercises expand on, or are somewhat related to, skills presented in the lessons. Each exercise provides a brief introduction, followed by instructions presented in a numbered-step format that are not as detailed as those in the Skill Drill exercises. You should complete these exercises in the order provided.

1. Open a New Window for a Destination

The home page of your golf supply Web site is complete; but you linked to a remote location from the home page, which is not exactly what the client expected. The client does not want the remote location to display in the original golfbusiness.com window. He wants to ensure that golfbusiness.com remains open in the original window. The client asked you to structure the site so a new window opens for this remote location.

1. From your WIP_04 folder, open golf.htm in a Web browser and text editor.

2. Add the **target="_blank"** attribute to the image link, as follows:

```
...

<a href=http://www.againsttheclock.com title="Golfbusiness.com"
target="_blank" >

<img src="golflogo.gif" alt="Golfbusiness Logo" alt="Logo" width="253"
height="84" border="0"  />

</a>

...
```

3. Save the changes to the text file. Refresh the document in the browser and view the result.

4. Click the image link.

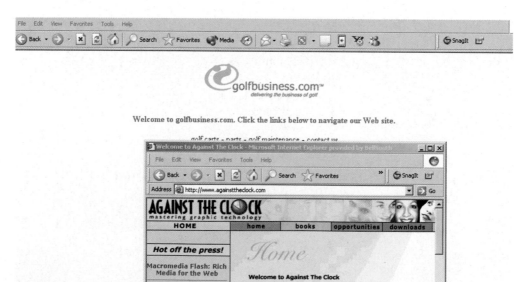

FIGURE 4.21

5. Leave the file open in both applications.

2. Send Email to Multiple Addresses

The owner of golfbusiness.com wants all emails to be sent to both the Webmaster and the "info" mailbox. Your task is to update the email links accordingly.

1. In the open file, add another email address to the email link.

    ```
    ...

    <a href="mailto:info@golfbusiness.com, webmaster@golfbusiness.com">contact
    us</a>

    ...
    ```

2. Save the changes to the text file. Refresh the document in the browser and view the result.

3. Click the Contact link to display both email addresses in the "To:" field of your email application.

FIGURE 4.22

4. Leave the file open in both applications.

3. Provide Additional Options for Email Links

The owner of golfbusiness.com wants a descriptive message in the subject line of any emails that come from the Web site, so the message can be identified quickly and easily. Your task is to add attributes to the email links on the site.

1. Add the **subject=""** attribute to the email link.

    ```
    ...

    <a href=mailto:info@golfbusiness.com,webmaster@golfbusiness.com
    subject=More information about Golfbusiness.com>contact us</a>

    ...
    ```

2. Save the changes to the text file. Refresh the document in the browser and view the result.

3. Click the Contact link to display the new subject line in the email application.

FIGURE 4.23

4. Keep the file open in both applications.

4. Add a Graphical Navigation

The text links are sufficient, but you feel that graphics would add to the overall effectiveness of the site. You decide to add graphical button links to the Web site.

1. In your WIP_04 folder, locate golfmaintbutton.gif, partsbutton.gif, contactusbutton.gif, and golfcartbutton.gif.

2. Insert the button images on the Web page.

   Use your best judgment on where the buttons should be located.

3. Set the images so they do not display borders.

4. Add the proper width and height information to each image.

5. Link each image to the appropriate target. Include a title.

6. Save the changes to the text file and refresh the document in the browser. View the result.

FIGURE 4.24

7. Close the file in both applications.

PORTFOLIO BUILDER

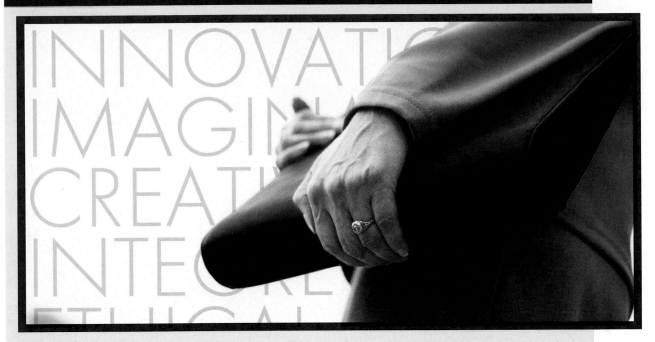

Develop a Personal Site

There is no doubt that as a Web site designer, you should publish your own Web site. Now is a good time to start thinking about the content you want to show potential clients. Offering your resume, an "about" page, and examples of your work are essential.

The first step in any Web site project is to create a storyboard. Next, you need to think about what each page on your storyboard should contain. Finally, you need to design the navigation system. To complete this exercise, you should do the following:

- Think about the type of content you want on your Web site. We suggest that you consider a main page that acts as the "about" page, a resume page, and a work page. The work page includes examples of your work.

- Create a storyboard of the pages you want to create for your Web site. Sketch image placement, content ideas, and color schemes.

- Create a flow chart of how you want the navigation of your Web site to flow. Small sites are easy, with each page linking to one another.

- Use images and text creatively. Choose a color scheme and make sure each page is consistent with the overall design of your Web site.

- Link each page on the site to every other page on the site. Make sure you supply some sort of text navigation, if you opt to use graphical images. Provide titles for your hyperlinks. If you link off of your site to other online work, think about linking the destination page into a new window. Provide email contact information, as well.

Working with Tables

OBJECTIVES

In this project, you learn how to

- Create a data table

- Enter data that spans multiple columns

- Change the dimensions of a table

- Align the data in table cells

- Apply styles to a table

- Add borders and colors to a table

- Change cellspacing and cellpadding

WHY WOULD I DO THIS?

The ability to include tables in HTML code was one of the first — not to mention important — enhancements that was made to the language. Before tables became available, Web page designers had virtually no way to align text vertically. Their only option was to use the **<pre>** tag to set their content to a monospaced font, and insert the necessary number of spaces to align content. The characters in a *monospaced font*, such as Courier, are all the same width. The characters in other fonts, such as Arial or Helvetica, are of variable widths. The **<pre>** tag displayed the content in the browser window exactly as it was placed in the source code. Achieving exact alignment was challenging, and the results were often far from aesthetically pleasing.

Since researchers were the original (and primary) Web users, the ability to format data was a definite advantage. Tables caught on quickly, despite the lack of universal browser support. In particular, the AOL browser has always been slow to adopt enhancements; Web authors must keep that in mind for the foreseeable future.

Today, tables are commonly used in Web page code. Unless you have targeted non-traditional audiences, such as PDAs or cell phones, you can be confident that your tables will display correctly and as intended on your pages.

Tables provide more control over the display of your content than any other XHTML element. Besides organizing your content in tabular format, you can design your page using tables as the underlying structure. In this project, you learn how to create basic tables to organize your content and Web page layout.

VISUAL SUMMARY

At the most basic level, tables are simply rows and columns of information. You place the information in the proper row and column in your table, and the browser takes care of the display on the Web page.

FIGURE 5.1

The table in Figure 5.1 has three rows. Each row has two cells and two columns, and each column has a header. A *row* extends horizontally across the table. A *column* extends vertically through the table. A *cell* is the intersection of a column and a row. A *header* is a cell whose text is formatted in bold and centered, and always appears at the top of the table. The table in Figure 5.1 displays as wide as the page because the width is set to 100%. You work with heights and widths in more detail later; but for now, understand that the width of a table can be set as a percentage of the available area, or it can be set as a fixed width that is measured in pixels.

Although tables were designed to organize data in a *tabular format* (data displayed in a table or grid), many designers use tables to control the layout of their Web pages. Consider the Web page in Figure 5.2. A table was used to position the images and text in the interface. This design could not have been achieved without the use of XHTML tables.

FIGURE 5.2

Figure 5.2 illustrates an image that was sliced into many smaller sections, and then pieced back together in a table. The smaller image slices are easy to work with, and they download faster than one large image. Tables allow you to create advanced layouts that would otherwise be impossible to design.

LESSON 1 Creating a Basic Data Table

To build a table, you create rows and columns, which in turn produce cells. Table rows are designated by the **<tr></tr>** (*table row*) tags. Each row contains data cells, which are designated by the **<td></td>** (*table definition*) tags. The entire set of rows and cells is enclosed in the **<table></table>** tags. These tags allow you to complete the basic setup for a data table.

To add a column, you add **<td></td>** to each row. To add a row, you add **<tr></tr>** and its associated **<td></td>** to the table. To remove a column or row, simply remove these tags and their content.

The following code creates a two-column, two-row, four-cell table that extends the entire width of the page.

```
<table border="1" width="100%">

<tr>

    <td>Cell 1</td>

    <td>Cell 2</td>

</tr>

<tr>

    <td>Cell 3</td>

    <td>Cell 4</td>

</tr>

</table>
```

The example code creates the following table.

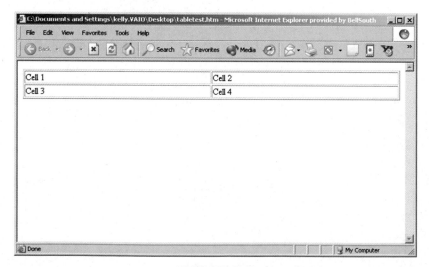

FIGURE 5.3

In the XHTML code for this example, all the text for each row is on a single line. While this may make it easier to see the individual rows, it is usually easier to read the XHTML when the data is divided into smaller chunks.

Notice in the code that a **width=""** attribute is provided for the **<table>** tag. Later in this project, you learn how to adjust the width of a table. For now, however, know that the width of a table can be set to a percentage of the screen — in this case, 100 percent.

Create a Basic Table

1   **Create a new hypertext document in your WIP_05 folder named "table.htm".**

You can use template.htm (located in the WIP_01 folder), rather than retype the document tags for table.htm. If you use template.htm to create a new document, make sure you change the title of the document to "Tables", as shown below.

2   **If you choose to create table.htm from scratch, add the basic document tags (including the title "Tables") to the file now, as shown below.**

Remember, using the basic template.htm file saves time because you don't have to manually type the document tags.

```
table - Notepad
File  Edit  Format  View  Help
<html>
<head>
<title>Tables</title>
</head>
<body>

</body>
</html>
```

FIGURE 5.4

3   **Open table.htm in your browser.**

4   **In the text editor, establish the table by inserting the table tags, as follows:**

```
<html>

<head><title>Tables</title></head>

<body>

<table>

</table>

</body>

</html>
```

The table tags tell the browser where to start and end a table.

5   **Add three rows with three cells each, as follows:**

```
<html>
<head><title>Tables</title></head>
<body>
<table>
    <tr> <td></td> <td></td> <td></td> </tr>
    <tr> <td></td> <td></td> <td></td> </tr>
    <tr> <td></td> <td></td> <td></td> </tr>
</table>
</body>
</html>
```

Three rows are created (**<tr>** tags), each containing three cells (**<td>** tags).

6   **Add data to the cells. In the first cell on the first row, enter "1". Enter "2" in the second cell on the first row. In sequence, continue to add data to the cells until you reach the third cell in the third row, and enter "9".**

```
<html>
<head><title>Tables</title></head>
<body>
<table>
    <tr> <td>1</td> <td>2</td> <td>3</td> </tr>
    <tr> <td>4</td> <td>5</td> <td>6</td> </tr>
    <tr> <td>7</td> <td>8</td> <td>9</td> </tr>
</table>
</body>
</html>
```

The numbers you inserted between the **<td>** tags become the content of the table cells. You can use anything as content, including images, large amounts of text, and other tables.

7   Save the file in the text editor and refresh the browser.

FIGURE 5.5

Notice how the browser displays this code. It shows your table of information, but it doesn't distinguish between the individual cells. You can expand the width of the table to separate the data and/or use borders to clearly define each cell.

8   Leave the file open in both applications. Continue to the next exercise.

Change the Table's Width

1   With table.htm active in the text editor window, make the table a little more spacious by setting the width to 75% of the page, as follows:

```
<html>

<head><title>Tables</title></head>

<body>

<table width="75%">

     <tr> <td>1</td> <td>2</td> <td>3</td> </tr>

     <tr> <td>4</td> <td>5</td> <td>6</td> </tr>

     <tr> <td>7</td> <td>8</td> <td>9</td> </tr>

</table>

</body>

</html>
```

This adds some space between the data in the cells. Although you change the table's width and height later in this project, adding the attribute now allows you to create a data table that is easier to read.

2   Save the changes in the text file and refresh the document in the browser.

FIGURE 5.6

3 To see the actual cells of the table, include a border for the table, as follows:

```html
<html>
<head><title>Tables</title></head>
<body>
<table border="1" width="75%">
    <tr> <td>1</td> <td>2</td> <td>3</td> </tr>
    <tr> <td>4</td> <td>5</td> <td>6</td> </tr>
    <tr> <td>7</td> <td>8</td> <td>9</td> </tr>
</table>
</body>
</html>
```

4 Save the file in the text editor and refresh the browser.

Adding a border creates lines between the columns and rows. This viewable grid allows you to see the individual cells more clearly. You can change the border's thickness by increasing the number of pixels in the border attribute.

FIGURE 5.7

5 Leave the file open in both applications and continue to the next exercise.

To Extend Your Knowledge...

CELL HEADERS

In the previous exercise, even though you didn't set any style information, the headers were automatically bolded and centered within their cells. Other than these simple formatting differences, header cells are the same as data cells. Originally, all three columns were the same width; now, however, the first column is slightly wider than the rest, allowing for the larger amount of text it contains. Remember, unless you specify otherwise, a table automatically adjusts to its widest and longest cells.

Add Table Headers

As you can see, the table consists of three rows, **<tr>**s, each of which contains three data cells, **<td>**s. You can use the **<th>** tag to create table headers for your columns of data.

1   **In the open file, add headers to the table using the <th> tags, as follows:**

```
<html>

<head><title>Tables</title></head>

<body>

<table border="1" width="75%">

    <tr>

        <th>First Column ...</th>

        <th>Second ... </th>

        <th>And Third</th>

    </tr>

    <tr> <td>1</td> <td>2</td> <td>3</td> </tr>

    <tr> <td>4</td> <td>5</td> <td>6</td> </tr>

    <tr> <td>7</td> <td>8</td> <td>9</td> </tr>

</table>

</body>

</html>
```

Headers are useful when you want to supply information for a column of data. Although you could have created the first row of text using the **<td>** tags and then applied formatting to differentiate the headings from the other text, using the **<th>** tags is faster and more convenient.

2   **Save the file in the text editor and refresh the browser.**

FIGURE 5.8

3   **Leave the file open in both applications.**

LESSON 2   Spanning Columns and Rows

Even if laying out grids of information were all you could do with tables, they would still be useful elements to include on Web pages. Luckily, you can do much more with tables: you can mix and match rows and columns, you can merge one table into another, and you can adjust alignments. For example, if you want to include a table header that applies to multiple columns in the table, you can add the **colspan=""** (*column span*) attribute to the header tag. The value contained within the quotes determines exactly how many columns the cell spans. If necessary, the **colspan=""** attribute can cause the cell to span the width of the entire table.

```
<table border="1" width="100%">

<tr>

    <th colspan="2">Title of the Table</th>

</tr>

<tr>

    <td>Cell 1<br>Cell 1<br />Cell 1<br />Cell 1</td>

    <td>Cell2Cell2Cell2Cell2Cell2Cell2Cell2Cell2</td>

</tr>

<tr>

    <td>Cell 3</td>

    <td>Cell 4</td>

</tr>

</table>
```

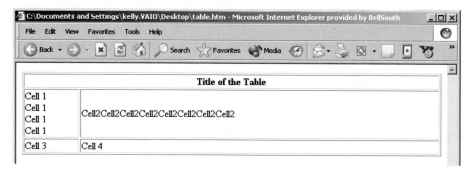

FIGURE 5.9

In Figure 5.9, notice that there is only one cell in the first row. That cell is set to span both columns of the table (**colspan="2"**). This single cell has the equivalent width of two cells, even though it appears to be one continuous cell. If another cell were added to this first row, it wouldn't make the first cell narrower. The additional cell would expand the width of the table and take the position of a new third column.

You can achieve a similar effect of expanding cells using the **rowspan=""** (*row span*) attribute, which extends the cell along a row vertically.

```
<table border="1" width="100%">

<tr>

    <th colspan="2">Title of the Table</th>

</tr>

<tr>

    <td rowspan="2">Cell 1<br>Cell 1<br />Cell 1<br />Cell 1</td>

    <td>Cell2Cell2Cell2Cell2Cell2Cell2Cell2</td>

</tr>

<tr>

    <td>Cell 4</td>

</tr>

</table>
```

FIGURE 5.10

In Figure 5.10, Cell 1 occupies the first column of the second row, so the second row contains only one additional cell, eliminating Cell 3. The reason for this change lies in the way that browsers construct tables. Each cell is placed in the first available position; although Cell 4 appears to occupy the first position in its row, it is actually placed in the second column.

Span the Row of a Table

1 | In the open table.htm in the text editor, add a row and use the `colspan=""` attribute to cause a single cell to span three rows, as follows:

```
<html>

<head><title>Tables</title></head>

<body>

<table border="1" width="75%">

<tr><td colspan="3"> </td></tr>

    <tr>

        <th>First Column ...</th>

        <th>Second ... </th>

        <th>And Third</th>

    </tr>

...
```

This creates a single cell that spans all three columns in the table.

2 | Add the header for the table, "Today's Objectives", in the row that spans across the table, as follows:

```
<html>

<head><title>Tables</title></head>

<body>

<table border="1" width="75%">

<tr><td colspan="3">Today's Objectives</td></tr>

    <tr>

        <th>First Column ...</th>

        <th>Second ... </th>

        <th>And Third</th>

    </tr>

...
```

Today's Objectives appears in the top expanded row. As you can see, however, the text displays at the default settings and offers no formatting, because you did not use the **<th>** tag. If you choose not to use the **<th>** tag for a table header, you can apply other formatting tags to emphasize the text (bold, italic, size).

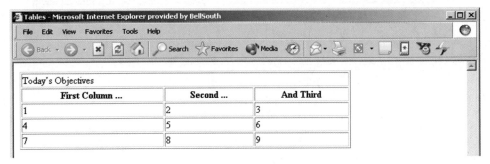

FIGURE 5.11

3 Format the table header using the Level 3 heading tag (**<h3>**) and center-align the text in the cell, as follows:

```
<html>

<head><title>Tables</title></head>

<body>

<table border="1" width="75%">

<tr><td colspan="3"><h3 align="center">Today's Objectives</h3></td></tr>

    <tr>

        <th>First Column ...</th>

        <th>Second ... </th>

        <th>And Third</th>

    </tr>

...
```

The text displays in the center of the expanded cell as a Level 3 heading.

4   Save the changes to the text file and refresh the document in the browser.

```
Tables - Microsoft Internet Explorer provided by BellSouth                    _ □ x
File   Edit   View   Favorites   Tools   Help                                   ●
○ Back ▾ ○ ▾ ✕ ② ⌂   ○ Search ☆ Favorites ● Media  ④ ⊗ ▾ ⤵ ◙ ▾ ▢ ▯ ⚐ ⤵

                        Today's Objectives
        First Column ...          Second ...           And Third
    1                        2                    3
    4                        5                    6
    7                        8                    9
```

FIGURE 5.12

Notice that there is a space beneath Today's Objectives. This is due to the **<h3>** tag, which automatically places a space beneath any contained text.

5   Leave the file open in both applications. Continue to the next exercise.

Span the Column of a Table

1   In the open table.htm in the text editor, add a column to the table using the **rowspan=" "** attribute, and change the **colspan="3"** to **colspan="4"**, as follows:

```
<html>

<head><title>Tables</title></head>

<body>

<table border="1" width="75%">

<tr><td colspan="4"><h3 align="center">Today's Objectives</h3></td></tr>

<tr><td rowspan="5"> </td></tr>

    <tr>

        <th>First Column ...</th>

        <th>Second ... </th>

        <th>And Third</th>

    </tr>

    ...
```

This adds an empty column to the left of the table. The column now spans 5 rows: it spans the 4 existing rows and 1 self-contained row.

2 Add descriptive text for the content of the expanded column, as follows:

```
<html>
<head><title>Tables</title></head>
<body>
<table border="1" width="75%">
<tr><td colspan="4"><h3 align="center">Today's Objectives</h3></td></tr>
<tr><td rowspan="5">Notes:</td></tr>
    <tr>
        <th>First Column ...</th>
        <th>Second ... </th>
        <th>And Third</th>
    </tr>
...
```

The text "Notes:" displays in the cell.

3 Save the changes to the file, and refresh the document in the browser.

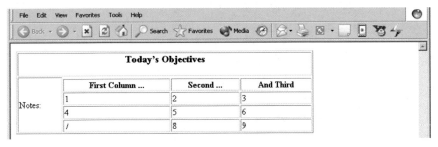

FIGURE 5.13

The table displays a column with the descriptive text "Notes:" in the middle of the cell. The text "Notes:" should display at the top of the cell, so any notes added to the table can fall beneath that text. Later in this project, you learn how to align text vertically and horizontally within cells.

4 Leave the file open in both applications.

To Extend Your Knowledge...

USING TABLES

You know how to create header rows using the **<th>** tag. You could have rendered the same effect by creating table rows and bolding the text within the table definitions, as follows:

`<tr><td><b>Some Text Heading Here</td></tr></table>`

LESSON 3 Height and Width

The most common reason to create a table is to fit content within a pre-defined area. In such cases, it's important to have as much control over sizing (height and width) as possible. In tables, height and width can apply to any of four items: cells, rows, columns, and/or the table itself.

You can use various methods to control height and width in tables. The first technique is using percentages, as you did earlier — you instruct the browser to use a particular percentage of the available area. This method enables you to set the height and width of a table based on the size of the area in which it resides. This technique is generally more useful for text than for images. Sometimes, however, a layout requires you to precisely set the size of the table (to an absolute number). In such a situation, you can use pixel measurements. For example:

```
<table width="300" height="200">

...

</table>
```

The code shown above produces a table that is 300 pixels wide and 200 pixels high, regardless of the size of the browser.

FIGURE 5.14

The table displays at this size only, even without units specified, because the pixel is the only unit of measurement these attributes render. On the other hand,

```
<table width="50%">

...

</table>
```

produces a table that adjusts to half the width of the browser window, whatever that width may be, as shown in Figure 5.15.

FIGURE 5.15

One exception to this rule is when the content of the table, such as an image, is larger than the specified table size. In that case, the browser displays the table as small as possible without compromising the content.

The height and width attributes are being phased out of XHTML (deprecated). For many browsers, however, these attributes provide the only way to control the height and width of a table; so, for now, they remain in use.

Controlling Column and Row Sizes

In addition to setting the size of the entire table, you can control the size of individual rows and columns. You do this by setting the size of the rows, or setting the size of the individual cells. In the sample table, you could set the height of the second row of data, as follows:

```
<table border="1" width="100%">

<tr>

   <th colspan="2">Title of the Table</th>

</tr>

<tr>

   <td width="100" height="150">Cell 1<br>Cell 1<br />Cell 1<br />
Cell 1</td>

   <td>Cell2Cell2Cell2Cell2Cell2Cell2Cell2Cell2</td>

</tr>

<tr height="100">

   <td>Cell 3</td>

   <td>Cell 4</td>

</tr>

</table>
```

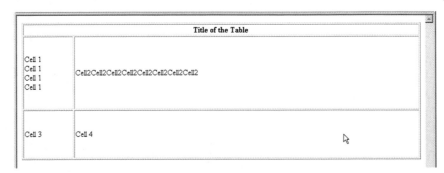

FIGURE 5.16

First, you set the width of the first cell (100 pixels). The width of the widest cell dictates the width of the column, so the width of the column is 100 pixels. Similarly, you set the height of the cell to 150 pixels, so the entire row expands to that height. You can also directly control the height of a row by setting the height attribute in the **<tr></tr>** tags.

You can also set the size of rows and columns based on percentages. If the size of the table is larger than necessary to display the content, the browser tries to render the table so the rows and columns are approximately the same size. For instance:

```
<table border="1" width="100%" height="100%">

<tr>

    <th colspan="2">Title of the Table</th>

</tr>

<tr>

    <td>Cell 1</td>

    <td>Cell 2</td>

</tr>

<tr>

    <td>Cell 3</td>

    <td>Cell 4</td>

</tr>

</table>
```

Here, all height and width attributes were removed, except those for the table itself.

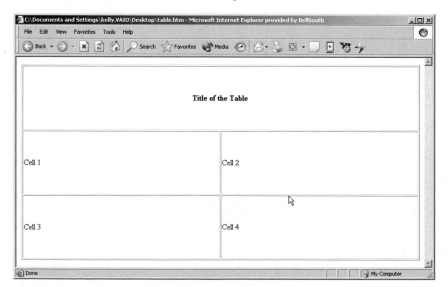

FIGURE 5.17

When you set height and width attributes using percentages, you can control the relative size of columns and rows, and still allow them to adjust as the table is modified. For example:

```
<table border="1" width="100%" height="100%">

<tr>

    <th colspan="2">Title of the Table</th>

</tr>

<tr>

    <td width="25%">Cell 1</td>

    <td>Cell 2</td>

</tr>

<tr height="50%">

    <td>Cell 3</td>

    <td>Cell 4</td>

</tr>

</table>
```

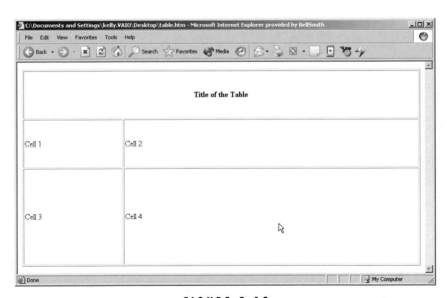

FIGURE 5.18

Another factor that can affect the size of columns and rows is the amount of content in a particular cell. While the browser normally tries to keep items evenly spaced in the absence of other instructions, a cell with more data requires more room in the table.

Change the Size of the Table

1   **With table.htm active in the text editor, change the table's width to 300 pixels, as follows:**

```
<html>

<head><title>Tables</title></head>

<body>

<table border="1" width="300">

<tr><td colspan="4"><h3 align="center">Today's Objectives</h3></td></tr>

<tr><td rowspan="5">Notes:</td></tr>

    <tr>

...
```

This sets the table's width to 300 pixels.

2   **Save the changes to the text file and refresh the document in the browser.**

FIGURE 5.19

3   **Return to the text file and change the table's width to 600 pixels, as follows:**

```
<html>

<head><title>Tables</title></head>

<body>

<table border="1" width="600">

<tr><td colspan="4"><h3 align="center">Today's Objectives</h3></td></tr>

<tr><td rowspan="5">Notes:</td></tr>

    <tr>

...
```

This sets the table's width to 600 pixels.

4 Save the changes to the text file and refresh the document in the browser.

FIGURE 5.20

5 Leave the file open in both applications. Continue to the next exercise.

Change the Size of Cells

1 In the open table.htm in the text editor, change the height of the header row to 100 pixels, as follows:

```
<html>
<head><title>Tables</title></head>
<body>
<table border="1" width="600">
<tr><td colspan="4"><h3 align="center">Today's Objectives</h3></td></tr>
<tr><td rowspan="5">Notes:</td></tr>
    <tr>
        <th height="100">First Column ...</th>
        <th>Second ... </th>
        <th>And Third</th>
    </tr>
...
```

Changing any cell (or header) in a row forces the other cells in that row to display that height, also.

2 Save the changes in the text file and refresh the document in your browser.

FIGURE 5.21

3 Return to the text editor and change the height of the header row to 75 pixels, as follows:

```
<html>

<head><title>Tables</title></head>

<body>

<table border="1" width="600">

<tr><td colspan="4"><h3 align="center">Today's Objectives</h3></td></tr>

<tr><td rowspan="5">Notes:</td></tr>

    <tr>

        <th height="75">First Column ...</th>

        <th>Second ... </th>

        <th>And Third</th>

    </tr>

...
```

The header displays 75 pixels in height.

FIGURE 5.22

4 | Leave the file open in both applications.

LESSON 4   Alignment

A significant part of the work involved in laying out a Web page is aligning the content. You can position the content to the right, left, or center; sometimes, you must ensure that content is at the top or bottom of a page section.

Similar to images, you can set text to flow around tables; the code for the table must be placed ahead of the coded text you want to flow around the table. In addition, entire tables can be aligned to the center, left, and right. For example:

```
<table border="1" align="right">

...

</table>
```

aligns the table on the right side of the browser window.

FIGURE 5.23

Aligning the Data

Just as the table can be aligned, each individual cell can have its own alignment attributes, both horizontal and vertical. Content can be aligned horizontally to the left (**align="left"**), right, or center, and can be aligned vertically to the top (**valign="top"**), bottom, or middle. With no instructions, a cell defaults to align horizontally to the left and vertically in the center.

Consider the following example, which results in a wide variety of alignments.

```
<title>Show Table</title>
<table border="1" width="100%" height="100%">
<tr>
   <th colspan="3">Title of the Table</th>
</tr>
<tr>
   <td align="right">Cell 1</td>
   <td align="left">Cell 2</td>
   <td align="center">Cell 3</td>
</tr>
<tr>
   <td valign="top">Cell 4</td>
   <td valign="bottom">Cell 5</td>
   <td valign="middle">Cell 6</td>
</tr>
</table>
```

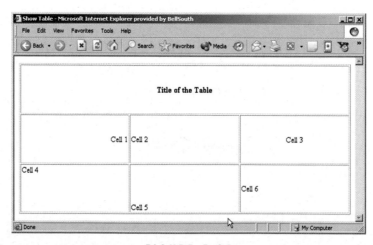

FIGURE 5.24

Notice that the alignments of Cell 1 and Cell 2 force the content to come together, no matter how much content is in either cell. This right/left alignment method can be useful when aligning different types of content, such as recipe ingredients and their associated amounts. Let's use "1/4 cup molasses" as an example: right-align "1/4 cup", and in the adjacent cell, left-align "molasses" to create two perfectly aligned columns of measurements and ingredients.

Align the Table

1   **With table.htm active in the text editor, center-align the table, as follows:**

```
<html>

<head><title>Tables</title></head>

<body>

<table border="1" width="600" align="center">

<tr><td colspan="4"><h3 align="center">Today's Objectives</h3></td></tr>

<tr><td rowspan="5">Notes:</td></tr>

    <tr>

...
```

This center-aligns the table on the Web page.

2   **Save the changes to the text file and refresh the document in the browser.**

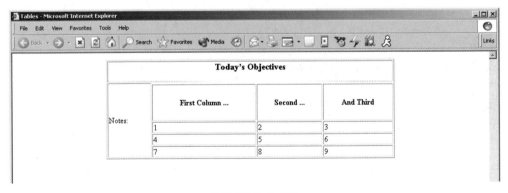

FIGURE 5.25

3 Return to the text editor and right-align the table on the Web page, as follows:

```
<html>

<head><title>Tables</title></head>

<body>

<table border="1" width="600" align="right">

<tr><td colspan="4"><h3 align="center">Today's Objectives</h3></td></tr>

<tr><td rowspan="5">Notes:</td></tr>

    <tr>

...
```

The table displays on the right side of the Web page.

4 Save the changes to the text file and refresh the document in the browser.

FIGURE 5.26

5 Leave the file open in both applications and continue to the next exercise.

Align Data in a Table

1 With table.htm active in the text editor, center-align the table, as follows:

```
<html>

<head><title>Tables</title></head>

<body>

<table border="1" width="600" align="center">

<tr><td colspan="4"><h3 align="center">Today's Objectives</h3></td></tr>

<tr><td rowspan="5">Notes:</td></tr>

    ...
```

The table displays in the center of the Web page.

2 Vertically align the text "Notes:" at the top of the page, as follows:

```
<html>
<head><title>Tables</title></head>
<body>
<table border="1" width="600" align="center">
<tr><td colspan="4"><h3 align="center">Today's Objectives</h3></td></tr>
<tr><td rowspan="5" valign="top">Notes:</td></tr>
    <tr>
        <th height="75">First Column ...</th>
        <th>Second ... </th>
        <th>And Third</th>
...
```

The text displays at the top of the cell, instead of the default center alignment.

3 Save the changes in the text file and refresh the document in the browser.

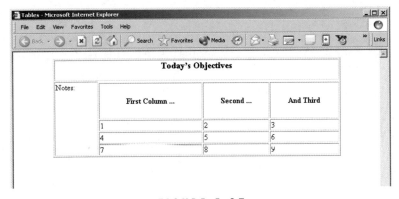

FIGURE 5.27

4 Leave the file open for the next exercise.

To Extend Your Knowledge...

THE IMPORTANCE OF TEMPLATES

For several reasons, the template is one of the most important concepts in Web site design. A template allows you to create a common look and feel for a site, which enhances the user's experience. You can include all the elements of the user interface in a template, so you can place more emphasis on creating content, rather than maintaining individual pages.

LESSON 5 Styling a Table

You can divide tables into three main sections: header, footer, and body. These parts are used in the same way as their counterparts in a word-processing program, with the header and footer appearing along the top and bottom of each printed page of a multi-page table.

You can set the header and footer to display before the body of the table has finished loading. To control the loading order (header, footer, and then body), you can place the footer code in front of the body code so the browser doesn't have to wait for the entire body to load before you can see the footer. To isolate the sections of a table, use the **<thead></thead>**, **<tbody></tbody>**, and **<tfoot></tfoot>** tags.

A table that loads the header, footer, and then body is constructed as follows:

```
<table border="1" width="100%" height="100%">
<thead>
   <tr>
      <th colspan="3">Title of the Table</th>
   </tr>
</thead>
<tfoot>
   <tr>
      <td colspan="3">The footer appears at the bottom, even though it
seems like it should be at the top.</td>
   </tr>
</tfoot>
<tbody>
   <tr>
      <td align="right">Cell 1</td>
      <td align="left">Cell 2</td>
      <td align="center">Cell 3</td>
   </tr>
   <tr>
      <td valign="top">Cell 4</td>
      <td valign="bottom">Cell 5</td>
      <td valign="middle">Cell 6</td>
   </tr>
</tbody>
</table>
```

Figure 5.28 shows you how the table looks in the browser.

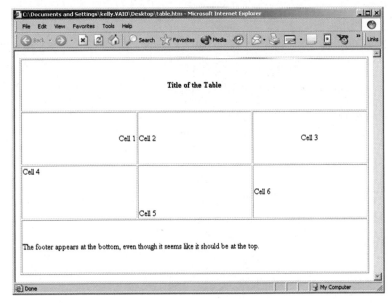

FIGURE 5.28

As of this writing, not all browsers fully support this function. In browsers that do not support header/footer control, the footer might appear at the top of the table, directly below the header. In most cases, this result is acceptable.

Style the Table

1   **With table.htm active in the text editor, add the table header, as follows:**

```
<html>

<head><title>Tables</title></head>

<body>

<table border="1" width="600" align="center">

<thead>

<tr><td colspan="4"><h3 align="center">Today's Objectives</h3></td></tr>

</thead>

<tr><td rowspan="5" valign="top">Notes:</td></tr>

    <tr>

        <th height="75">First Column ...</th>

        <th>Second ... </th>

        <th>And Third</th>

...
```

2   **Add descriptive column headers.**

```
...
</thead>
<tr><ld rowspan="5" valign="top">Notes:</td></tr>
    <tr>
        <th height="75">Call List</th>
        <th>To Do</th>
        <th>Groceries</th>
    </tr>
    <tr> <td>1</td> <td>2</td> <td>3</td> </tr>
    <tr> <td>4</td> <td>5</td> <td>6</td> </tr>
    <tr> <td>7</td> <td>8</td> <td>9</td> </tr>
</table>
...
```

These are the descriptive column headers for your Today's Objectives list.

3   **Add the table body section.**

```
...
<thead>
<tr><td colspan="4"><h3 align="center">Today's Objectives</h3></td></tr>
</thead>
<tbody>
<tr><td rowspan="5" valign="top">Notes:</td></tr>
    <tr>
        <th height="75">Call List</th>
        <th>To Do </th>
        <th>Groceries</th>
    </tr>
    <tr> <td>1</td> <td>2</td> <td>3</td> </tr>
    <tr> <td>4</td> <td>5</td> <td>6</td> </tr>
    <tr> <td>7</td> <td>8</td> <td>9</td> </tr>
</tbody>
</table>
...
```

These tags identify the body of the table. We chose not to add an expanded row along the bottom of this table as a footer, so we excluded the **<tfoot>** tag. If you were to add a footer to the bottom of the table, it would be beneficial to contain it within the **<tfoot>** tags.

4   **Save the changes to the text file and refresh the document in the browser.**

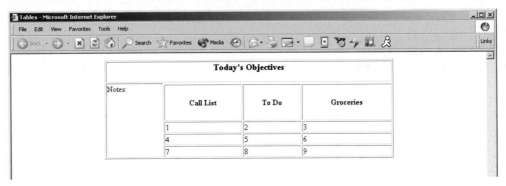

FIGURE 5.29

5   **Leave the file open in both applications.**

To Extend Your Knowledge...

PLANNING A TABLE

The easiest way to create a table (considering all of the coding involved) is to plan your idea on paper *before* you begin coding. This method works best for tables you are designing for page layout, rather than for structuring data, but it's useful for both.

If you are working in a tabular format to align data into columns and rows, creating a paper version ensures that you remember to include all the necessary data, such as headers. If you need to use tables to achieve a particular visual result, sketching the layout of the page helps you know how to structure the tables, where to place the tables, how many tables you need, where to place supporting images, and other design elements.

LESSON 6 Borders and Colors

You can change the ***border color*** of a table, which is, by default, the black border around the rows and columns of the table. You can use the **bordercolor=""** attribute to change the color of the table border to a flat uniform color. Internet Explorer (the only browser that supports this feature) allows you to specify the attributes **bordercolorlight** and **bordercolordark** to set the color of the light and dark sides to create a chiseled 3-D effect.

The **bordercolor=""** attribute has been deprecated in XHTML 1.0, and removed altogether from XHTML 2.0. An alternative is to use CSS to control the color and effects of table borders. The following code shows how to change the border color of the table:

```
<table bordercolor="green">
```

produces the following border in a browser.

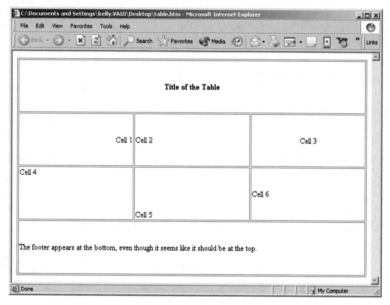

FIGURE 5.30

You can use any of the 16 pre-defined colors or hexadecimal colors when changing the color of your table border.

Changing the Background Color

You can change the ***background color*** of the entire table, a row, or an individual cell. The **bgcolor=""** attribute works with the **<table>**, **<tr>**, and **<td>** tags. This method of changing the background color has been deprecated in XHTML 1.0, and completely removed from XHTML 2.0. Nonetheless, you can use CSS to change the background color in a table, row, or individual cell.

To change the background color in a table to red, you would enter the following code:

```
<table bgcolor="red">
```

To change the background color in a row to blue, you would enter:

```
<tr bgcolor="blue">
```

To change the background color in a cell to green, you would enter:

```
<td bgcolor="green">
```

Change the Table Colors

1   **With table.htm active in the text editor, change the background color of the table to yellow.**

```
<html>
<head><title>Tables</title></head>
<body>
<table border="1" width="600" align="center" bgcolor="yellow">
<thead>
<tr><td colspan="4"><h3 align="center">Today's Objectives</h3></td></tr>
</thead>
...
```

You can use the pre-defined color Yellow, or you can choose any shade of yellow from the hexadecimal color system.

2   **Change the background color of the heading row to green.**

```
<html>
<head><title>Tables</title></head>
<body>
<table border="1" width="600" align="center" bgcolor="yellow">
<thead>
<tr><td colspan="4" bgcolor="green"><h3 align="center">Today's
Objectives</h3></td></tr>
</thead>
...
```

The entire row changes to green.

3 Change the cell color that contains the text "Notes:" to gray.

```
...
</thead>
<tbody>
<tr><td rowspan="5" valign="top" bgcolor="gray">Notes:</td></tr>
    <tr>
        <th height="75">Call List</th>
        <th>To Do </th>
...
```

The cell's background color changes to gray. Even if an entire table is set to a particular color, the modified cell color takes precedence over the table's background color.

4 Change the border color to gray.

```
<html>
<head><title>Tables</title></head>
<body>
<table border="1" width="600" align="center" bgcolor="yellow"
bordercolor="gray">
<thead>
<tr><td colspan="4" bgcolor="green"><h3 align="center">Today's
Objectives</h3></td></tr>
    ...
```

The border changes to gray.

5 Save the changes to the text file and refresh the document in the browser.

FIGURE 5.31

6 Leave the file open in both applications.

LESSON 7   Cellspacing and Cellpadding

Cellspacing is the gap between the cells in a table. *Cellpadding* is the space between the content of a cell and its borders. Both are used to fine-tune the appearance and alignment of content in a table. These attributes are both set on the table itself, and can be used independently or together. For example:

```
<table cellpadding="15" border="1">
```

creates a space around the content of a cell.

FIGURE 5.32

Cellspacing works in a similar manner, but actually controls the width of the interior borders themselves. For example:

```
<table cellspacing="15" border="1">
```

produces the following table.

FIGURE 5.33

In many cases, the positioning is the same whether you use cellpadding or cellspacing; the difference lies in whether you can see what is behind the table.

Change Cellspacing and Cellpadding

1   With table.htm active in the text editor, change the cellspacing of the table.

```
<html>

<head><title>Tables</title></head>

<body>

<table border="1" width="600" align="center" bgcolor="yellow"
bordercolor="gray" cellspacing="10">

<thead>

<tr><td colspan="4" bgcolor="green"><h3 align="center">Today's
Objectives</h3></td></tr>

</thead>

...
```

This places 10 pixels between each cell.

2   **Change the cellpadding of the table.**

```
<html>

<head><title>Tables</title></head>

<body>

<table border="1" width="600" align="center" bgcolor="yellow"
bordercolor="gray" cellspacing="10" cellpadding="10">

<thead>

<tr><td colspan="4" bgcolor="green"><h3 align="center">Today's
Objectives</h3></td></tr>

</thead>

...
```

This places 10 pixels between the content of the cell and the cell wall.

| **3** | Save the changes to the text file and refresh the document in the browser. |

FIGURE 5.34

| **4** | Leave the file open in both applications. |

To Extend Your Knowledge...

ADDING SPACERS

Some designers use transparent images called *spacers* to expand cells to a specific size. Spacers are transparent, so the viewer cannot see them on the Web page. Spacers are usually 1 pixel in width, so they separate cells by 1 pixel; they are often much longer in height than width.

As you become more comfortable working with tables in your Web page layouts, you'll work with transparent spacers to create precise layouts and apply exact spacing to achieve a desired result.

LESSON 8 Nested Tables

Although using tables for advanced layout techniques (such as mortised Web pages) is not within the scope of this book, it is necessary to discuss *nested tables* (one table is contained within another). Nesting one or two tables within a larger table is rather simple; but the idea behind *mortised Web pages* is to use many tables to piece together images and other elements that would be impossible using other XHTML features. Mortised Web pages are usually created in a Web editor; simple nested tables, however, can be hand-coded in XHTML.

Consider the following example of a simple nested table:

```
<table>
 <tr>
  <td>
   <table>
    <tr>
     <td>


     </td>
    </tr>
   </table>
  </td>
 </tr>
</table>
```

Nest a Table

1   With table.htm active in the text editor, add a table to the Notes section.

```
...
</thead>
<tbody>
<tr><td rowspan="5" valign="top" bgcolor="gray">
<table>
    <tr><td>Notes:</td></tr>
    <tr><td>1. </td><tr>
    <tr><td>2. </td><tr>
    <tr><td>3. </td><tr>
    <tr><td>4. </td><tr>
    <tr><td>5. </td><tr>
    <tr><td>6. </td><tr>
</table>
```

```
</td></tr>

    <tr>

        <th height="75">Call List</th>

        <th>To Do </th>

        <th>Groceries</th>

    </tr>

...
```

2   **Save the changes to the text file and refresh the document in the browser.**

The table displays with the nested table in the Notes section. You can format nested tables in a wide variety of ways. Remember to plan the display of your content prior to coding the table/s to save time and (possible) errors.

FIGURE 5.35

3   **Close the file in both applications.**

To Extend Your Knowledge...

TABLES AND POSITIONING

Before tables became the norm on the Web, very few page-layout options were available. Tables allow designers to turn a page into a literal grid in which they can puzzle together a professional-looking design and apply precise positioning.

Using mortised design techniques has become a very popular strategy for many Web designers. CSS also offers advanced positioning; but as CSS is not as well supported as tables, designers opt for using tables.

SUMMARY

In Project 5, you learned that tables allow Web page authors to vertically align content on a Web page. Before the use of tables, authors could place text and images horizontally, but they had little control over vertical placement; at most, authors could control vertical alignment of images using the **align=""** attribute.

You learned how to create basic data tables to arrange text in easy-to-read tabular format. You also learned to expand rows and columns to create customized tables. You learned how to format tables using borders, border sizes, background colors, cellspacing, and cellpadding. You discovered that you can merge two or more tables to create a nested table, which offers increased flexibility and control over the display of the content.

KEY TERMS

Background color	Monospaced font	Table
Cell	Nested table	Table definition tag
Cellpadding	<pre> tag	Table row tag
Cellspacing	Row	Tabular format
Column	Row span	<table> tag
Column span	Spacer	

CHECKING CONCEPTS AND TERMS

MULTIPLE CHOICE

Circle the letter that matches the correct answer for each of the following questions.

1. Why are tables useful?
   a. They provide a way to display content vertically.
   b. You can organize data in tabular format.
   c. You can design page layouts that would be impossible with other XHTML elements.
   d. All of the above.

2. What basic tags create a table?
   a. <table> tag only
   b. <table>, <tr>, and <td> tags
   c. <tr> and <td> tags

3. A table row is defined by the <td> tag.
   a. True
   b. False

4. What tag do you use to create the table header?
   a. <td>
   b. <tr>
   c. <th>
   d. None of the above.

5. The default width of the table is determined by the content of the table.
   a. True
   b. False

6. What element is used to expand a row?

   a. colspan

   b. rowspan

   c. merge

   d. None of the above.

7. You can specify the height and width of a table using exact pixels or percentages.

   a. True

   b. False

8. You can align data in a table and you can align the table itself.

   a. True

   b. False

9. To change the space between cells, you can use the _____.

   a. cellspacing attribute

   b. cellpadding attribute

   c. non-breaking space element

   d. You cannot change the spacing.

10. Why are footers and headers beneficial?

   a. They make the page load faster.

   b. They load the appropriate information in order.

   c. They provide important information about the table.

   d. None of the above.

DISCUSSION QUESTIONS

1. What are some of the most common uses of tables on Web pages today, and why?

2. Why did tables become so popular?

3. Why is it important to use CSS to format your tables, rather than use XHTML elements?

SKILL DRILL

Skill Drills reinforce project skills. Each skill reinforced is the same, or nearly the same, as a skill presented in the lessons. Detailed instructions are provided in a step-by-step format. You should complete these exercises in the order provided.

1. Create a Table

1. Open template.htm from your WIP_01 folder. Save it as "skilltable.htm" in your WIP_05 folder.

2. Create a basic table using the **<table>** tags.

3. Add a table header row that spans two columns and contains the text "Student Grade".

4. Create a second row with two cells. Add the content "Name" to the first cell, and add "Pass/Fail" to the second cell.

5. Create 5 more rows with 2 cells in each row, as follows:

```
<table>
    <tr>
      <td width="100%" colspan="2">
Student Grade
</td>
    </tr>
    <tr>
      <td>Name</td>
      <td>Pass/Fail</td>
    </tr>
    <tr>
      <td></td>
      <td></td>
    </tr>
    <tr>
      <td></td>
      <td></td>
    </tr>
    <tr>
      <td></td>
      <td</td>
    </tr>
    <tr>
      <td></td>
      <td></td>
    </tr>
    <tr>
      <td></td>
      <td></td>
    </tr>
  </table>
```

6. Create a final row that spans across two cells and contains the text "Spring Semester". Center-align Spring Semester and apply bold styling.

7. Add a border to the table. Set the size to 1.

8. Set the table's width to 75% of the screen size.

9. Save the changes to the text file. Open the document in your browser and view the result.

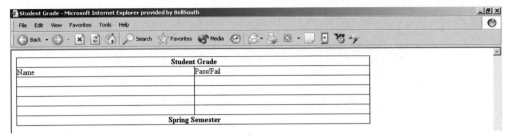

FIGURE 5.36

10. Leave the file open for the next exercise.

2. Change the Table Display and Alignment

1. In the open document, align the table in the center of the browser window.

2. Center-align the cells that contain Name and Pass/Fail.

3. Center-align the content in the empty cells beneath the table headers.

4. Save the changes to the text file. Refresh the document in the browser and view the result.

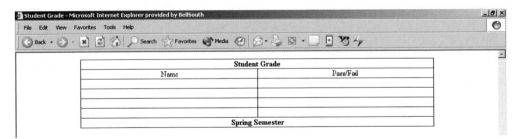

FIGURE 5.37

5. Leave the file open for the next exercise.

3. Add Headers, Footers, and Body

1. In the open document, contain the header cell within the **<thead>** tags.

2. Contain the body of the table within the **<tbody>** tags.

3. Contain the footer of the table within the **<tfoot>** tags.

4. Save the changes to the text file. Refresh the document in the browser.

5. Leave the file open for the next exercise.

4. Format the Table's Color

1. In the open file, change the background color of the entire table to Gray.

2. Change the table header's background color to Black.

3. Format the font inside the header cell to White.

4. Change the border color of the table to Dark Gray.

5. Save the changes to the text file. Refresh the document in the browser and view the result.

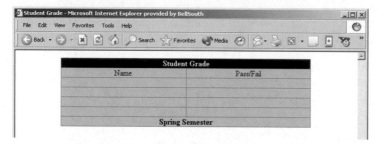

FIGURE 5.38

6. Close the file in both applications.

CHALLENGE

Challenge exercises expand on, or are somewhat related to, skills presented in the lessons. Each exercise provides a brief introduction, followed by instructions presented in a numbered-step format that are not as detailed as those in the Skill Drill exercises. You should complete these Challenge exercises in the order provided.

1. Create a Simple Page Layout

You know how to create a basic table. You want to use your knowledge to create a page layout that includes tables. You decide to create an ad about an online XHTML course that includes tables, formatted text, and images.

1. Copy the content of the Project_05 folder into the WIP_05 folder.

2. Create a new hypertext document with the appropriate document tags. Save it as "course.htm" in your WIP_05 folder.

3. Create a table that displays 3 rows.

4. Set the table to center-align, with no borders, and is 80% of the screen size.

5. Expand the top and bottom rows.

6. Open the text file named project5content.txt.

7. Copy the text beneath the Top Row section of the text file into the first row of the table.

8. Copy the text beneath the Bottom Row section of the text file into the last row of the table.

9. Save the changes to the file. Open the document in your browser and view the result.

10. Leave the file open for the next exercise.

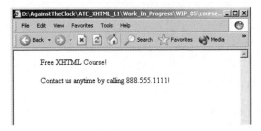

FIGURE 5.39

2. Nest Tables

Your next task is to add additional course information in tabular format. Create a nested table in the left cell, and position the data into columns and rows. (In the next exercise, you add an image that aligns to right of the text; positioning the table to the left will not affect the location of the image.)

1. In the open document, position your cursor in the first cell of the second row.

2. Create a table within this cell that has 2 columns and 3 rows.

3. Add a header that spans across the table.

4. Add the text "Take the Online Course and Learn:" in the header row.

5. In the second row, add the following items (one item per cell): "XHTML 1.0", "Browser Support", and "Web Server".

6. In the third row, add the following items (one item per cell): "CSS Basics", "Intro to Images", and "and More!".

7. Center-align the table within the cell. Make sure no border displays.

8. Leave the file open for the next exercise.

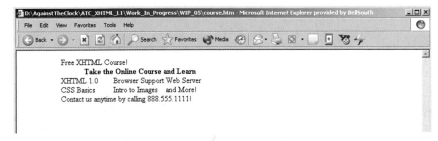

FIGURE 5.40

3. Create an Image Layout

An image will liven up this rather lackluster Web page. Positioning an image on the right of the text will fill in a lot of the extra white space, and create a more balanced design.

1. In the open document, position your cursor in the second row of the main table.

2. Create a nested table with two rows and two columns.

3. In the first cell of the nested table, insert ad1.gif.

4. Insert ad2.gif in the cell next to ad1.gif.

5. Move down to the first cell in the third row and insert ad3.gif.

6. Insert ad4.gif in the cell next to ad3.gif.

7. Link all four images to the Against The Clock Web site, www.againsttheclock.com. Make sure you remove any borders from the images.

   Against The Clock's Web site is used only as an example site for the links.

8. Leave the document open for the next exercise.

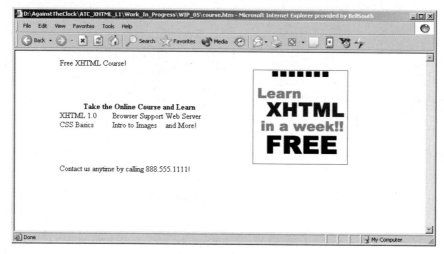

FIGURE 5.41

4. Format Table Data

The final step is to format the text. You can change the default text and add some background color to parts of the table. You can also format other elements in the table by containing the content within format tags.

1. In the open document, change the heading of the table to a suitable color, font, and text size.

2. Add your email address in the last row.

3. Format the background color of the header row. Use any color you prefer.

4. Change the font style throughout the document to any font you prefer.

5. In the main table, second row, second cell (the one that contains the image table), change the cell's width to 210 pixels.

6. Change the alignment of all the cells' contents, however you prefer.

7. Save the changes in the text file. Refresh the document in your browser and view the result.

8. Close the file in both applications.

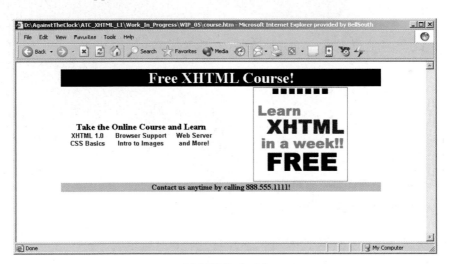

FIGURE 5.42

PORTFOLIO BUILDER

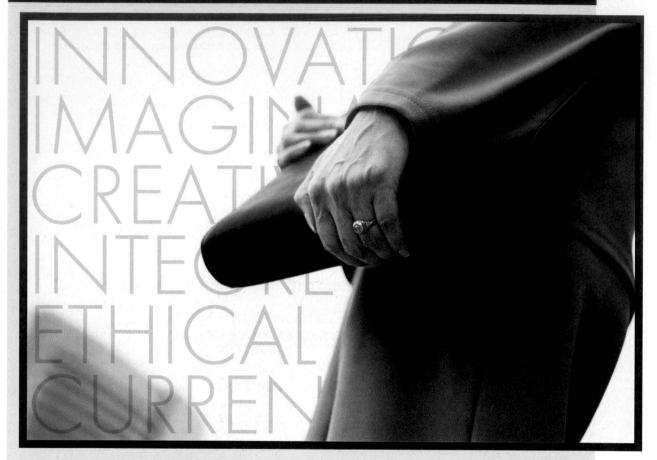

Create a Sports Schedule

A local sports club hired you as a Web design consultant. The club's manager wants an online sports schedule that features the next season of professional football games. The club hired you to create a Web page that offers next season's schedule in tabular format. They want you to maintain the scoring of each game. To complete this exercise, you should do the following:

- Log on to the National Football League's Web site at http://www.nfl.com/.

- View their schedule and scoring information. Decide how you can create a Web page layout (using tables) that will allow you to display this information in an easy-to-read format. Consider future updates while you design the site.

- Identify which teams are playing, where, and when. In addition, you might want to include empty cells for future scoring information for a particular game.

- When you create the Web page, consider the table's formatting. Think of creative ways to format, such as using team colors when supplying information about a particular team. You can also link to a team's official Web site.

Creating XHTML Forms

OBJECTIVES

In this project, you learn how to

- Create a basic form

- Work with form data

- Submit forms

- Create text and password fields

- Insert radio buttons and check boxes

- Include selection menus

- Generate multi-line text areas

- Incorporate hidden fields

- Produce form buttons

WHY WOULD I DO THIS?

Site designers willingly spend considerable time and effort on the presentation of information *to* their viewers; but they often overlook the benefits of acquiring information *from* viewers. As the Web is an interactive medium, it can be used as a tool to collect significant amounts of data, on a variety of topics, from all types of users.

Obtaining information from users is important for a number of reasons:

- You can monitor users' behavior on your sites, and interact with their actions and preferences. These interactions can be subtle, such as customizing the information that is presented to a particular user, based on what he looked at previously. This customized information can be presented dynamically.

- Interactions can also be more overt, such as surveys about users' tastes and interests.

- E-commerce is a practical reason to collect information. How else can you know the types of products and services your users want to order? You could probably acquire some information with hyperlinks, but that wouldn't help you safely obtain credit card information for users' purchases.

- Internet would be impossible if users couldn't indicate the topics of their searches.

In this project, you learn how to create forms for your Web pages, which allow you to collect useful information from your viewers, and ultimately use that information to enhance the content on your sites.

V I S U A L   S U M M A R Y

The purpose of an *online form* is to acquire information from the user and send it to the server. The server can then perform a variety of actions with the information (or store it in a database for retrieval later). The information is then processed using server-side applications or scripts, the most popular being CGI scripts. (Advanced scripts, such as CGI, are outside the scope of this book. A wealth of information on scripts is available on the Web.)

Forms can contain many different types of input fields, including text boxes and drop-down menus. In Figure 6.1, you see a basic form with input fields that collect and submit user data. Certain types of input fields are more appropriate in one situation than another. You explore a number of these input options in this project.

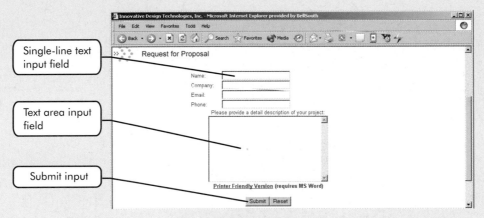

FIGURE 6.1

Standard forms, similar to the one shown above, are created using XHTML or HTML. CSS, however, provides additional control over the presentation of forms because it allows you to change the field colors, background colors, and so forth, as shown below.

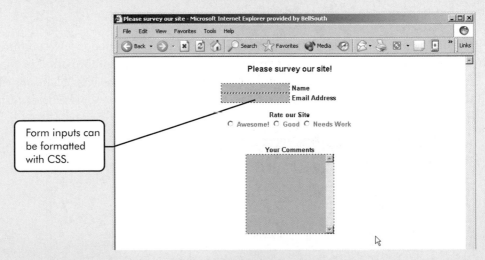

FIGURE 6.2

LESSON 1 Creating a Basic Form

A form consists of a **<form>** tag with one or more input tags. The **<form>** tags tell the browser where a form begins and ends. The "on" **<form>** tag also contains useful information, such as where the form data will be sent, how the form data is submitted, and the name of the form.

The *input fields* (also called input types) can be designed as text boxes ("text") or submit buttons ("submit"). An input tag can also have a name attribute, which helps the server identify the information when it is submitted by the browser. For example, if you were building a form that asked for a user's telephone number, you might use **name="phone"** to tell the server exactly what it is receiving.

The following code is the basic format for a form that includes a text field:

```
<form>

Enter your information here:

<input type="text" name="myTextField" />

</form>
```

This code would produce a simple Web page, as shown below.

FIGURE 6.3

Unlike a typical Web form, there is no submit button in this example; because there is only one text box, the user can press Enter/Return to submit this form. Many viewers would not realize that they could press the Enter/Return key to submit their input, so it's best to include a submit button on every form you create. You learn more about buttons throughout this project.

The example form in the previous illustration does not include any other instructions; so submitting the form simply returns the browser to the same page. When you submit the form, the information in the text field is added to the URL (the Address or Location field of the browser). In this case, the text "blah" was entered in the text field, and then the Enter/Return key was pressed. This placed "blah" in the Address field, as shown below.

FIGURE 6.4

The text "blah" displays in the Address field.

FIGURE 6.5

In a real-world scenario, you would use a Web server combined with other scripting technologies to perform some sort of action with the form data. We cannot provide a server for you to work with, but we provide a script that allows you to see the form in action.

Create the Form

1 **Copy the content of your Project_06 folder to your WIP_06 folder.**

2 **Open forms.htm in a text editor and in a Web browser.**

The source code shows the basic document tags.

3 **In the text editor, position your cursor beneath the `<body>` tag, and enter the `<form>` tags, as follows:**

```
<html>

<head><title>Form Test Page</title></head>

<body>

<form>

    <input />

</form>

</body>

</html>
```

The **`<form>`** tags tell the browser where to expect the form to start and end. The input fields for each form you include on a Web page must be placed within the **`<form>`** tags. Note that the input field is an empty tag.

4   Save the change to the text file and refresh the document in the browser.

FIGURE 6.6

The form displays a single input field in the browser. The input's type is not yet defined; you have not described the input field as a text field or check box. You learn more about defining the types of inputs you can use with forms later in the project.

5   Return to the text file. Include a name for the input field, as follows:

```
<html>

<head><title>Form Test Page</title></head>

<body>

<form>

    <input name="welcome" />

</form>

</body>

</html>
```

6   Save the change to the text file and refresh the document in the browser.

There are no changes to the input field; the document looks the same as before. The idea behind including the **name=""** attribute is to identify the field so you can easily transfer its content later.

7   Click your cursor in the input field. Type "Hello World".

FIGURE 6.7

8   **Press the Enter/Return key.**

Nothing happens to the page; however, "Hello World" displays in the Address field.

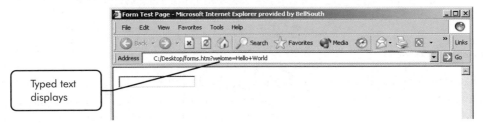

Typed text displays

FIGURE 6.8

9   **Close the file in both applications.**

To Extend Your Knowledge...

THE NEXT GENERATION OF WEB FORMS

The W3C recommends the new XForms model as an XML application and a replacement for standard HTML/XHTML forms. **XForms** offer everything that HTML/XHTML forms offer — plus a lot more. Currently, XForms is at version 1.0. Although XForms is not within the scope of this book, we recommend that you visit www.w3c.org to find out more about this new technology.

You will find that using XHTML in combination with CSS allows additional control over form display than using XHTML alone. You must decide which technology is more suitable for the project at hand — XHTML and CSS, or XForms.

LESSON 2   Form Data

Form data is the information that the user types into the form fields. Once the user types information into a simple form (that does not contain submission instructions) and presses Enter/Return, the information in the Address/Location field in the browser changes; it displays the file path and the information that was submitted with the form.

For example, in the preceding exercise, the URL in the Address/Location field includes a question mark toward the end of the line. The question mark tells the server that what follows is data. The data could be one piece of information or multiple pieces. In either case, the data is sent as a name-value pair to a specified location, such as a database on a server. Remember that a name-value pair is a combination of two elements: a name, which identifies the information; and a value, which is the information itself.

All form information is submitted in name-value pair format. The browser strips the data from the name-value pair and attaches it to the URL. If our sample form were on an actual Web server, the URL might be:

```
http://www.againsttheclock.com/login.htm?username=Nick
```

This data could be extracted from the URL and used in some way, such as displaying the form results to the user. To retrieve the data, however, you need to use a script. In addition, if you want to send the user to another location, you must specify that, as well. As you work through this project, you learn how to accomplish all of these operations.

The Form Action

Our sample page isn't very useful yet, since it doesn't actually do anything. What you need to do next is create a page to receive your information, once it has been sent by the browser. The receiving page is called the *form action*, because sending the information to the receiving page is the "act" the browser performs with the information.

The action is used with a relative or absolute URL in the **action=""** attribute of the form element, such as in the following form:

```
<form action="myFormAction.asp">

   Enter your information here:

   <input type="text" name="myTextField" />

</form>
```

In this case, when you submit the form, the browser would try to open the URL

```
file:///<yourpathhere>/myFormAction.asp?myTextField=myinfo
```

In almost every case, this URL represents some sort of program, such as an Active Server Page (which uses the file extension .asp) or a CGI script. The Web server executes the program and usually performs an action, such as processing an order or adding user information to a database, and then returns an HTML page to the browser.

Creating Active Server Pages and CGI scripts are separate disciplines; entire books are dedicated to the subjects. Some ISPs provide their own CGI scripts to serve these functions, and require that you use their scripts. You can talk with your ISP about their policies and what scripts they provide, if any. Other service providers allow you to add scripts that you create yourself, or download from resources such as:

```
www.cgiforme.com/

www.cgiscripts.net/

www.worldwidemart.com/scripts/
```

Since we don't have the luxury of using a Web server with this book, the script we provide executes and displays the values you type in the form. The script shows you these values in the URL in the Address/Location field. Any URL can be used as the action of a form, and the browser takes over from there.

Add the Action Attribute

1   **From the WIP_06 folder, open login.htm in a text editor and browser.**

The code displays with a script tag and the necessary attribute to call an outside script for the form processing. Working with advanced scripts is outside the scope of this book. We use this particular script to illustrate form action.

2   **Add an action to the form that calls on a script to process the data.**

```
<html>

<head><title>Form Test Page</title></head>

<body>

<script src="scriptvalues.js" language="Javascript"
type="text/javascript"></script>

<h2>Please Log In</h2>

<form action="login_action.htm">

    <input name="username" />

</form>

</body>

</html>
```

3   **Save the file in the text editor and refresh your browser.**

FIGURE 6.9

You don't see a change, but the browser does.

4   **In the browser window, type any text into the text field, and then press Enter/Return.**

FIGURE 6.10

Notice that the browser goes to login_action.htm, which you specified as the form's action in Step 2. While you did receive messages telling you that the username and password were incorrect, that's not important right now. The important point is the URL; notice that it's not login.htm anymore — it's login_action.htm. The script processed the data it obtained from the form's input field, and then displayed the result on the next page.

5   **Leave the file open in both windows.**

To Extend Your Knowledge...

A PLETHORA OF METHODS FOR PROCESSING FORMS

The examples provided in this project for data collection and form processing are just a few of the many ways you can work with forms. A number of technologies are available to you, from advanced programming languages to the mail protocol.

As you continue to increase your abilities in creating forms, keep in mind the myriad options available to you.

LESSON 3   Text Inputs

As you now know, you can create a form that submits information to a URL that is designated as the form action. You also know that you must use name-value pairs because only inputs that have names are submitted to the form action. Next, let's examine the variety of input types that allow you to create powerful forms.

Text input is the most familiar type of form input. You used a text input form — a text box — in the previous exercise. A ***text input*** is a single-line option that allows users to enter alphanumeric text (letters and numbers).

You have some control over these text fields. Using attributes, you can control the size of the field, the number of characters the user can type into it, and the values that you want the field to contain when the page first loads. For example, you can make our sample form load with an initial value that includes explanatory text. You can also set the size of the field (`size=""`) to 15 characters, and the maximum number of characters that the user can type (`maxlength=""`) to 30, as shown below.

```
<form action="myFormAction.asp">

   Enter your information here:

 <input type="text" name="myTextField" value="your name here" size="15"
maxlength="30" />

</form>
```

The above code results in the following page.

FIGURE 6.11

You can provide an initial value by adding the **value=""** attribute to your input tag. The copy between the quote marks displays when the page is loaded, as shown in the previous illustration.

As its name suggests, this copy is only the initial value. When the user types his information into the box, the new copy replaces the original (initial value) text.

Add Text Fields

1 **In the open document, return to the text editor. Make the input a text box, add explanatory text, set the size, change the page title, and add WIP_06>images>soaplogo.jpg as the top image, as follows:**

```
<head><title>SoapToShawls.com Administration Suite</title></head>

<body>

<script src="scriptvalues.js" language="Javascript"
type="text/javascript"></script>

<img height="133" width="246" src="images/soaplogo.jpg" alt="Logo" />

<br />

<center>

<h2>Please Log In</h2>

<form action="login_action.htm">

    Please enter your username: <input type="text" size="20"
name="username" />

</form>

</center>

</body>

</html>
```

This changes the page considerably. A more descriptive title displays, the image logo offers more appeal to the page, and a text input box is included to collect a username from a viewer.

2   **Save the file in the text editor and refresh your browser.**

Click your browser's Back button or reload login.htm if login_action.htm is still open.

FIGURE 6.12

The text box is now somewhat smaller than before.

3   **Type some words in the box.**

If you type more than 20 characters, the text scrolls to the left, but allows you to continue to type.

4   **Press Enter/Return to submit the form.**

5   **Look at the URL in the Address/Location field.**

All of your text was submitted.

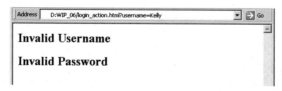

FIGURE 6.13

The page tells you that this information is invalid. This happened because the script that is processing your data is looking for a specific username and password — which you have not yet supplied.

6   **Leave the file open in both windows.**

Limit the Number of Characters

Although you can set the number of characters that display in a text field, it doesn't control the amount of text that can be submitted. While this is not generally a problem, programmers often need to limit the amount of text that is returned. For instance, the text may be destined for a database that allows only a certain number of characters. You can use the **maxlength=""** attribute to control the number of characters entered.

1 In the open file, set the maximum number of characters in the text box to 10.

```
...

<form action="login_action.htm">

    Please enter your username: <input type="text" size="20"
name="username" maxlength="10" />

</form>

...
```

2 Save the file in the text editor and refresh your browser. Type 12 characters in the text box in the browser.

While there appears to be room in the box, the browser allows you to type only 10 characters.

FIGURE 6.14

You cannot go beyond the limit defined in the **maxlength=""** attribute. In addition to assigning a maximum number of characters to text fields, you can also establish an initial value.

3 Use the **value=""** attribute to add explanatory text to the text box. Change the maximum length to allow for all of the text, which in this case is 20.

```
...

<center>

<h2>Please Log In</h2>

<form action="login_action.htm">

    Please enter your username: <input type="text" size="20"
name="username" maxlength="20" value="Enter Your Userid" />

</form>

</center>

</body>

</html>
```

4   **Save the file and refresh the browser.**

The text you typed as the value appears in the text box.

FIGURE 6.15

You specified this initial value by adding the **value=""** attribute to your input tag. The copy between the quote marks displays when the page is loaded, as shown in the previous example. When the user types her information into the box, the new copy replaces the original (initial value) text.

5   **Leave the file open in both windows.**

To Extend Your Knowledge...

FORM SUBMISSION OPTIONS

Before scripting languages became popular, there were very few options for form submission. If you used a scripting language such as CGI, it could have been costly, too, depending on your hosting account.

One option that was often used to submit forms without an advanced script (and is still used today) is the mailto: command. The mailto: command was used with the **action=""** attribute with an email address as the value. For example:

<form action="mailto:name@domain.com">

When the user submitted the form, the result from the name-value pair was sent to the address via the mail protocol. This method was not perfect — the data was sent unsecured, and it was difficult to read once retrieved. In addition, the mailto method offered less flexibility to perform other actions on the data.

LESSON 4 Passwords

In addition to taking login information, online forms can also take the user's password. The difficulty in acquiring a user's password is the need to hide the information from onlookers to ensure the security of the user's account. For example, ATM machines do not display password text; instead, the text is replaced with placeholder characters. You can do the same with password input on an online form.

Password input is similar to text input, with one exception: the characters that the user types display as asterisks or bullets (depending on the user's browser and operating system), rather than actual text characters. For example, you can change the sample form to use password input instead of text input, as follows:

```
<form action="myFormAction.asp">

Enter your information here:

<input type="password" name="myTextField" value="your name here" size="20"
maxlength="30" />

</form>
```

When you use this code, the browser obscures the initial value, as well as anything that the user types, as shown in Figure 6.16.

FIGURE 6.16

If you submit this form, however, the URL shows the flaw in this plan.

```
file:///<your path here>/myFormAction.asp?myTextField=mysecretinfo
```

As you can see, password boxes don't really encrypt the information — they just hide it from someone who may be watching the user as he types. If the above sample form were submitted, the password would be visible to anyone who knew where to look (in the URL field). Later in this project, you learn how to resolve this particular problem. For now, however, remember that information is not necessarily secure just because it's in a password box.

Adding a Submit Button

A second complication that arises when adding a password box to the login form is unrelated to security: How do you submit information when you have multiple information fields on your form? Up to now, you pressed the Enter/Return key to submit the sample form. This method worked perfectly because there was only one text box in the form. Now that you have multiple information fields on your form, however, that method no longer works properly. You need another way to submit the form — you need to add a submit button.

A *submit button* is just another type of input, which is coded as follows:

```
<input type="submit" />
```

The submit button displays on your Web page with the words Submit Query, as shown below.

FIGURE 6.17

The browser interprets this as a form button that, when clicked, submits the form. You work with submit buttons in detail later in the project.

Create a Password Field

1   **In the open login.htm file, add a password input box that is 20 characters wide.**

```
...

Please enter your username: <input type="text" size="20" name="username"
maxlength="20" value="Enter Your Userid" />

<br />

    Please enter your password: <input type="password" size="20"
name="password" />

<br />

</form>

...
```

2   **Beneath the password field, place a submit button.**

```
...

Please enter your username: <input type="text" size="20" name="username"
maxlength="20" value="Enter Your Userid" />

<br />

    Please enter your password: <input type="password" size="20"
name="password" /><br />

<input type="submit" />

</form>

...
```

3   Save the changes to the text file and refresh the document in the browser.

FIGURE 6.18

The form displays what seems to be a basic text field and a submit button. Notice that you used the line break tag to force the button down to the next line. Similar to any other XHTML element, you can control the display of form elements on the page.

4   Type random letters in the password box in the browser window.

FIGURE 6.19

Rather than the actual characters you type, bullets or asterisks display in the text field. This leads you to believe the information is secure — but don't be fooled.

5   Type the username "sandra" and password "bunnies", and then click the Submit Query button to submit the form. Look at the URL in the Address/Location field.

FIGURE 6.20

The username and password display in the browser's Address field.

6   Save your changes and close the file.

LESSON 5   Radio Buttons and Check Boxes

A typical online form that you have probably seen many times is the order form. An online *order form* allows a user to buy (order) items from a Web site, usually on a secure server. A *secure server* ensures that any information it receives, as well as any information it sends, is encrypted so others cannot steal (hack) the information.

The most familiar type of input field on an order form is the *radio button*. Radio buttons are also known as *radio groups* because, in most cases, they're only useful when there's more than one option from which to choose. Use radio buttons when you want to allow users to choose from several options, but make only one selection at any given time.

For example, we can use a radio group ("radio") on our sample form, as follows:

```
<form action="myFormAction.asp">
  What is your choice?
  <br />
  <input type="radio" name="choice" value="Y" checked="checked">Yes
  <input type="radio" name="choice" value="N">No
  <input type="radio" name="choice" value="M">Maybe
  <br />
  <input type="submit" />
</form>
```

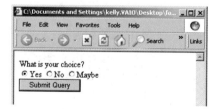

FIGURE 6.21

There are a couple of points to notice about radio groups. Contrary to what you might think, radio buttons are not grouped according to where they are located on the page. Radio buttons in different areas of the page can be grouped together by assigning the same name to each of the buttons. Notice that all three of the buttons in the sample code have the same name — which is what defines a radio group. Buttons in a different group have a different name.

In a button group, one button is denoted as "checked." The reason for the strange notation (**checked="checked"**) is because in older versions of HTML, you simply included the word "checked" to designate which button was selected by default. With the advent of XHTML, however, all attributes must have an assigned value.

Clicking another button selects it and deselects the previous button. This means that you must make a selection in a radio group — the default button remains selected if you don't select another button. You can be certain that a value will be submitted — as long as you make sure that a value is selected initially. (If not, the user may submit the form without making a choice, which defeats the purpose of a radio group.)

The last point to remember about radio groups is that the value submitted is the data in the value attribute, not the text next to the radio button. For example, if the user were to submit our sample form as is, the value passed would be "Y", not "Yes".

Check Boxes

Check boxes are often used to indicate something to which the user must agree, or a group of items from which the user must choose. Check boxes ("checkbox") are similar to radio groups — if they aren't clicked, their values are not submitted. The difference is that check boxes can provide several different values for the same name; the user can select more than one choice without removing the check from the previous choice.

You can change your sample radio buttons to check boxes, as follows:

```
<form action="myFormAction.asp">
  What is your choice?
  <br />
  <input type="checkbox" name="choice" value="Y" checked="checked">Yes
  <input type="checkbox" name="choice" value="N">No
  <input type="checkbox" name="choice" value="M">Maybe
  <br />
  <input type="submit" />
</form>
```

This changes your form slightly, as shown in Figure 6.22.

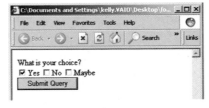

FIGURE 6.22

The primary differences between check boxes and radio buttons are that check boxes can be left completely unselected, and more than one check box can be selected at one time.

Create Radio Buttons

1   Open WIP_06>order.htm in the text editor and browser.

2   In the text editor, add three radio buttons named "shipping" to the Shipping Methods section, and add three radio buttons named "card_type" to the Credit Card Type section. Add the appropriate values, as follows:

```
...
<b>Shipping Method:</b>
<input type="radio" value="1" name="shipping" checked="checked" />
Overnight    
<input type="radio" value="2" name="shipping" />
Second Day    
<input type="radio" value="3" name="shipping" />
Standard Mail
<br /><br />
<b>Credit Card Type:  </b>
<input type="radio" value="1" name="card_type" />
American Express    
<input type="radio" value="2" name="card_type" />
Mastercard    
<input type="radio" value="3" name="card_type" />
Visa    
<br /><br />
...
```

3 Save the file and refresh the browser.

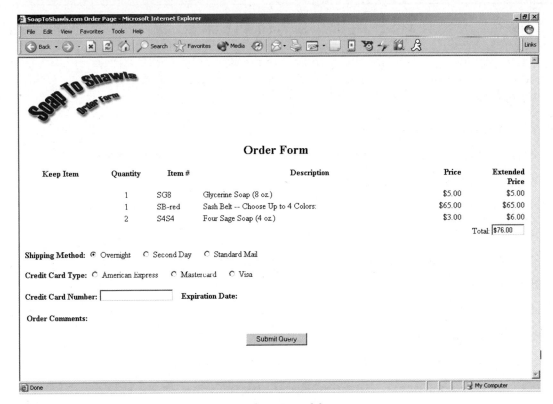

FIGURE 6.23

You have two groups of buttons, but only one of them has values.

4 Submit the form exactly as it is, and look at the values that are passed.

While the value for the selected button was passed, no value was passed for card_type, because none was selected.

Remember that radio buttons are grouped according to their name, not where they are located on the page. Radio buttons in different areas of the page can be grouped together by assigning the same name to each of the buttons.

5 Leave the file open in both windows.

Check the Radio Groups

1   In the open order.htm file, swap the names of one of the shipping buttons and one of the card_type buttons.

```
...
<br />
<b>Shipping Method:</b>
<input type="radio" value="1" name="shipping" checked="checked" />
Overnight    
<input type="radio" value="2" name="card_type" />
Second Day    
<input type="radio" value="3" name="shipping" />
Standard Mail
<br /><br />
<b>Credit Card Type:  </b>
<input type="radio" value="1" name="card_type" />
American Express    
<input type="radio" value="2" name="shipping" />
Mastercard    
<input type="radio" value="3" name="card_type" />
Visa    
<br /><br />
<b>Credit Card Number: </b> <input type="text" name="ccnumber" />
   
...
```

2 Save the file in the text editor and refresh your browser. Experiment with the two groups of buttons.

FIGURE 6.24

At one moment, one button may be selected in each of the two rows; at the next moment, two buttons may be selected in one row and none in the other row. This is due to the changes you made to the button groups.

3 Undo the last change in the text editor so each button belongs to the proper group.

4 Leave the file open in both windows.

To Extend Your Knowledge...

TABBING THROUGH FORMS

You can enable your visitors to tab through your form fields simply by adding `tabindex=""` to your input tags, as follows:

<input type="text" name="name" size="20" maxlength="30" tabindex="1" />

The above example shows that the user tabs to a text box the first time he presses the Tab key.

The `tabindex=""` value determines the order you tab through text boxes and other fields on the Web page. If you want the tab order to skip a field, use a negative value beginning with "-1," then "-2," and so on. Each negative value is bypassed when the user tabs through your form.

Add Check Boxes

1   **In the open order.htm file, add a check box name item for each of the three products in the table at the top of the page.**

```
...

<tr>

        <th>Keep Item</th><th>Quantity</th>

        <th>Item #</th><th>Description</th><th>Price</th>

        <th>Extended<br />Price</th>

</tr>

<tr>

        <td><input type="checkbox" name="item" value="SG8"
checked="checked" /></td><td>1</td><td>SG8</td>

        <td>Glycerine Soap (8 oz.)</td><td>$5.00</td><td>$5.00</td>

</tr>

<tr>

        <td><input type="checkbox" name="item" value="SB"
checked="checked" /></td><td>1</td><td>SB-red</td>

        <td valign="top" >Sash Belt — Choose Up to 4 Colors</td>

        <td>$65.00</td><td>$65.00</td>

</tr>

<tr>

        <td><input type="checkbox" name="item" value="S4S4"
checked="checked" /></td><td>2</td><td>S4S4</td>

        <td>Four Sage Soap (4 oz.)</td><td>$3.00</td><td>$6.00</td>

</tr>

...
```

2   Save the file and refresh the page in your browser.

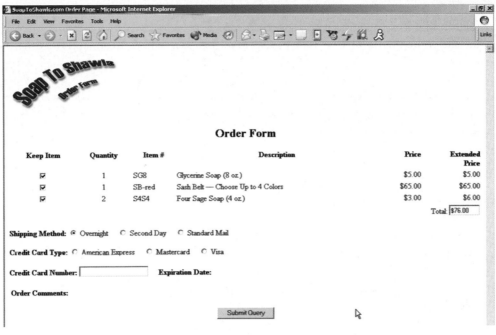

FIGURE 6.25

The check boxes appear at the start of each line, and all of them are checked.

3   Uncheck one of the boxes and submit the page.

FIGURE 6.26

The items that were checked were submitted, but the item that was unchecked was not submitted.

4   Leave the file open in both windows.

LESSON 6 Select Boxes

Select boxes (also known as pull-down menus, drop-down boxes, drag-down menus, or drop lists) are radio-button-and-check-box hybrids. One type of select box acts as a radio button, and the other type behaves as a check box.

A select box is not simply another type of input. Instead, it is a select element that contains one or more option elements. The traditional select box shows only one value at a time, and allows the user to select only one option (through the selected attribute or through user action). For example:

```
<form action="myFormAction.asp">

  What is your choice?

  <br />

  <select name="choice">

     <option value="Y" selected="selected">Yes</option>

     <option value="N">No</option>

     <option value="M">Maybe</option>

  </select>

  <br />

  <input type="submit" />

</form>
```

FIGURE 6.27

What you see in Figure 6.27 is a select box that consists of a **<select></select>** element that contains one or more **<option></option>** elements. The select box is the overall object, so that's where the name of the form belongs. The values, on the other hand, are contained in the **<option>** elements. A select box can have any number of options; but remember, users scroll only so far before giving up and moving to another page, so you should attempt to restrict your options to a reasonable number.

As with check boxes and radio buttons, the browser doesn't care about the label (the description of the field) for a particular option; the browser is only concerned with the value assigned to the option. To avoid potential problems, however, it is best to specify a value on each option, even if the value is the same as the label.

You can also set a size on the select box, which displays the number of options by default. For example:

```
<select name="choice" size="3">

</select>
```

With a select box, only one value can be submitted at a time, similar to a radio group. To make the select box act as a set of check boxes, you can add the **multiple=""** attribute. Similar to checked and selected, the **multiple=""** attribute used to be written without a value in HTML; but now, XHTML 1.0 requires that a value is included.

```
<form action="myFormAction.asp">
   What is your choice?
   <br />
<select name="choice" size="3" multiple="multiple">
     <option value="Y" selected="selected">Yes</option>
     <option value="N">No</option>
     <option value="M">Maybe</option>
   </select>
   <br />
   <input type="submit" />
</form>
```

FIGURE 6.28

The page looks the same in the browser, but now users can hold down the Shift key to choose more than one option, and hold down the Control key to select multiple adjacent options.

Add a Select Box

1   In the open order.htm file, add select boxes for the credit card expiration month and year.

```
...
<input type="radio" value="3" name="card_type" />
Visa    
<br /> <br />
<b>Credit Card Number: </b> <input type="text"
name="ccnumber" />   
<b>Expiration Date: </b>
<select name="exp_month">
<option value="1">January</option>
<option value="2">February</option>
<option value="3">March</option>
<option value="4">April</option>
<option value="5">May</option>
<option value="6">June</option>
<option value="7">July</option>
<option value="8">August</option>
<option value="9">September</option>
<option value="10">October</option>
<option value="11">November</option>
<option value="12">December</option>
</select>
/
<select name="exp_year">
<option value="2001">2001</option>
<option value="2002">2002</option>
<option value="2003">2003</option>
<option value="2004">2004</option>
</select>
<br /><br />
<table><tr><td valign="top"><b>Order Comments:
</b></td><td></td></tr></table>
...
```

? If you have problems...

In HTML, it was very common to leave the <option> tag open and to omit the value. Early browsers used the label in this case, but some newer browsers use the "index" of the choice. For instance, if the second choice is selected, it might pass the value "1." (Lists are *zero-based*, meaning that the first choice is the number "0.") To avoid potential misunderstandings and problems, you must specify a value on each option, even if it is the same as the label.

2   Save the file and refresh the browser.

FIGURE 6.29

The select boxes appear. Without a value designated as selected, the first value in the list is selected by default.

3   Leave the file open in both windows.

Add a Multiple-Choice Select List

A second type of select element is more of a list than a menu. This list, which looks the same as the select boxes above, allows users to select multiple values.

1   **In the open order.htm file, add the color select list to the Sash Belt item.**

```
...

<tr>

    <td><input type="checkbox" name="item" value="SB" checked="checked"
/></td><td>1</td><td>SB-red</td>

    <td valign="top" >Sash Belt — Choose Up to 4 Colors

    <br />

    <select name="colors" size="3" multiple="multiple">

    <option value="red">Red</option>

    <option value="blue">Blue</option>

    <option value="green">Green</option>

    <option value="black">Black</option>

    <option value="yellow">Yellow</option>

    <option value="purple">Purple</option>

    <option value="other">Other (add comments)</option>

    </select>

    </td><td>$65.00</td><td>$65.00</td>

</tr>

...
```

2   **Save the file and refresh the browser.**

FIGURE 6.30

Notice the select list. You created a select box, but by giving it a size attribute — even if you set the size to 1 — you tell the browser to render it as a list (with a scroll bar, if necessary), as shown here.

3   **Scroll through the values in the list and choose a few of them.**

Notice the multiple values for colors.

4   **Leave the file open in both windows.**

LESSON 7   Text Areas

Now that you have explored text inputs, you can work with a second type of text box: the *text area* ("textarea"), which is a multi-line text box. A text area is an excellent choice when you want to provide an area for free-form comments from users.

A text area allows users much more latitude in what they input. Instead of being limited to writing in a single one-line window, users can see all (or most) of what they type, depending on the size that the Web page author sets for the text area. The **\<textarea\>** tag includes attributes that indicate how many columns and rows it should take up on the page, but this doesn't limit the number of characters it can hold.

For example, you can add a **\<textarea\>** tag to your sample form, as follows:

```
<form action="myFormAction.asp">

   What is your choice?

   <br />

   <textarea cols="60" rows="5">

   The initial text for a textarea goes into the textarea element.

   </textarea>

   <br />

   <input type="submit" />

</form>
```

The following results are displayed in the Web browser.

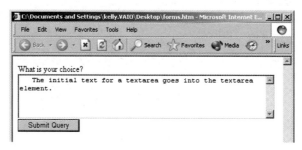

FIGURE 6.31

Not only did you retain the initial text, you retained the spaces at the beginning of the text, as well. Spaces and line feeds are preserved with this input option.

One issue with using text areas is that you cannot easily limit the number of characters that a user inputs. If the application executed by the form action has a size limitation, the data must be checked against that limit before being used. When too much data (a very large file) is passed to a Web server, the server may crash. You should discuss this issue with the system administrator for your Web server and plan accordingly. He may tell you there is a size limit on the data that can be safely sent to your server.

Add a Text Area

1 In the open order.htm file, add a text area for order comments, including some text to explain how to use the text area.

```
...

<table><tr><td valign="top"><b>Order Comments:   </b></td><td>

<textarea name="comments" rows="5" cols="40">

    Enter any comments here.

</textarea>

</td></tr></table>

...
```

2 Save the file and refresh the browser.

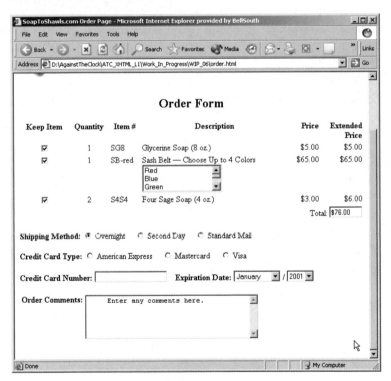

FIGURE 6.32

Notice the text area and its initial text.

3 Leave the file open in both windows.

To Extend Your Knowledge...

ASP

Active Server Pages (ASP) is another scripting language that programmers use to create Web pages. Similar to ColdFusion MX, ASP integrates with XHTML code, and affects a Web page in one way or another — such as sending data to a server for processing. ASP is a bit more difficult to learn than ColdFusion, but both languages were designed for the same purpose — to create Web pages/sites.

LESSON 8 Hidden Elements

We already discussed most of the visible elements on the page; but what if you want to include information on the form that the user doesn't need to see? It's not that the user shouldn't know this information — it's just that the information may not be relevant at that moment, and displaying it would only confuse the user and clutter the page. For example, you might want to:

- Include a session number that identifies this particular user, which you need on the script that processes the form.

- Include information about which pages this user already visited.

- Include information on which page the user visited immediately before coming to the form.

- Provide additional information about a product that would be required for packaging.

None of this information should be shown to the user, but it must be submitted with the rest of the information on the form. In these situations, you should use hidden fields. A *hidden field* ("hidden") is a type of input that doesn't actually appear on the page, but is submitted to the server with the form. For example:

```
<input type="hidden" name="myFieldName" value="myFieldValue" />
```

Hidden input fields allow you to include hidden data in a form for submission.

Add a Hidden Field

1   **In the open order.htm file, add the order number to a hidden field on the page.**

```
...
<h2 align="center">Order Form</h2>
<form action="order.htm">
<input type="hidden" name="order_id" value="1234" />
<table width="100%" border="0">
...
```

2   **Save the file in the text editor and refresh your browser.**

There should be no change in how the page appears in the browser.

3   **Submit the page.**

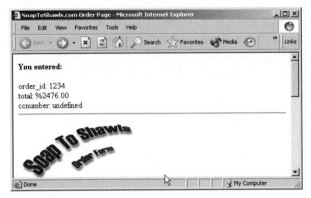

FIGURE 6.33

Notice that the hidden field was also submitted.

4   **Leave the file open in both windows.**

To Extend Your Knowledge...

HIDDEN FIELDS

Not only is the so-called "hidden" field submitted with the page, it is also in plain view in the URL. As with passwords, hidden fields are a convenience, but they are not substitutes for security.

One of the most common security errors made on the Web today is leaving sensitive or important information in hidden fields. Information in hidden fields is visible to anyone who chooses "View Source" on the page. It would be a simple matter for an experienced programmer to change hidden information. In the case of an e-commerce site, he could lower the price on an item he wants to purchase.

LESSON 9 Buttons

Now that the rest of your sample page is in place, you can focus on submit buttons. You had a brief introduction to the submit button when you created password fields. Now, let's take a closer look.

Submit buttons allow the user to click a button to submit a form. Order forms often include a pair of submit buttons — click one button to submit the order, click the other button to cancel it. If you include two buttons on the page, however, how will your users distinguish one from the other if they both are labeled "Submit Query?" (And what do queries have to do with orders, anyway?)

Fortunately, you can set the value on a submit button, just as you can with reset and other buttons. You can also name buttons. Naming buttons causes the name value to be passed to the server, where the program can decide what action to take based on which button was clicked.

If you were to name the submit button in your sample form as follows:

```
<input type="submit" name="submitButton" value="Submit Form" />
```

the name and value would be added to the URL and submitted to the server.

FIGURE 6.34

As you see, the submit button changed from the default text "Submit Query" to the text that is specified in the **value=""** attribute.

Reset Buttons

Reset buttons ("reset") are similar to submit buttons, but they have a completely different purpose. Rather than submitting the form, a reset button returns the form to its original state. Notice that we didn't say a reset button *clears* the form — it doesn't, unless the form was empty originally. Instead, a reset button restores the initial values that you set in the form.

A reset button looks very similar to a submit button, and the two are coded in a similar fashion. For example:

```
<input type="reset" value="Undo Changes To Form" />
```

displays as follows.

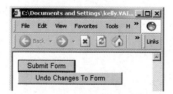

FIGURE 6.35

Add Form Buttons

1   In the open order.htm file, name the existing submit button and change the default text that displays on the button.

```
...
<center>
<input type="submit" name="submitorder" value="Submit Order" />
</center>
...
```

This code changes the text on the button to display a descriptive option.

2   Add a reset button next to the submit button.

```
...
<center>
<input type="submit" name="submitorder" value="Submit Order" />
<input type="reset" name="cancelorder" value="Cancel Order" />
</center>
...
```

This provides the user with the option of clearing the form.

3   Save the changes in the text file and refresh the document in the browser.

FIGURE 6.36

The buttons display next to each other at the bottom of the Web page.

4 Clear the form, and then enter random information into the fields.

5 Submit the form.

FIGURE 6.37

All the values display on the next page, even the hidden values. This form is processed with a script; to achieve the same results as in these exercises, you must use a special script or program, such as ASP or ColdFusion.

6 Save your changes. Close the file in both applications.

C A R E E R S   I N   D E S I G N

CERTIFICATION

The nature of your project determines whether you should consider any sort of Web certification. If you are simply dabbling in Web design, or using it for personal use, then certification is probably not important to you — although learning the principles could prove useful later.

A variety of popular certifications is available to you. The CIW (Certified Internet Webmaster) certification series offers different types of Web development certification. You can choose one or several paths of study to obtain certification. Some of the certifications offered include CIW Associate, CIW Security Analyst, Master CIW Designer, and Master CIW Enterprise Developer. To learn more about the CIW series, log on to www.ciwcertified.com.

SUMMARY

In Project 6, you learned that forms allow you to collect information from your viewers. You can create simple forms that collect a few lines of text data, or you can create elaborate forms that gather a wide variety of data — as well as provide users with selection options.

As you worked with forms, you learned that many attributes are provided for the form itself and the elements it contains. These attributes allow developers to control the kind of form data they collect, including text fields, password fields, selection fields, and text areas. You also learned that "hidden" data is not always well hidden, especially from an experienced hacker who knows where to look.

Although basic XHTML forms are very useful, forms that include advanced scripts to collect and manipulate data are much more powerful. A number of technologies are available to perform these advanced actions, including the new XForms standard, CGI scripts, and ASP scripts.

KEY TERMS

Check box	Password input	Text area
Form	Radio button	Text input
Form action	Radio group	Username input
Form data	Reset button	XForms
Hidden input	Secure server	Zero-based
Input field	Select box	
Online order form	Submit button	

CHECKING CONCEPTS AND TERMS

MULTIPLE CHOICE

Circle the letter that matches the correct answer for each of the following questions.

1. Which tag creates a form?
   a. <form>
   b. <input>
   c. <submit>
   d. <submitform>
   e. None of the above.

2. Why is it important to name your form and form fields?
   a. To identify the field when you are looking at the source code.
   b. Naming the fields identifies the input.
   c. You can transfer the value of a field through a URL.
   d. Both b and c.

3. Why would you limit the number of characters allowed in a text field?

   a. To save space on the page.

   b. Because the information is being placed in a database.

   c. You can enter as many characters as you want.

   d. None of the above.

4. Using password fields automatically secures the data.

   a. True

   b. False

5. Radio buttons are used for _____.

   a. single-option choices

   b. multiple choices

   c. collecting text

   d. All of the above.

6. Radio groups allow the user to _____.

   a. make only one choice at any given time

   b. make as many choices as he wants

   c. choose nothing from the list of options

   d. None of the above.

7. Check boxes allow the user to _____.

   a. make multiple choices at a given time

   b. make only one choice at a give time

   c. choose nothing from the list of options

   d. All of the above.

8. Selection fields are excellent when you need to choose from a long list of options.

   a. True

   b. False

9. Hidden fields allow you to transfer values without the user's knowledge.

   a. True

   b. False

10. What form button should always be available to the user?

   a. Submit button.

   b. Go button.

   c. Reset button.

DISCUSSION QUESTIONS

1. What are some of the benefits of using forms?

2. Why would you want to collect form data in a database?

3. When would you want to require a user to input data?

4. Discuss how tables might be useful when creating forms.

SKILL DRILL

Skill Drills reinforce project skills. Each skill reinforced is the same, or nearly the same, as a skill presented in the lessons. Detailed instructions are provided in a step-by-step format. You should complete these exercises in the order provided.

1. Create a Basic Form

1. Open the file named teaform.htm from your WIP_06 folder.

2. Add the basic form tags to the file.

3. Name the form "teaorder".

4. Include descriptive text in a paragraph, as follows: "We will process your order in 48 hours or less."

5. Save the changes to the file. Load the Web page in a browser.

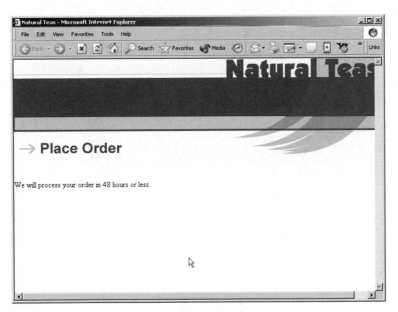

FIGURE 6.38

6. Keep the file open for the next exercise.

2. Add Text Inputs

1.   In the open file, beneath "We will process your order in 48 hours or less," type "Account Information". Insert two line breaks after the text.

2.   On the next line after the two line breaks, type "Full Name:".

3.   Next to "Full Name:" create a text box that is 30 characters in length. Name the text box "full_name".

4.   Add the value "Enter full name here" to the full_name field. Include a line break after the input.

5.   After the line break, type "Email".

6.   Add another text box that is 30 characters in length. Name the new field "email". Include a line break after the input.

7.   Add the descriptive text "Password" after the line break.

8.   Add a password input field that is 30 characters in length. Name the field "password". Include two line breaks after the input.

9.   Save the changes and load the Web page in a browser.

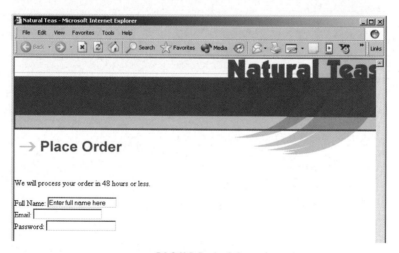

FIGURE 6.39

10.   Keep the file open for the next exercise.

3. Create Select Options

1.   In the open file, beneath the last entry in the source file, type "Select Tea(s)". Include two line breaks.

2.   After the line breaks, create a check box named "raspberry". Press the spacebar. Next to the check box, type the text "Raspberry - 6.00". Include a line break after the text.

3.   After the line break, create a check box named "lemonbalm". Press the spacebar. Next to the check box, type the text "Lemon Balm - 6.00". Include a line break after the text.

4. Repeat Steps 2 and 3 for the following flavors, naming each input accordingly: Anise, Peppermint, and Green Tea. After the last line of text, include two line breaks.

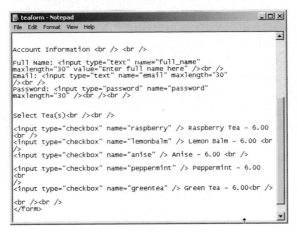

FIGURE 6.40

5. After the line breaks, type "Payment", and then include two line breaks.

6. After the line breaks, create a radio group. Name it "pay". Include three payment options: COD, Credit Card, and Check Card. Label each option accordingly. Include two line breaks.

7. After the line breaks, type "Shipping". Include two line breaks.

8. After the line breaks, create a pull-down menu named "ship" with the following options: Standard, 2nd Day, and Overnight. Include two line breaks.

9. Save the changes and refresh the document in the browser.

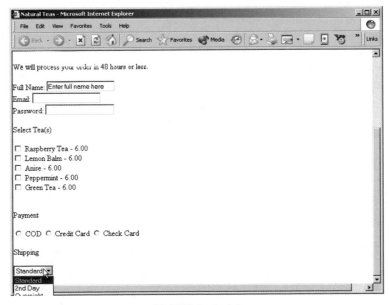

FIGURE 6.41

10. Keep the file open for the next exercise.

4. Provide a Comment Section and Create Form Buttons

1. After the last entry in the open file, type "Comments and Suggestions". Include two line breaks.

2. Create a text area that is 10 lines in length and includes 20 rows.

3. Include the initial text, "Please provide any comments, suggestions, or instructions for your order."

4. After the text area, include two line breaks.

5. Include a submit button with the value "Send Order".

6. Next to the submit button, create a reset button with the value "Clear Form".

7. Save the changes in the file and refresh the document in your browser.

FIGURE 6.42

8. Close the file in both applications.

CHALLENGE

Challenge exercises expand on, or are somewhat related to, skills presented in the lessons. Each exercise provides a brief introduction, followed by instructions presented in a numbered-step format that are not as detailed as those in the Skill Drill exercises. You should complete the exercises in the order provided.

1. Create a Form Action

In the Skill Drills, you created a simple order form for Natural Teas. In this exercise, you include form information, such as where to submit the form when the user clicks the submit button.

1. Open teaform.htm from your WIP_06 folder.

2. In another text editor window, open login.htm.

3. Copy the script code (the **<script>** tags and content) from login.htm and paste it beneath the **<body>** tag in teaform.htm.

4. Close login.htm.

5. In the **<form>** tag in teaform.htm, add an action to submit the form to teaform.htm (**action="teaform.htm"**).

6. Save the changes to the file and refresh the document in the browser.

7. If you want, fill in the fields and submit the form.

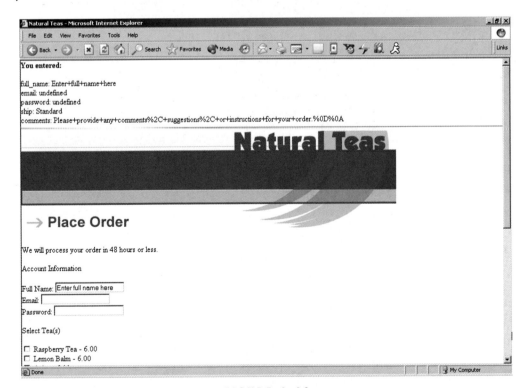

FIGURE 6.43

8. Reload (do not click the Back button) teaform.htm in the browser.

9. Leave the file open for the next exercise.

2. Put the Form into a Table

1. In the open file, beneath Account Information, create a table that is 300 pixels wide, with two columns, three rows, and no borders.

2. Cut and paste Full Name and place it in the first cell on the top row.

3. Cut and paste the text input, fullname, into the second cell on the top row.

4. Repeat Steps 2 and 3 for the Email text input and the Password input.

5. Bold the descriptive text for the text inputs and the password inputs.

6. Save the changes in the file and refresh the document in the browser.

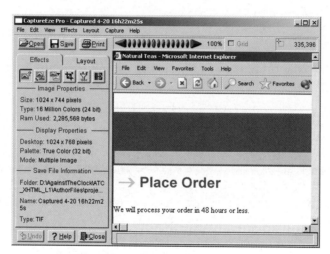

FIGURE 6.44

7. Leave the file open for the next exercise.

3. Format the Form Content

1. In the open file, bold the tea flavor options next to the check boxes.

2. Bold the payment options next to the radio buttons.

3. Bold the sentence, "We will process your order in 48 hours or less."

4. In the section headings (e.g. Payment), increase the font size, change the font color, and bold the text.

5. Format the document however you prefer. Place elements into tables, change colors, and change font attributes.

6. Save the changes to the file and refresh the document in the browser.

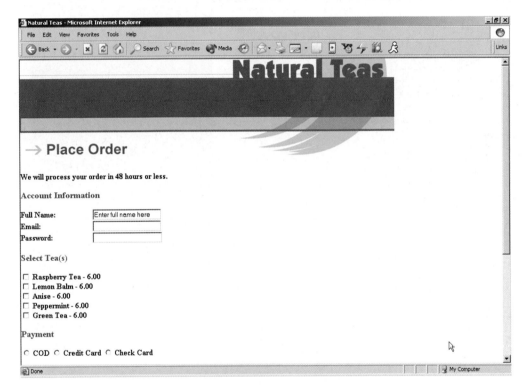

FIGURE 6.45

7. Leave the file open for the next exercise.

4. Reset the Document and Print

1. In the open file, click the reset button on the form.

2. In the Full Name field, type your full name.

3. Complete the rest of the form as if you were placing an order.

4. Choose Print>Print Preview to preview the document.

5. If you have access to a printer, print the document.

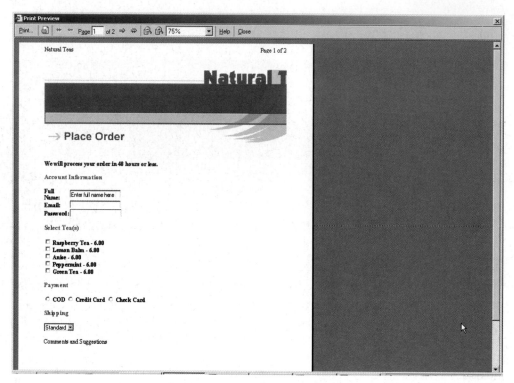

FIGURE 6.46

6. Close the file in both applications.

P O R T F O L I O   B U I L D E R

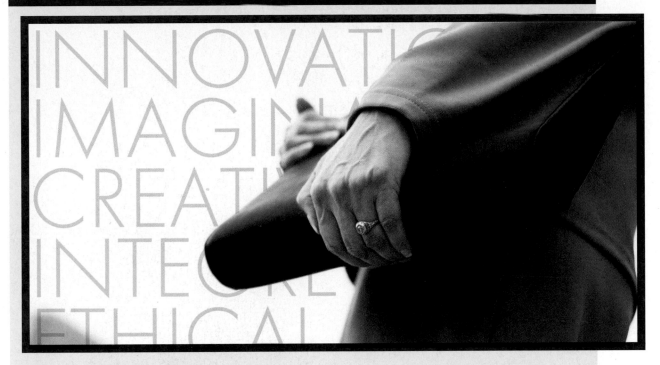

Create a Survey Form

The owners of a local ice cream store, JiJi's Ice Cream, want to collect information from their customers. They decided to publish an online survey so they can save on printing costs. As an incentive, they will give a free ice cream sundae to any customer who submits an online survey. JiJi's hired you to create the online form and set it up so the information is sent to their email address. To complete this exercise, you should do the following:

- Think about what type of important information could be collected from ice cream store customers. Obvious information would be name and contact information. Other information would be favorite ice cream flavors, favorite frozen yogurt flavors, how often they buy ice cream, and what other types of frozen treats they enjoy. It would be helpful to know if they purchase ice cream from other locations, as well as what kind of ice cream they have at home.

- Create a storyboard for your Web page. The heading for the page should be "JiJi's Ice Cream Give-Away".

- Knowing what type of information you need to collect, consider the type of form elements you should use to accomplish your task. Make notes on these elements next to the sections in the storyboard.

- Create the form using a variety of form elements. If necessary, use a table for alignment. Consider other formatting methods, and what graphical elements you can use to enhance the form. Research other methods of submitting this form, such as CGI scripts.

Working with Frames

OBJECTIVES

In this project, you learn how to

- Create a frameset page
- Include nested frames
- Work with individual frames
- Control content location and borders
- Create targets
- Work with parent frames
- Provide an alternative page for browsers that do not support frames

WHY WOULD I DO THIS?

Most Web users enjoy the convenience of seeing all of the content of a page without having to scroll. Web users also appreciate sites that make it easy for them to find everything they need, quickly and easily; this particularly applies to finding the navigation buttons. Users want navigational systems to be obvious, and to be available at all times — on every page of a site. Frames were designed to address these user requirements.

The idea behind *frames* was to subdivide a Web page into logical sections. Certain sections of a page, such as the navigational elements and menus, would be fixed; every page on a site would display those elements in exactly the same place. The user would know where to find those elements, regardless of what page she was on. Other sections of the window would be scrollable, and would contain content that changed dynamically (based upon user choices), or was updated on a regular basis.

This structure served more than one purpose. First, the user could view a long page and always keep sight of the navigational elements. Second, only the part/s of the page that change need to be loaded by the browser; this, of course, allows the page to load faster than if every element on the page were unique. At the height of their popularity, frames were most commonly used to add a logo and navigational elements to the top of the page, and a menu along the left side.

In this project, you learn all about the benefits, as well as the drawbacks, of using frames when designing a Web page.

V I S U A L   S U M M A R Y

Frames allow you to divide the browser window into parts (sections), with each part displaying a different document. Dividing a browser window into sections allows designers to create navigational systems quickly and easily. It also provides more control over the organization and display of the content, much the same as tables.

The following illustration shows a Web site's navigational system that was set up using frames.

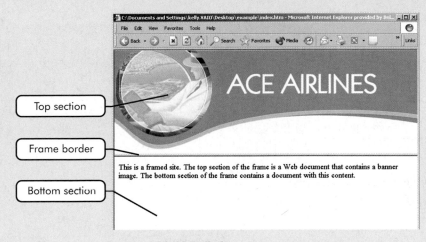

FIGURE 7.1

Notice the horizontal line that separates the two sections. This default border displays whenever you use frames. If you prefer, you can remove the border to provide a seamless and unified appearance on your page. You learn how to modify frames later in this project.

The following illustration shows the same page set up using tables.

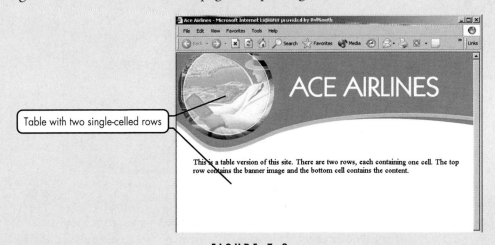

FIGURE 7.2

It's clear that these two methods offer much more control over the layout of the page than XHTML. Most of the time, designers use a combination of frames and tables when designing navigational elements.

LESSON 1   The Frameset

When building a frame-based site, you work with two kinds of pages: the frameset and the frames. A *frameset* is very similar to the layout of a printed document; it tells the browser how to lay out the page and what frames to include in each section. Each frame, in turn, tells the browser what content to put into its particular area on the page.

Consider the following framed site. Look closely at its structure.

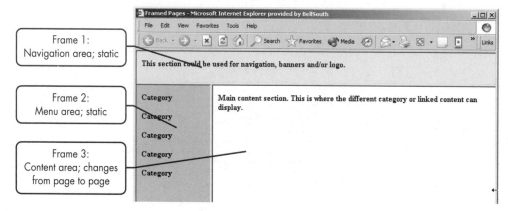

FIGURE 7.3

To build this page, you would create a frameset that divides the window into three sections: the navigation at the top, the featured categories on the left side (the menu), and the content on the right side. There are several ways to achieve this result, all of which involve dividing the page into rows and columns. Some sites take this concept a step further, and subdivide the rows and columns into smaller units.

The following example is a simple page with two columns, each of which displays a different page.

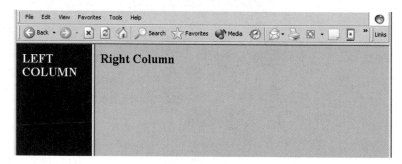

FIGURE 7.4

This page was created by building a frameset using the **<frameset>** tag, which split the page into two columns. Then, a frame with content (a page) was assigned to each of those columns. In the following code, notice the column attribute, **cols=""**. In this case, it divides the page into two sections — one 20% of the page, and the other 80% of the page. The frameset code does not include the **<body></body>** tags. If the **<body>** tags were present, the frameset page would not work properly. The frameset page is used strictly for dividing the screen, so multiple Web pages can display at the same time.

```
<html>

<head><title>Frames</title></head>

<frameset cols="20%, 80%">

        <frame src="left.htm" />

        <frame src="righ.htm" />

</frameset>

</html>
```

The above files, left.htm and right.htm, are regular XHTML files — there is nothing special about them. The content assigned to a row or column can be the XHTML file of your choice.

As you learned earlier, you can divide framesets into columns or rows, each of which can be further subdivided into columns or rows. You can specify the width of columns and height of rows in percentages or pixels. You can also use the asterisk (*) character to indicate that you want a particular row or column to take up the balance of the page.

For instance, to create a page with two rows, the first of which is 100 pixels high, and the second of which occupies the rest of the page, you would write the following code:

```
<html>

<head><title>The Winter and the Summer</title></head>

<frameset rows="100, *">

        <frame src="winter.htm" />

        <frame src="summer.htm" />

</frameset>

</html>
```

FIGURE 7.5

Measurements in percentages are *relative sizes* — they represent a percentage of the page, or of the frame in which the column or row resides. Measurements in pixels are *fixed sizes*. If you want a frame to be a specific size to match the height or width of an image, you should use pixels as the units of measurement for the rows or columns. The result of the type of measurement applied is most apparent when you resize a window. A frame size specified as a percentage (relative size) adjusts to match the new window size, whereas a frame size specified as pixels (fixed size) remains the same size.

Create the Frameset

1 In the WIP_07 folder, create a new folder named "frames".

? If you have problems...

This project uses some non-standard XHTML 1.1 attributes associated with frames. To achieve the desired effect without using CSS, the pages you create in this project will not produce a valid XHTML document. We note which attributes have been deprecated.

2 Copy all of the content in your Project_07 folder to the WIP_07>frames folder, except the skilldrill folder.

The skilldrill folder is specifically for the Skill Drills at the end of this project.

3 Open your text editor and create a new file. Save it in the WIP_07>frames folder as "frameset.htm".

This document acts as a canvas upon which you build framed pages. You divide the page into sections, and within those sections, indicate what content to display.

4 Create the shell of the frameset (the empty frameset). Create two rows and allot a portion of the window to each (25% to one, and 75% to the other), as follows:

```
<html>
<head><title>Frameset Page</title></head>
<frameset rows="25%,75%">
</frameset>
</html>
```

Later, you can subdivide the second row into two columns.

5   **Add frames of content, menu.htm and listing.htm, as follows:**

```
<html>
<head><title>Frameset Page</title></head>
<frameset rows="25%,75%">
    <frame src="menu.htm" />
    <frame src="listing.htm" />
</frameset>
</html>
```

This content page displays in the sections you allotted on your frameset page. In standard HTML, the end **</frame>** tag is not required; to be a valid XHTML element, however, you must close the **<frame>** tag.

6   **Save the page. Open frameset.htm in your browser.**

FIGURE 7.6

You created two rows and assigned a relative size to each. In fact, the size of the rows (not the frames you added) determined the number of rows.

7   **Resize the window and watch the row sizes change.**

This is acceptable in some situations, but not here. The top frame needs to remain the same size as the menu elements, which means a fixed size should be applied to the top row.

8   Change the height of the top row to 125 pixels, and set the second row to take up the balance of the space, as follows:

```
<html>

<head><title>Frameset Page</title></head>

<frameset rows="125, *">

    <frame src="menu.htm" />

    <frame src="listing.htm" />

</frameset>

</html>
```

9   Save the file, and refresh the browser.

FIGURE 7.7

Some browsers have difficulty refreshing frames. If you don't see a difference in your browser, you may need to open a new browser window and reopen the page. In the refreshed/new browser window, notice that the top frame matches the size of the menu, even when you resize the window.

Later in the project, you remove the borders of the frames to create a seamless design. Setting the height any higher than 125 pixels would create too much white space on the page.

10   Leave the file open in both windows.

To Extend Your Knowledge...

FRAME CONTENT

Some sites use frames to incorporate content from other sites into their own pages. For instance, www.ask.com presents the sites it finds during a search in the bottom frame, while displaying the ask.com logo and navigation in the top frame. Ask.com makes no secret about what it is doing. Some companies were less than honest when they used this process; they attempted to hijack content and endured litigation as a result.

LESSON 2   Nested Framesets

When creating a frameset, you must choose between rows and columns; both cannot reside in the same frameset. You can, however, replace a row with a frameset that defines columns (or vice versa). Adding one frameset to another is called nesting the framesets. Any number of framesets can be nested within another.

You can use two methods to add a nested frameset: you can add it directly, or through a separate framed document that contains a frameset. The direct method adds a second frameset within the code where one frame would normally be placed, as follows:

```
<html>

<head><title>The Winter and the Summer</title></head>

<frameset cols="50%, 50%">

        <frame src="winter.htm" />

        <frameset rows="25%, *">

              <frame src="summer.htm" />

              <frame src="spring.htm" />

        </frameset>

</frameset>

</html>
```

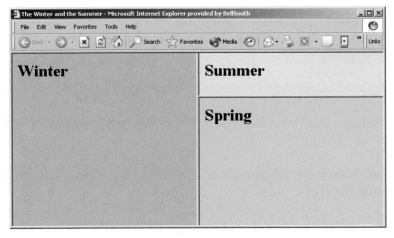

FIGURE 7.8

As an alternative, you can retain your original frameset, but make the content of one of its frames another frameset. For instance, the original frameset is:

```
<html>

<head><title>The Winter and the Summer</title></head>

<frameset cols="50%, 50%">

          <frame src="winter.htm" />

          <frame src="warm.htm" />

</frameset>

</html>
```

where the content of warm.htm is:

```
<html>

<head><title>The Warm Months of the Year</title></head>

<frameset rows="50%, 50%">

          <frame src="summer.htm" />

          <frame src="spring.htm" />

</frameset>

</html>
```

This code creates the same result as the previous example.

Subdivide the Second Row

1   **Double-check that frameset.htm is open in both the text editor and browser.**

2   **In the text editor, create a new file. Name it "subframe.htm" and save it in the WIP_07> frames folder.**

3   **Create a second frameset in subframe.htm. This time, instead of specifying rows, specify columns, as follows:**

```
<html>

<head><title>Subframe Page</title></head>

    <frameset cols="25%, 75%">

        <frame src="featurecat.htm" />

        <frame src="listing.htm" />

    </frameset>

</html>
```

4   **Save subframe.htm.**

5   **Open frameset.htm and make the following change.**

```
<html>
<head><title>Frameset Page</title></head>
<frameset rows="125, *">
    <frame src="menu.htm" />
    <frame src="subframe.htm" />
</frameset>
</html>
```

6   **Save the file and refresh frameset.htm in the browser.**

FIGURE 7.9

The bottom frame was replaced with a document that defined its own frameset.

7   **Leave the windows open for the next exercise.**

Nest the Framesets

1   In the open frameset.htm file in the text editor, replace the second frame with the same frame-set that is in subframe.htm.

```
<html>

<head><title>Frameset Page</title></head>

<frameset rows="125, *">

    <frame src="menu.htm" />

    <frameset cols="25%, 75%">

        <frame src="featurecat.htm" />

        <frame src="listing.htm" />

    </frameset>

</frameset>

</html>
```

2   Save the file and refresh the browser.

FIGURE 7.10

You shouldn't see any change.

3   Leave the file open in both windows.

To Extend Your Knowledge...

CSS VS FRAMES

Even though tables and frames can be used for horizontal and vertical content display, there are many unresolved issues regarding frames (which you discover at the end of this project).

CSS offers powerful positioning features that allow finer control over page layout than tables or frames. With the promise of XHTML 2.0 on the horizon, it's important that you begin to consider using CSS.

LESSON 3 Controlling Individual Frames

The frameset is only half the story. You also need to work with individual frames. You can control the appearance of frames, such as their size and scrolling, with the addition of attributes.

Attributes don't affect the content of a frame; they only affect the presentation of a frame. For instance, you can control the size of a frame (with the height and width attributes), whether the user can change the size (using the *noresize attribute*), and whether a scroll bar is available (using the *scrolling attribute*). To create a fixed-size frame that cannot be resized by the user and has a scroll bar, you would write the following tag:

```
<frame src="mypage.htm" height="200" scrolling="yes" noresize="noresize" />
```

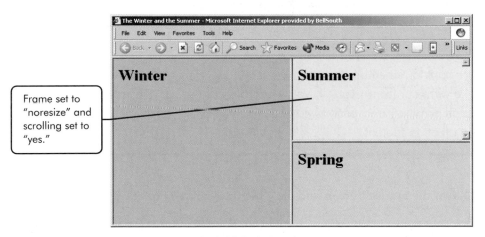

FIGURE 7.11

The **scrolling=""** attribute has three permissible values: yes, no, and auto (auto adds a scroll bar only if it's needed). These values apply to both vertical and horizontal scroll bars.

The **noresize=""** attribute, similar to the **checked=""** attribute you learned about in Project 6, is normally written without a value. To create a well-formed XHTML page, however, you must assign a value to the **noresize=""** attribute. This accounts for the seemingly redundant appearance of **noresize="noresize"**.

Control the Size of a Frame

1 In the open frameset.htm in the browser, position the cursor over the horizontal line separating the top frame from the rest of the page.

FIGURE 7.12

The cursor changes to a two-sided vertical arrow.

? If you have problems...

It's important to remember that your users will use monitors of various sizes, many of which could be quite different from yours. If you were to create a frame using a percentage, and your users turned off scrolling and prohibited resizing, you could inadvertently create a frame that did not display all of its content.

---

2 Hold down the mouse button and drag the frame border to resize the frame.

If a user resized a page this way, it would ruin your layout. Let's add the **noresize=""** attribute to prevent the user from being able to do so.

3 | In the text editor, add the `noresize=""` attribute to the first frame.

```
<html>
<head><title>Frameset Page</title></head>
<frameset rows="125, *">
    <frame src="menu.htm" noresize="noresize" />
    <frameset cols="25%, 75%">
        <frame src="featurecat.htm" />
        <frame src="listing.htm" />
...
```

4 | Save the file and refresh the browser. Try to resize the frame.

The two-sided arrow doesn't appear. This solves one problem, but creates another. At this size, you see a scroll bar on the window, even though it's not necessary.

5 | Eliminate the scroll bar with the `scrolling=""` attribute.

```
<html>
<head><title>Frameset Page</title></head>
<frameset rows="125, *">
    <frame src="menu.htm" noresize="noresize" scrolling="no" />
    <frameset cols="25%, 75%">
        <frame src="featurecat.htm" />
        <frame src="listing.htm" />
...
```

The noresize and scrolling attributes are optional, and not apart of the XHTML 1.1 standard. A document that contains these attributes is not considered a valid XHTML document. You can control these elements using CSS in combination with the XHTML 1.1 Frameset.

6   Save the file and refresh the browser.

FIGURE 7.13

The scroll bar disappears from the top row.

7   Leave both windows open for the next exercise.

To Extend Your Knowledge...

FORMATTING FRAMES

Some of the formatting features used in frames (such as the border attributes) are supported in some browsers, but not all. As an alternative, you should consider other methods of page layout than standard HTML frames. If you choose to use frames, you should comply with the XHTML 1.1 standard and use CSS as a presentational tool. Another alternative is to explore using XFrames, which we discuss in greater detail at the end of this project.

LESSON 4   Controlling Content Location and Borders

In additional to controlling the size of a frame, you can also control the location of the content within the frame, and whether the frame has a border. You control these features of the frame's appearance with the **marginheight=""**, **marginwidth=""**, and **border=""** attributes.

For instance, you could add a 5-pixel margin around the top and bottom of a frame, as well as a 10-pixel margin on the left and right, by writing:

```
<frame src="mypage.htm" marginheight="5" marginwidth="10" border="0" />
```

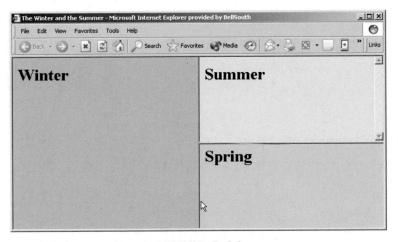

FIGURE 7.14

In Figure 7.14, the border was removed from the particular frame (**border="0"**). All the other frames in the frameset still have borders. Be careful when you use this process, since it can sometimes result in a "half" border if one neighboring frame has a border, but the other doesn't.

Neither the **marginheight=""** nor the **marginwidth=""** attribute is supported in the XHTML 1.1 standard. These attributes have been replaced with features from CSS.

Set the Margins and Border

1 In the text editor of the open frameset.htm file, set the `marginheight=""` attribute on the top frame.

```
<html>

<head><title>Frameset Page</title></head>

<frameset rows="125, *">

    <frame src="menu.htm" noresize="noresize" scrolling="no"
marginheight="4" />

    <frameset cols="25%, 75%">

        <frame src="featurecat.htm" />

        <frame src="listing.htm" />

...
```

2 Save the file and refresh the browser.

FIGURE 7.15

This adds a 4-pixel separation between the content of the top frame (menu.htm) and the frame border.

3 | Next, let's remove the borders from the top and left frames.

```
<html>

<head><title>Frameset Page</title></head>

<frameset rows="125, *" >

    <frame src="menu.htm" noresize="noresize" scrolling="no"
marginheight="4" frameborder="0" />

    <frameset cols="25%, 75%">

        <frame src="featurecat.htm" frameborder="0" />

        <frame src="listing.htm" />

    </frameset>

</frameset>

</html>
```

4 | Save the file and refresh the browser.

FIGURE 7.16

The frame border is removed from only one frame; the other frame border is still intact. The border attribute isn't actually specified for the frameset element, but browsers currently support it. Remember, this attribute is not included in the XHTML 1.1 standard.

5 | Remove the borders completely.

```
<html>

<head><title>Frameset Page</title></head>

<frameset rows="125, *" border="0">

    <frame src="menu.htm" noresize="noresize" scrolling="no" margin-
height="4" frameborder="0" />

    <frameset cols="25%, 75%">

        <frame src="featurecat.htm" frameborder="0" />

...
```

6 | Save the file and refresh the browser.

FIGURE 7.17

All frames are now border-free. The page display is unified and seamless. The user is unaware that the "page" is actually several pages framed together. This method of framing is used specifically for navigation. The menus at the top and left remain in the same positions as the user navigates through the pages of the site.

7 | Leave the file open in both windows.

LESSON 5   Targets

In the first four lessons in this project, you used frames to determine the appearance of a Web page, as well as its layout; but the real power of frames is yet to be seen — enabling you to click a link in one frame, which causes new content to display in another frame, leaving the overall layout intact.

You can create this structure by adding a target to a link. The ***target attribute*** tells the browser where to display the new content. There are several ways to add a target; the most common is to name your frames. Once named, you can target the frames directly. You can name a frame anything you want, but the name can't start with an underscore; that character is used for special purposes, as we discuss later.

Let's see how named frames work. You can, for instance, structure your familiar seasonal frameset with named frames, as follows:

```
<html>
<head><title>The Winter and the Summer</title></head>
<frameset cols="50%, 50%">
            <frame src="winter.htm" name="winterframe" />
            <frameset rows="25%, *">
                    <frame src="summer.htm" name="summerframe" />
                    <frame src="spring.htm" name="springframe" />
            </frameset>
</frameset>
</html>
```

If you then add a target to the link in spring.htm that references the winter frame, such as:

```
<a href="spring.htm" target="winterframe">winter</a>!
```

FIGURE 7.18

you can change the content of the winter frame. The `target=""` attribute tells the browser where to send the content.

FIGURE 7.19

If you click the new link, the browser displays spring.htm as the content in the frame called winterframe.

Set a Target

1   In the open browser that shows frameset.htm, click the See All Categories>Sports and Recreation link.

FIGURE 7.20

The content displays in the same frame as the link.

2   **In frameset.htm, assign names to all frames.**

```
<html>

<head><title>Frameset Page</title></head>

<frameset rows="125, *" border="0">

    <frame src="menu.htm" noresize="noresize" scrolling="no" margin-
height="4" frameborder="0" name="menu" />

    <frameset cols="25%, 75%">

        <frame src="featurecat.htm" frameborder="0" name="categories"  />

        <frame src="listing.htm" name="content" />

    </frameset>

</frameset>

</html>
```

3   **Save frameset.htm in the text editor, and then open featurecat.htm in the text editor.**

4   **Add a target to the Sports and Recreation link, as follows:**

```
...

    <tr><td class="basefont"><b><a href = "art.htm" >Art</a></b></td></tr>

    <tr><td class="basefont"><b><a href = "baby.htm" >Baby
Needs</a></b></td></tr>

    <tr><td class="basefont"><b><a href = "playground.htm"
target="content">Sports and Recreation</a></b></td></tr>

    <tr><td> </td></tr>

    <tr><td class="basefont"><b><a href="allcat.htm">See All
Categories</a></b></td></tr>

    </tbody>

  </table>

...
```

5   **Save the file and refresh the browser.**

6   Click the Sports and Recreation link.

FIGURE 7.21

The new page opens in the frame on the right. The most common method for adding a target is to name the frames, and then add the **target=""** attribute that references the named frames.

7   Close both applications.

LESSON 6   Using a Base Target

Using named targets enables you to send content to the frame of your choice. If every link on a page had the same target, however, such as a list of links that all send their information to the "content" frame, setting the targets on the links could become quite tedious. The sample page you are using in this project has only four links, which is certainly not a burden. Consider, however, a page with hundreds of links, all of which have the same target. Retyping the same target hundreds of time would take up a considerable amount of your valuable development time.

To avoid this problem, you can utilize the **<base>** tag that you used in the beginning of this book to specify a base URL; you can use the same **<base>** tag to specify a base target. If you want to direct all links without a target to the frame called "main," you can add a **<base>** tag, as follows:

```
<base target="main" />
```

Add a Base Target

1   Open WIP_07>frames>featurecat.htm in the text editor.

FIGURE 7.22

2   Add a **\<base>** tag to the list of featured categories, and remove the target from the Sports and Recreation link.

```
<html>

<head>

<title>Free 'Til It Sells!</title>

<link href="images/SearchFourm.css" type="text/css" rel="stylesheet" />

<link href="images/Style1.css" type="text/css" rel="stylesheet" />

  <base target="content" />

</head>

<body>

  <table cellspacing="0" cellpadding="0">

    <tbody>

    <tr>

...
```

3   **Save the file. Open frameset.htm in the browser.**

If your browser was already open before Step 3, refresh the left frame so the changes in featurecat.htm take effect. You should see no change.

4   **Click the Sports and Recreation link.**

The new page still takes you to the content frame.

5   **Leave both windows open for the next exercise.**

To Extend Your Knowledge...

REFRESHING FRAMES

Refreshing the overall page doesn't always refresh individual frames. To refresh an individual frame on the Macintosh, hold down the mouse button in the particular frame, and then choose the Refresh Page (or Refresh Frame) option. On a Windows system, right-click the frame you want to refresh, and then choose the Refresh Frame option from the pop-up menu.

LESSON 7   Using Targets for Special Cases

Using a base target can save you the time and effort of adding a target to each link individually. Doing so can, however, raise a new problem: What do you do when you want one or two links to replace the content in the same frame? Fortunately, there are special targets that you can use for this and other special cases. These targets include:

- The _self target replaces the content in the same frame.

- The _parent target sends the content to the parent document of the frame. (You'll learn about parents in a moment.)

- The _blank target opens a new window for the content.

- The _top target replaces the main frameset.

Add the _self Target

In our sample Free 'Til It Sells page, if you click the See All Categories link, the linked document moves to the content frame; but that's not what you want to happen. You want the original page that displays the text link, "See All Categories," to stay where it is. Not only that, you want the page to remain in place no matter where the original page starts. Let's add a _self target to solve this problem.

1   **Open featurecat.htm in the text editor.**

2   **Add the _self target to the See All Categories link, and remove the content target.**

...

```
    <tr><td class="basefont"><b><a href="playground.htm">Sports and
Recreation<a></b></td></tr>

    <tr><td> </td></tr>

    <tr><td class="basefont"><b><a href="allcat.htm" target="_self">
See All Categories</a></b></td></tr>

    </tbody>

  </table>

</body>

</html>
```

3   **Save the file. Open frameset.htm in your browser, and then refresh that frame.**

A scroll bar does not separate the left and right panels — which happens when the long list of category links displays — because there is not enough content in these sections to automatically generate a scroll bar.

FIGURE 7.23

4 Click the Sports and Recreation link to verify that the new content still goes to the content frame.

5 Click the See All Categories link.

The list appears in the left frame, even though the base target indicates that it should go to the content frame.

6 Leave both applications open.

Open a New Window

Another option for creating targets is to open an entirely new window. This can be useful if the content to which you're linking is not directly related to what's on the current page, or if you want to display content from another site. When you open a new window, you avoid sending users away from your site. When they finish looking at the other page, your original page remains open and in view.

1 Double-check that featurecat.htm is open in the text editor, and frameset.htm is open in the browser.

If necessary, click the browser's Back button to return to the Featured Categories page.

2   Change the `<base>` tag to a `_blank` target.

```
...
 <base target="_blank" />
</head>
<body>
  <table cellspacing="0" cellpadding="0">
...
```

3   Save the file. Refresh the category frame in your browser.

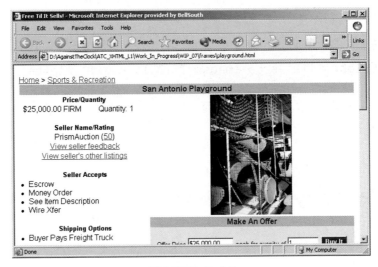

FIGURE 7.25

4   Click the Sports and Recreation link to open a new window.

You might also choose to open a new window if you have an extensive list of items, such as the results of a search. With a new window, the user would not have to continually click the Back button to reload the list page.

5   Close the new Sports and Recreation window. Leave the original browser window and the featurecat.htm (text editor) open.

Link the Logo to the Main Window

Rather than opening a new window, you can replace the current window (as opposed to the current frame) with new content. You can do so by targeting the top window. This is normally done to "break a user out" of frames — that is, take the user from a subdivided page back to a single page with no frames.

1   Open WIP_07>frames>menu.htm in the text editor, and open frameset.htm in the browser.

2   Target the link on the logo to the **_top** frame.

```
...
<tbody>
 <tr>
  <td valign="top" width="144" rowspan="4">
    <a href="home.htm" target="_top">
     <img height="112" src="images/FTIS_logo.gif" width="144" border="0" />
    </a>
  </td>
...
```

3   Save the file. Refresh the **_top** frame in the browser.

4   **Click the logo.**

FIGURE 7.26

The page no longer includes any framed sections.

5   **Close both windows, but leave the applications open.**

To Extend Your Knowledge...

WEB SITE FLOW CHARTS

As if linking a large Web site isn't cumbersome enough, linking and targeting frames can be a nightmare without proper planning. Before beginning any Web project that consists of three or more pages, you should consider creating a flow chart to help guide you through the process. A **flow chart** is a diagram that shows the navigational flow of a Web site. It identifies the pages that will be linked together and in what manner. It also identifies the external links that will be provided, as well as the areas of the site that will be limited to specific viewers.

Flow charts can be elaborate computer-generated diagrams or simple sketches on paper. To prevent broken links and incorrect targeting, we recommend that you create a flowchart of your Web site before actually creating and linking the site's pages.

LESSON 8 Parents

Another common way to manage content in a frameset is to send content to the *parent*, which is the actual frameset document. Identifying a frameset as a parent allows you to target that frameset, instead of a specific frame. For instance, when you sent the Sports and Recreation page to its own window in the previous exercise, it didn't look very good because the top interface disappeared.

Instead, you could have sent the Sports and Recreation page to the bottom two frames. These two frames are part of a single frameset that can be considered the "parent" of each frame. To replace these bottom frames with linked content (and keep the top frame), you can send the content to the parent of the link page. For instance, let's look at the frameset:

```
<html>

<head><title>Frameset Page</title></head>

<frameset rows="125, *" border="0">

    <frame src="menu.htm" noresize="noresize" scrolling="no"
marginheight="4" frameborder="0" name="menu" />

    <frameset cols="25%, 75%">

        <frame src="featurecat.htm" frameborder="0" name="categories" />

        <frame src="listing.htm" name="content" />

    </frameset>

</frameset>

</html>
```

You are working with a link in featurecat.htm in the categories frame; logically, the "parent" would be the frameset enclosing that frame, shown in bold above.

Check the Parent

1 Open featurecat.htm in the text editor.

2 Set the base target as **_parent**.

```
...

<link href="images/SearchFourm.css" type="text/css" rel="stylesheet" />

<link href="images/Style1.css" type="text/css" rel="stylesheet" />

  <base target="_parent" />

</head>

<body>

...
```

3   Remove the `target="_self"` attribute from the See All Categories link.

4   Save the file and refresh the frame.

5   Click the Sports and Recreation link.

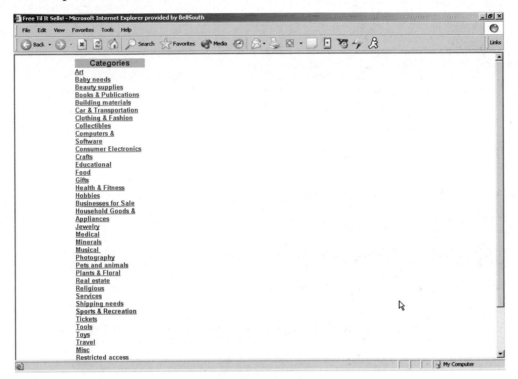

FIGURE 7.27

The entire window was replaced. Think about why this occurred.

6   Close featurecat.htm in the text editor. Leave the browser open.

Change the Parent

The result in Step 5 of the previous exercise may, at first, seem to make little sense. Why would the entire window be replaced if you specified only the parent? This happened because of the definition of "parent." The parent of a frame is not actually the frameset containing the frame, but the document containing that frameset. If you want to send the listing to the bottom half of the window, you need to return to your original frameset. In the following exercise, you restructure the Free 'Til It Sells framesets.

1   Open frameset.htm in the text editor. Replace the second frameset with a frame containing subframe.htm.

```
<html>

<head><title>Frameset Page</title></head>

<frameset rows="125, *" border="0">

    <frame src="menu.htm" noresize="noresize" scrolling="no" margin-
height="4" frameborder="0" name="menu" />

    <frame src="subframe.htm" name="content" />

</frameset>

</html>
```

2   Save the file and refresh the browser.

3   Click the Sports and Recreation link.

FIGURE 7.28

The content now occupies the entire bottom portion of the page.

4   Close both applications.

LESSON 9 The "Future" of Frames

With all that you now know about frames, you probably think that Web designers must find them indispensable. You may also wonder why you don't you see them used more often — even FreeTilItSells.com, the site we used as the example in this project, doesn't use frames on the actual site.

Why Frames Have a Bad Reputation

When frames were first used on Web pages, browsers were (fairly) primitive, and Web page authoring tools even more so. There were few WYSIWYG editors, and the features they provided were quite basic. Even Netscape, the innovative company that created frames, didn't support them in the original Netscape Navigator Gold — their own authoring tool.

As a result, authors learned how to work with frames in the same way they learned to do everything else in HTML — they copied existing code. At that time, the accepted method for learning HTML was to examine sites that you liked, study the source code, and then do the best you could to develop code of your own. Without any formal education in HTML coding, and without knowing any better, many Web authors inadvertently developed non-standard code that caused problems for viewers. (The strict XHTML guidelines were put in place to rectify this problem.)

The majority of the early frame-based sites could only be viewed with the Netscape browsers; all other browsers (and there were quite a few of them) were unable to display frames — or the content they contained. While it makes sense that frames wouldn't appear in the browsers that did not support the frames technology, why did those browsers also fail to display the content? The answer lies in the source code.

Take a moment to examine the source code of frameset.htm. You can see that there is no actual content in the code, only instructions that a non-frames browser doesn't understand, and therefore, ignores. A non-frames browser would "see" a blank window instead of the planned page, and that is exactly what it would display to the viewer.

Over the past couple of years, this problem has become much less of an issue, as virtually every modern browser supports frames. Now that we're moving toward designing pages for PDAs and cell phones, however, the issue of successfully displaying framed pages is being examined, once again.

Additional problems can arise when you index search engines, as well as when external sites link to your pages. Sometimes a search engine indexes one of the pages within a frame, but does not index the actual frameset page. When this happens, the page displays outside the frameset, and the rest of the pages and their content are not indexed.

Accommodating the Frameless: the <noframes> Tag

Fortunately, you can use the **<noframes>** tag to provide content to browsers that don't recognize frames. For instance, you could add some explanatory text to frameset.htm, as follows:

```
<noframes>

  <body>

    Thank you for visiting our Web site. We are currently working on a
frameless version of this site.

  </body>

</noframes>
```

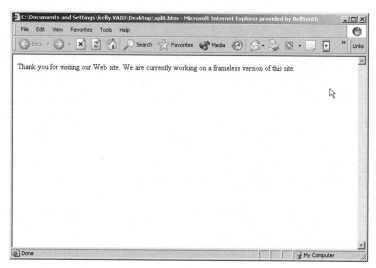

FIGURE 7.29

We omitted the **<body>** tag from the sample code used earlier in the project, since it would have prevented the frames from working. Now, you can restore it.

Any browser that understands frames also understands the **<noframes>** tag, and knows to ignore the content within it. Any browser that doesn't understand frames doesn't understand **<noframes>**, either; such a browser ignores the **<frameset>**, **<frame>**, and **<noframes>** tags, displaying only (in this case) the body content.

Add <noframes> Tags

1   Open frameset.htm in the text editor. Add the **<noframes>** tags beneath the frameset code.

```
...
<frameset rows="125, *" border="0">

    <frame src="menu.htm" noresize="noresize" scrolling="no" margin-
height="4" frameborder="0" name="menu" />

    <frame src="subframe.htm" name="content" />

</frameset>

<noframes>

  <body>

    Thank you for visiting our Web site. We are currently working on a
frameless version of this site.

  </body>

</noframes>

</html>
```

2   Save the changes and refresh the document in the browser.

FIGURE 7.30

The page displays as a framed site because the browser supports frames. If you were using a browser that did not support frames, the content between the **<noframes>** tags would display.

3   Close the file in both applications.

To Extend Your Knowledge...

THE ELIMINATION OF FRAMES

All of our discussion on frames will become a moot point when XHTML 2.0 becomes the standard. In their effort to separate content from presentation, the authors of XHTML 2.0 removed frames from their recommendation (as of this writing). Frames are relegated, instead, to a separate module that may (or may not) be supported by browsers.

Removing frames from the standard is not necessarily a loss. Many of the features of frames, such as creating multiple independent sections on a page, and being able to change content in only one section, can be duplicated using other features. XHTML 2.0 offers one solution, **XFrames**, which promises to answer the frames problems. For more information on XFrames, visit www.w3.org/TR/xframes/.

SUMMARY

In this project, you learned how to create framed pages. You discovered how to create a frameset and lay it out on the page. You became familiar with manipulating the appearance of individual frames. You also learned to direct content to a specific frame, to the entire window, or to a new window. You became familiar with some of the issues regarding frames, and the alternatives for non-frames-savvy browsers — including the XFrames solution.

KEY TERMS

Fixed size	Nested frame	Scrolling attribute
Flowchart	Noframes attribute	Subframe
Frames	Noresize attribute	Target attribute
Frameset	Parent	XFrames
Name frame	Relative size	

CHECKING CONCEPTS AND TERMS

MULTIPLE CHOICE

Circle the letter that matches the correct answer for each of the following questions.

1. What tag creates a "canvas" where you can build framed pages?
   a. <frame>
   b. <frame target="">
   c. <frameset>
   d. <noframes>
   e. None of the above.

2. Which of the following is a relative size?
   a. 50
   b. 50%
   c. both a and b
   d. None of the above.

3. How is the asterisk (*) symbol used when creating a frameset?

   a. It represents the "rest of the screen" when sizing a frame.

   b. It represents the entire screen when sizing a frame.

   c. It means, "start at the end of the screen."

   d. It means, "start of the beginning of the screen."

4. Nested frames allow you to specify both rows and columns for framed content.

   a. True

   b. False

5. Why would you remove a frame border?

   a. To make the page appear seamless.

   b. To allow the Web designer to add content that stretched from one margin all the way to the other.

   c. To ensure that all browsers could correctly display the content.

   d. All of the above.

6. What attribute prevents a framed paged from scrolling?

   a. scrolling="no"

   b. scrolling="auto"

   c. scrolling="yes"

   d. You cannot control the scrolling.

7. What target method would you use to place a destination page in a new window?

   a. target="_newwindow"

   b. target="_self"

   c. target="_blank"

   d. target="_parent"

8. What is the purpose of the base target?

   a. It saves you the work of adding the target to each link individually.

   b. No matter where you are on the page, you can return to the base target.

   c. When you click the home page icon, it accesses the base target.

   d. All of the above.

9. Why are frames being eliminated in XHTML 2.0?

   a. Some browsers do not support frames.

   b. Framed pages can display differently than the author intended, depending on the computer used to view the page.

   c. You can have legal problems linking to outside Web sites when these sites display within the framed pages.

   d. All of the above.

10. To prevent problems with browsers that do not support frames, you can _____ .

   a. use a base target

   b. use the <noframes> tag

   c. create pages without frames

   d. use the _self target

DISCUSSION QUESTIONS

1. What are some of the benefits of using frames?

2. What are some of the problems associated with using frames?

3. What other alternatives to frames can you foresee, besides the up-and-coming XFrames?

4. Why do mainstream sites use frames? Do you agree with their method? Why/why not?

SKILL DRILL

Skill Drills reinforce project skills. Each skill reinforced is the same, or nearly the same, as a skill presented in the lessons. Detailed instructions are provided in a step-by-step format. You should work through the exercises in the order provided.

1. Create a Frameset Page

You want to create a Web site that displays some of your favorite poetry from various poets. You opt to create a framed site so your visitors can easily navigate the content. Start by creating the frameset page.

1. Create a new folder in the WIP_07 folder called "skilldrill". Copy the content of the Project_07>skilldrill folder into the WIP_07>skilldrill folder.

2. Create a new XHTML document named "index.htm". Save it in the skilldrill folder.

3. In index.htm, create a frameset that creates two framed columns.

4. Set the left frame to 150 pixels. Set the right column to fill up the rest of the screen.

5. Use WIP_07>skilldrill>links.htm as the content of the left frame.

6. Use WIP_07>skilldrill>main.htm as the content of the right frame.

7. Save your changes. Load index.htm in a browser.

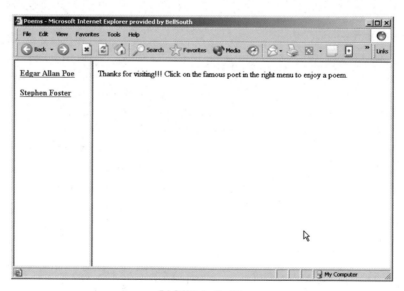

FIGURE 7.31

8. Keep the file open for the next exercise.

2. Define Frame Attributes

In order for the browser to display your pages correctly, you must define the frames in the frameset. In this exercise, you name each frame.

1. In the open file, name the links.htm frame "links", and name the main.htm frame "main".

2. Set the links frame to have no margins.

3. Make sure the links.htm frame does not scroll.

4. Remove the frame borders from links.htm.

5. Change the background color of links.htm to a light gray.

6. Save the changes to the file. Refresh the document in the browser.

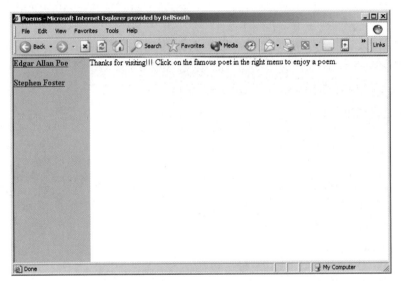

FIGURE 7.32

7. Keep the file open for the next exercise.

3. Create Targets

In addition to naming the individual frames, you need to provide targets for the links; when the link is clicked, the page is sent to the proper target — which is the named frame.

1. In the open file, add a base target to index.htm that links to itself.

2. Target the link to Edgar Allan Poe to display in the main frame.

3. Target the link to Stephen Foster to display in the main frame.

4. Add a link to poe.htm and foster.htm that links back to main.htm.

5. Provide a target for the links to main.htm to display in the main frame.

6. Save the changes to the file. Refresh the document in the browser.

7. Test the links.

FIGURE 7.33

8. Keep the file open for the next exercise.

4. Provide a Browser Alternative

To make sure all visitors can access your Web pages, you need to provide an alternative for browsers that do not support frames.

1. In the open index.htm file, create a noframes section.

2. Include a paragraph that explains why the content of the page does not display (because the user's browser does not support frames).

3. Change the target of the links in the frameset page to open in a new window.

4. Save the changes. Test the links in the browser.

5. Switch back to index.htm in the text editor. Change the links back to targeting the main frame.

6. Save the changes. Test the links in the browser.

7. Close the file in both applications.

FIGURE 7.34

CHALLENGE

Challenge exercises expand on, or are somewhat related to, skills presented in the lessons. Each exercise provides a brief introduction, followed by instructions presented in a numbered-step format that are not as detailed as those in the Skill Drill exercises. You should work through the exercises in the order provided.

1. Create an Alternative Page

In this Challenge, you create an alternative page for the poem page you worked with in the Skill Drill exercises.

1. Create a new XHTML document named "alter.htm". Save it in the WIP_07>skilldrill folder.

2. Create a table that displays the links in a column on the left, and displays the main content on the right side of the screen.

3. Create two links, "Edgar Allan Poe" and "Stephen Foster". Link them to the corresponding pages.

4. Place the content from main.htm in the section of the table on the right.

5. Save the changes to the file. Open the file in a browser.

FIGURE 7.35

6. Leave the file open for the next exercise.

2. Add the A Noframes Solution

In this exercise, you add the content for the **<noframes>** tag.

1. Open the index.htm frameset page in a new text editor window.

2. Remove the content in the **<noframes>** section.

3. In the alter.htm file, copy the code between the opening **<body>** tag and the ending **</body>** tag.

4. Paste the code in index.htm. Save your changes.

5. Open index.htm in your browser. The content between the **<noframes>** tags should not display.

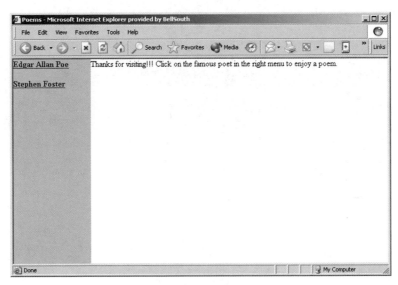

FIGURE 7.36

6. Leave the file open for the next exercise.

3. Create a Banner

Next, you add a banner section to the frameset.

1. In the open index.htm, create another frame across the top of the page.

2. Set that frame size to 100 pixels.

3. Create an XHTML document named "banner.htm". Save it in the skilldrill folder.

4. Insert WIP_07>skilldrill>banner.gif into the banner.htm file.

5. Remove all borders, and make sure the banner frame does not scroll.

6. Save the changes to the file. Refresh the document in the browser.

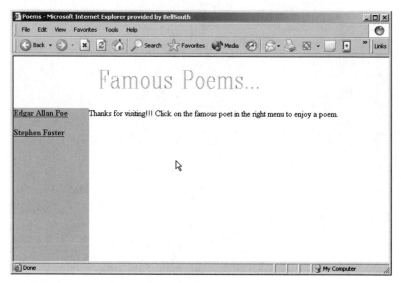

FIGURE 7.37

7. Leave the file open for the next exercise.

4. Provide a Linked Logo

In this exercise, you modify the design and add more content.

1. Create three additional pages of content in the main frame of index.htm.

   You link to this content later. This content does not have to be poems. The idea is simply to get used to adding content to a framed site.

2. Add the links to the links.htm page. Target the links to the main frame.

3. Create a link on links.htm that links to a remote URL. It can be any site of interest, such as www.againsttheclock.com.

4. Link to an email address.

5. Change the format and layout of the site to appear more aesthetically appealing.

6. Add more content to the main page.

7. Refresh index.htm in your browser. Test the links.

8. Close the file in both applications.

FIGURE 7.38

PORTFOLIO BUILDER

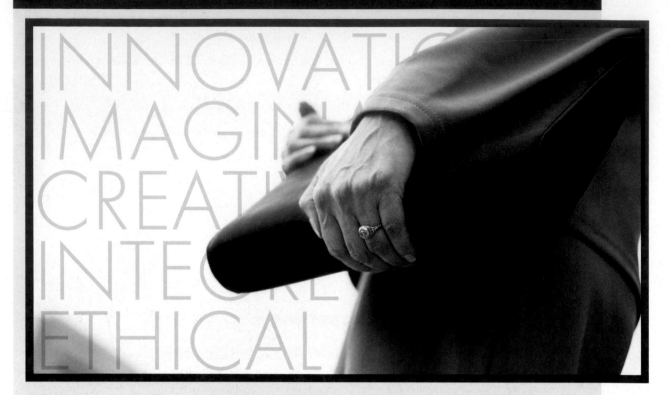

Create an Image Catalog

A stock photo company hired you to create an online image catalog. They specialize in three categories of images. They want an intuitive navigation system, a simple home page, and three additional pages to display their images. You decide that using frames is the best choice for the layout of the Web site.

To complete this exercise, you should do the following:

- Find a Web site that allows you to use free stock images, such as www.sxc.hu. Pick three categories of images, and download four images for each category.

- Consider how you want to create the framed layout of the site. You need to create one page for each category, a main page, and a menu page.

- Build the Web site. Include a main page as the original load page, and provide a menu page so visitors can navigate through the site.

- Consider what kind of menu page you want to use. Will you offer text navigation, or will you provide buttons? On each category page, place four images that relate to that category.

- Consider how to link all the pages within the site. Be sure to test the links to ensure they display in the correct frame.

Prepping and Publishing a Web Site

OBJECTIVES

In this project, you learn how to

- Add comments to content and code
- Work with special character entities
- Add meta data to your pages
- Include a document type definition

- Validate a Web site
- Register a domain name
- Work with hosting companies
- Submit a page to search engines

WHY WOULD I DO THIS?

As you completed the lessons and exercises in the first seven projects in this book, you learned the essentials of creating Web documents. Now that you understand how to create basic XHTML files, you can focus on the final stages of building and publishing a Web site. Part of this work involves adding comments to your code. *Comments* make it easier to update the code, as well as provide useful information about the content of the code to members of your team or others who might want to reuse your code.

Another important aspect of finalizing a site is adding keywords and descriptions to the pages. *Keywords* are the subject words used by online databases and search engines that help Web surfers locate your site quickly and easily.

You also need to register your own domain, validate your XHTML documents, and upload your site to a Web server. You concentrate on all of these key subjects in this final project of the book, as you learn how to successfully create a fully functional Web site.

V I S U A L   S U M M A R Y

 The diagram in Figure 8.1 shows the step-by-step process of publishing a Web site. In general, you should have a good idea of the type of site you want to build, as well as the content you want to include, before you begin the site-creation process.

We recommend that you sketch a site layout (storyboard) and flowchart as the first step in the design process. A *storyboard* is a series of sketches that illustrates your site on a page-by-page or section-by-section basis. In your storyboard, you can include notes about navigation, content, types of graphics, audio, and any other information that would be helpful to you and your team during development. Storyboards can prove invaluable in keeping you on track during every stage of development.

FIGURE 8.1

After the storyboard is complete, you develop and test the site. Then, you add comments and `<meta>` tags, followed by site validation. After you make the decision on whether to purchase Web space on someone else's domain, or register your own domain name, the final step is to upload your site to the Web. Once posted (uploaded), you should consider how best to promote your Web site so the viewing public knows that it is available for access and use.

LESSON 1 The Comment Tag

Some Web projects are so large that several programmers are needed to complete the scripting. Oftentimes, programmers located in different cities (or countries) work on the same project simultaneously. You must not overlook those occasions when a programmer starts a project, goes on vacation, and turns over the coding to someone else while he is away from the office. How can you ensure that all these disparate individuals who are involved in your project understand what has already been scripted, and why?

The answer is to write comments (notes) within the code. Commenting allows you to write anything about the code or project that you think is important, or that you might forget when you resume coding later. You can use comments to "comment out" sections of the document you don't want to display in the browser, but you don't want to delete (people can look at these sections if they view the source code). You do not have to remove your comments from the code before uploading the site to the Web; comments do not change the code in any way, nor do they display in the browser.

Commenting is the perfect communication mechanism for teams of programmers. The group leader can specify the goals of the script within the coding environment itself. Everyone on the team sees the same comments and can follow the same directions.

The **<comment>** tag doesn't look the same as other XHTML tags. For example:

```
<!-- this is a comment -->
```

The exclamation point followed by two dashes indicates the beginning of a comment. Another set of two dashes indicates the end of the comment. The HTML/XHTML parser ignores the content between the dashes, and hides the content from the Web page display.

Add a Comment Line

1 Copy the files from the Project_08 folder into your WIP_08 folder.

2 Open PoetrySite>index.htm in your text editor and Web browser.

The main page displays a complete Web site.

FIGURE 8.2

3 In the source file, add a comment at the top of the page to identify the author's contact information.

```
<html>

<head>

<title>My Favorite Poems</title>

<!--Contact author of site: Kelly Valqui - kvalqui@hotmail.com. -->

</head>

<body topmargin="0" bgcolor="#ffffff">

...
```

You can provide your contact information for those who view your source code.

4   **Add a comment to the bottom of the file indicating copyright information.**

```
...

<!-- The design of this Web site is copyrighted by Kelly Valqui.
Please contact me at kvalqui@hotmail.com if you wish to use any of the
content. -->

</body>

</html>
```

Providing important copyright information can warn viewers about your policy for copying content or code from your Web pages.

5   **Save the changes to the file. Refresh the document in your browser.**

FIGURE 8.3

The content placed within the **<comment>** tags does not display in the body of the Web page.

6   **Leave the file open in both applications for the next exercise.**

To Extend Your Knowledge...

COMMENTING TECHNIQUES

You can use comments as reminders of when and where to place content updates. When you edit XHTML code, comments allow you to identify where a particular section of content begins and ends.

LESSON 2 Adding Character Codes

At times, the Web browser does not display standard characters because the browser assumes that they are part of a command. For example, under normal circumstances, the browser would not display an actual XHTML tag on a Web page (such as **<p>**). Instead, the browser would insert a paragraph break at that point in the document because that is what the **<p>** tag usually means.

The way around this problem is to use special character references. You encode the actual ASCII value of the character in the document by prefixing the character with an ampersand (**&**) and a hash mark (**#**), and following it with a semi-colon (**;**).

- The ampersand tells XHTML that what follows is a special character definition.

- The hash mark says that the character is being represented by its *ASCII value,* which is the numeric representation of a character on a computer system. If you omit the hash mark, the browser expects a special character name, called a *character entity*, not its ASCII value.

- Special character references end with semi-colons; when the browser reaches a semi-colon, it knows it has reached the end of the character.

The following illustration shows some of the character references and how they display on a Web page.

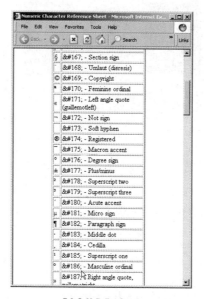

FIGURE 8.4

Some characters also have entity names that allow you to specify that character entity instead of the ASCII value. For instance, the left and right brackets around an HTML command have the ASCII values of **060** and **062** respectively; but they are also called "**lt**" and "**gt**." Therefore, the character "<" can be represented as either **<** or **<**, and the character ">" can be represented as either **>** or **>**.

A list of ASCII values and character entity names is included at the back of this book.

Using the numeric ASCII values is preferred to using the entity names because not all browsers support all entity names. Browsers must, by definition, support all ASCII values, since ASCII is how the computer interprets the characters. It is safe to include commonly used entity names for characters such as **<**, **>**, and **"** (for quotes). These names are easier to recognize in the code than their numeric equivalents.

XHTML Strict only recognizes the following special character names:

- **&** Ampersand (&)
- **<** Less than, open bracket (<)
- **>** Greater than, close bracket (>)
- **"** Double quote (")
- ** ** Non-breaking space (hard space) ( )

Add Copyright Information

1 In the open file, switch to the text editor window.

2 Add copyright information to the bottom of the page.

```
...

<p><font size="2" face="verdana">

Please join our mailing list to receive poems and updates by email.

</font></p>

<p align="center"><font face="verdana" size="2">Copyright &#169; 2004.
Kelly Valqui.</font></p>

</td>

</tr>

</table>

...
```

This provides the character code for a copyright symbol.

3 Save the changes to the file. Refresh the document in the browser.

FIGURE 8.5

The copyright symbol displays in the string of text along the bottom of the screen. The copyright symbol is not available on your keyboard. You can create the copyright symbol using the entity name "**©**". The entity name is not supported in XHTML, however, so the numeric value should be used instead.

4 Switch to the text editor window. Add the following quoted material.

```
...

<p><font size="2" face="verdana">

Welcome to my site. Here you'll find my favorite poems by my favorite
poets. There are other useful links to web sites that offer popular
poems.</font></p>

<p><font size="2" face="verdana">&quot;Success is counted sweetest by those
who ne'er succeed.&quot; - Emily Dickinson </font></p>

<table border="1" cellpadding="0" cellspacing="0" width="100%">

...
```

The character reference used an entity name. Remember that **"** is one of the character entities supported by XHTML.

? If you have problems...

The character entity only displays if the font you selected is also loaded on the viewer's machine. The viewer might experience problems if the browser does not interpret the encoding correctly.

5   **Save the changes to the file. Refresh the document in the browser.**

FIGURE 8.6

The paragraph is placed within quotes. Although you could have used the actual quote characters from your keyboard, using the character entity ensures the quotes display properly.

6   **Leave the file open in both applications for the next exercise.**

LESSON 3 Working with Meta Information

Meta information is literally information about information; *<meta> tags* provide useful information about the content of your Web site. **<Meta>** tags allow you to boost your site's ranking in some search engines and online directory listings by providing additional keywords and descriptions of the site. You can assign many attributes to **<meta>** tags. The most important attributes for search engine submission are **name="description"** and **name="keywords"**.

Normally, a search engine displays the first sentence of a page that it finds during a search. While this is certainly accurate, you might prefer that something more meaningful displays when a search engine returns a hit on your page. The *description value* tells the search engine precisely what to return as the description of the page, rather than the first sentence of the page.

As you know, keywords are words or phrases that a user is likely to type into a search engine when looking for information on the Web. The best way to develop a list of keywords for your site is to think about what you would type into a search engine if you were looking for information on your particular topic. When accurate keyword values are assigned to a site, the site receives a much higher ranking than one with poor keyword assignment. Below is some sample code that illustrates description and keyword values:

```
<html>

<head>

<title>Example of a Web page using Meta tags.</title>

<meta name="description" content="Learn how to use meta tags to increase
your chances of high rankings in search engine results pages." />

<meta name="keywords" content="example, Meta, tags" />

</head>
```

Add <meta> Tags to the Home Page

1   In the open document, switch to the text editor window.

2   Add keywords to the document using the `meta name=""` attribute.

```
<html>

<head>

<title>My Favorite Poems</title>

<meta http-equiv="keywords" content="famous poets, emily dickinson, robert
frost, T.C. Eliot, Walt Whitman, favorite poems">

<!--Contact author of site: Kelly Valqui - kvalqui@hotmail.com.-->

</head>

...
```

3   Add a description to the document.

```
<html>

<head>

<title>My Favorite Poems</title>

<meta http-equiv="description" content="The My Favorite Poems Web site is a
collection of favorite famous poems. Join the mailing list to receive site
updates.">

<meta http-equiv="keywords" content="famous poets, emily dickinson, robert
frost, T.C. Eliot, Walt Whitman, favorite poems">

<!--Contact author of site: Kelly Valqui - kvalqui@hotmail.com. -->

</head>

...
```

The description provides a detailed overview of the content of a site. The description displays in the search engine results page.

For now, do not add the closing slash to the **<meta>** tags. Later in the project, you validate the tags and correct this error.

4 | **Modify the page title so it's more descriptive.**

```
...

<title>My Favorite Poems - a collection of popular poems by famous
poets.</title>

...
```

The new title provides a more descriptive explanation of the Web site. This is important for viewers scanning several links to similar sites.

5 | **Save the changes to the file. Refresh the document in the browser.**

FIGURE 8.7

The document display remains unchanged. The Title bar reflects the modification.

6 | **Leave the file open for the next exercise.**

To Extend Your Knowledge...

RANKING HIGH IN A SEARCH

A search engine query often returns hundreds (sometimes thousands) of matching Web pages. In most cases, the 10 most likely matches are displayed first. These matches are called the "top 10." Of the hundreds of listings provided, most viewers look at about 30 listings. If your Web site is not included in the first 30 listings, it will probably be overlooked. Here are some techniques you can use to improve your chances of a higher ranking.

1. Pick Strategic Keywords. Decide what words you predict users will type into the Search field when looking for a site such as yours. Those are your strategic keywords, which should accurately reflect the content of your Web page. Your keywords should be two or more words long. Too many sites will be relevant for a single word, such as "dogs." Such stiff competition reduces your chances of success.

2. Position Your Keywords Carefully. Make sure your keywords appear in strategic locations on your Web pages — the most important of which is the page title. Failure to put tactical keywords in the page title is one of the primary reasons entirely relevant Web pages receive poor rankings.

Use keywords for your page headlines, if possible. They should also appear in the first paragraph of a page. Search engines read Web pages from top to bottom, assigning lesser importance to information as it moves down the page. Keep in mind that tables can push your text farther down the page (because tables break apart when search engines read them), assigning less relevance to keywords in the lower sections of the page.

LESSON 4   Validating a Web Site

Web page validation is an essential final step in Web page development, particularly when you use XHTML to code your documents. Web page *validation* checks your XHTML source code against a particular document type definition to ensure you properly coded your Web pages.

Although validation is not required when using HTML (it is advised), XHTML documents must be validated before they can be defined as XML applications. Since XHTML is the new standard for the Web, you should become familiar with the three document types.

Document Type Definitions

Applications such as browsers use *document type definitions* (*DTD*) to specify the "rules" that apply to a document's source code. DTD tags are required in XHTML. The tags tell the browser what kind of XHTML source code it can expect to render.

XHTML 1.0 specifies three document types: Strict, Transitional, and Frameset. You had a brief introduction to these document types in Project 1. Let's take a moment to review them.

Use the XHTML 1.0 Strict DTD tag when you do not include any of the deprecated tags from previous versions (namely presentational tags such as **`<b>`** and **`<font>`**) in your document. You can use XHTML Strict with cascading style sheets (CSS). The XHTML Strict DTD tag is:

```
<!DOCTYPE html
PUBLIC "-//W3C//DTD XHTML 1.0 Strict//EN"
http://www.w3.org/TR/xhtml1/DTD/xhtml1-strict.dtd />
```

Use the XHTML 1.0 Transitional DTD tag when you include some of the HTML presentational features, either with or without CSS. The XHTML Transitional DTD tag is:

```
<!DOCTYPE html
PUBLIC "-//W3C//DTD XHTML 1.0 Transitional//EN"
http://www.w3.org/TR/xhtml1/DTD/xhtml1-transitional.dtd />
```

Use the XHTML 1.0 Frameset DTD tag when you want to use HTML frames. The XHTML Frameset DTD tag is:

```
<!DOCTYPE html
PUBLIC "-//W3C//DTD XHTML 1.0 Frameset//EN"
http://www.w3.org/TR/xhtml1/DTD/xhtml1-frameset.dtd />
```

Let's look at the first example of a DTD tag — the XHTML Strict DTD.

- The first line, <!DOCTYPE html, indicates the document type to the Web browser. Even though you used XHTML, the document is still considered hypertext.

- The second line, PUBLIC "-//W3C//DTD XHTML 1.0 Strict//EN", indicates the type of XHTML you used, which in this example is Strict. Remember, in XHTML Strict, you cannot include presentational tags in the code.

- The third and final line, http://www.w3.org/TR/xhtml1/DTD/xhtml1-frameset.dtd, is the URL for the DTD. Here, the code in your page is compared against the actual DTD.

The DTD tag is placed above all the other tags in your document. It indicates which type of XHTML is used, as well as the location of the actual DTD, so the document can be compared to that language reference. You can use the W3C's validators to validate HTML, XHTML, and CSS files. To do so, include a link to http://validator.w3.org/ in your document, and then simply click the link to validate the document.

Validate the Home Page

1   **In the text editor of the open document, define index.htm as an XHTML Transitional document by providing the proper DTD at the top of the document, before the `<html>` tag.**

```
<!DOCTYPE html
PUBLIC "-//W3C//DTD XHTML 1.0 Transitional//EN"
http://www.w3.org/TR/xhtml1/DTD/xhtml1-transitional.dtd />

<html>

...
```

Your document includes presentational elements, including the **`<font>`** tag, which is why you must define index.htm as an XHTML Transitional document.

2   **Save the changes to file. Refresh the Web browser.**

The display remains the same, since you only added information about the XHTML DTD.

3   **If you have an active Internet connection, log on to http://www.htmlhelp.com/tools/validator/upload.html.**

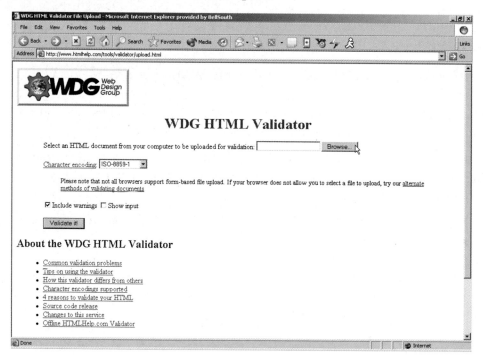

FIGURE 8.8

Htmlhelp.com offers an excellent XHTML validation service. You can upload documents from your machine, or provide a URL.

4   **Click the Browse button to display the Choose File dialog box.**

FIGURE 8.9

5   **Choose index.htm from the list of files in the PoetrySite folder. Click the Open button.**

The file uploads and displays in the text field on the Web page.

6   **Click the "Validate it!" button on the Validation page.**

Validate it!

FIGURE 8.10

Error: end tag for meta omitted; end tags are required in XML for non-empty elements; empty elements require an end tag or the start tag must end with />

- Line 8, character 1:

  `<meta name="description" content="The My Favorite Poems Web  ...`
  `^`

  start tag was here

- Line 9, character 120:

  `... lt Whitman, favorite poems" >`
  `                                ^`

  Error: end tag for meta omitted; end tags are required in XML for non-empty elements; empty elements require an end tag or the start tag must end with />

- Line 9, character 1:

  `<meta name="keywords" content="famous poets, emily dickinson ...`
  `^`

  start tag was here

Validate by URL ~ Validate by file upload ~ Validate by direct input

Developed and maintained by Liam Quinn <liam@htmlhelp.com>

FIGURE 8.11

The results page returns some errors. We intentionally included errors in the code so you would have the opportunity to correct them and revalidate.

7   **Leave the file open in both applications.**

Correct Validation Errors

1 In the text editor of the open file, make the following minor corrections at the ends of the `<meta name="">` lines in index.htm.

```
...

<head>

<title>My Favorite Poems - a collection of popular poems by famous
poets.</title>

<meta name="description" content="The My Favorite Poems Web site is a col-
lection of favorite famous poems. Join the mailing list to receive site
updates." />

<meta name="keywords" content="famous poets, emily dickinson, robert frost,
T.C. Eliot, Walt Whitman, favorite poems" />

<!--Contact author of site: Kelly Valqui - kvalqui@hotmail.com. -->

</head>

<body bgcolor="#ffffff">

...
```

The lack of the closing "/" at the end of each `<meta>` tag resulted in the `<meta>` tags remaining open. With the added "/" on each `<meta>` tag, the tags are now properly closed and the code complies with the XHTML standards. Keep in mind that sometimes one error might cause the validation program to report another error. More often than not, correcting an obvious error prevents other errors from showing.

To Extend Your Knowledge...

MORE ON <META> TAGS

As you know, meta keywords and descriptions are the most popular meta information used today. You should include them on every Web page. Search engines, such as AltaVista, use these `<meta>` tags to help identify and catalog your pages (as you learn later in this project). These are not the only `<meta>` tags available to you. Here are some other tags you can use:

<meta name="revisit" content="15days" /> This tag tells the search engine how often it should revisit your page. This is especially helpful if you update your pages on a regular basis. Every time the search engine visits your site, it updates its index with your new content.

<meta name="robots" content="nofollow" /> This is useful if you have a "linear" Web site — you want visitors to see the main page first, and then navigate the site in a specific manner, rather than find your site through one of the other individual pages. The content values include all, index, nofollow, and noindex.

For more information on `<meta>` tags, visit searchenginewatch.com/webmasters/article.php/2167931.

2   Save the changes to index.htm in the text editor.

3   Click the Back button in the Web browser to return to the original validation page.

4   Re-upload the document.

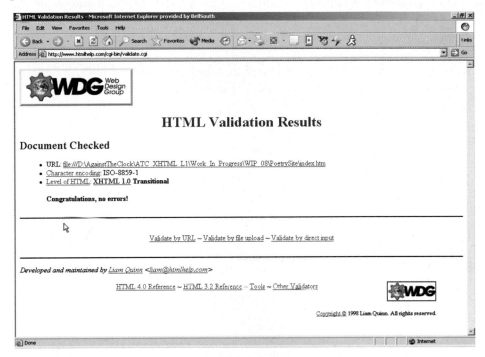

FIGURE 8.12

These minor corrections resolved the errors.

5   Close the file in the text editor.

LESSON 5 Publishing a Web Site

There are still many tasks to complete before you are ready to publish your Web site, one of which is to decide if you are going to register your own domain name. Domain names are not required, but they are certainly very beneficial, especially if you are building a commercial site (.com). *Domain names* are used in URLs to identify specific Web pages. For example, in the URL http://www.againsttheclock.com, the domain name is againsttheclock.com.

Every domain name has a suffix (usually three letters) that indicates which top-level domain it belongs to. The most commonly used suffixes and the associated top-level domains are listed below:

- **.com** for commercial business

- **.edu** for educational institutions

- **.gov** for government agencies

- **.mil** for the military

- **.net** for network organizations

- **.org** for nonprofit organizations

The Importance of a Domain Name

The primary reason to own a domain name is that it always stays with you, regardless of where the site is hosted. For example, if you change your Web hosting service, you don't need to worry that your regular visitors will no longer be able to find your site. If they know your site name as www.mywebsite.com on one Web host, that is exactly how it remains on every other Web host — as long as you own your domain name. Users simply enter your Web address as usual, and they are directed to your new site.

Registering a Domain Name

Securing a domain name involves searching for an available name, and then registering that name with InterNIC through a domain registrar. A *domain registrar* is a company that allows you to register domain names through them, and then they update *InterNIC*, which is the organization that indexes domain names.

Once you choose a domain name, such as mygreatwebsite.com, you must go to a registrar and pay a registration fee that ranges from $15 to $35 (annually). Once registered, you have rights to the name for a year, or however long you registered the name. Renewals are optional.

Although many hosting providers suggest that you list them as the technical contact, you might prefer to list yourself as the technical contact. Doing so makes it much easier to transfer your domain name to a new Web host. You don't have to wait for your old host to approve the transfer; instead, the new host contacts you directly.

When you register your domain name, be prepared to pay your fee with a credit card (it's a requirement). Two popular places to register your domain name are NetworkSolutions.com and Register.com.

Your Hosting Service Provider

Selecting a Web site hosting provider that best suits your needs can be a confusing (and sometimes frustrating) task. As you sift through the multitude of hosting options, you will find that hosting prices vary significantly, as do the supplied technologies. You must decide if you need a simple account, database support, FrontPage extensions, and much more.

While all Web hosts experience downtime, it is important to identify the extent of these lapses in service. Your host's downtime greatly affects your site. When your host is down, your Web site is down, too. You should expect your host to have at least 95% uptime (or better). Don't fall for the 100% uptime that some providers boast. It doesn't exist. A good host alerts you about problems before your viewers have a chance to notice them.

Your host should have a strong customer-care and technical-support team. Be sure to ask about the availability of commercial technical support. Often, if you are paying an unbelievably low hosting price, your host is cutting corners somewhere. In addition, beware of the hosting provider that does not offer a telephone number for technical support.

It is important to question both high- and low-cost hosting packages. When evaluating prices, be sure to find out exactly what is (and is not) included in the price. Look at other factors driving the price. Are you paying for a package that you don't really need? Does the package provide all the technologies you require? If you don't need the technologies in one package, find another package.

Check Domain Name Availability

1 **If you have an active Internet connection, log on to www.register.com.**

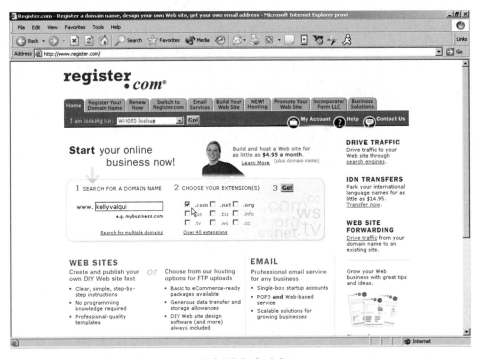

FIGURE 8.13

2 Look for the text box that allows you to search for a domain name.

It's located below the Start arrow.

3 Type in your preferred domain name. Check the domain name extension, such as .com or .edu.

4 Click the Go button to submit the search.

Register.com searches for this domain name. If it is available, you have the option to reserve it; if it is not available, alternate domain names and extensions are provided.

5 Leave the Web browser window open for the next exercise.

To Extend Your Knowledge...

UPLOADING YOUR SITE AND GOING LIVE

When development is complete, and your Web site is ready, all your files are stored only on your computer. To make your Web site available to the public, you need to transfer your files to a computer (your Web host's server) that has a special connection to the Internet — which is, of course, a Web server.

Once you have established a hosting account, and your hosting provider has given you the necessary information about the Web server so you can transfer your domain name, you can upload your pages to the Web server and "go live." (Remember, you don't have to register your domain name to publish your site.) If you are not comfortable transferring your domain name, most hosting providers will transfer the domain for you.

The most common method of copying/moving files from your computer to the Web server is to use **FTP**, which stands for **File Transfer Protocol.** To access an FTP server, you need an FTP address, a username, and a password, all of which your hosting service or server administrator should provide to you. Many hosting services provide FTP instructions and/or software for you to use.

LESSON 6   Search Engine Registration

At one time or another, you have probably used a search engine (such as yahoo.com, google.com, altavista.com, or ask.com) to locate specific information on the Web, or to locate a particular Web site. A **search engine** is actually an online URL database or index. When you log on to a search engine, you enter specific keywords, click the Search button, and the search engine looks through its index to locate Web pages that match your keywords. The pages the search engine returns are ordered according to how relevant they are to your **search criteria** (your keywords); the most relevant sites are placed at the top of the list, and sites of lesser relevance are placed lower in the list.

Submitting to a Search Engine

Getting your page to display in the top 10 on a search return isn't easy. Don't be discouraged if you have trouble locating your Web page in a search return after you register your site. Most likely, many other sites pertain to the same subject as yours, especially if yours is a commercial Web site. Even though `<meta>` tags are supposed to bring your Web site to the top of every search list, there are no guarantees.

An excellent source of information for search engine submission is www.searchenginewatch.com. The site includes information on how search engines work, alternative ways to register your sites, as well as online marketing resources.

Registering Your Web Site

In order for a search engine to return a site in its list of results, the site must first be registered with the search engine. You can register your site with each individual search engine, or you can register your site with a submission service that, in turn, registers your site with multiple search engines. Keep in mind that each search engine is different. Some require information about the site, others allow you to resubmit or edit your site, and some ask you to place a reciprocal link to their search engine. To ensure correct registration, be certain you understand the requirements of each search engine before you register your site.

The actual registration process is quite simple. After you upload your site to a Web server, log on to various search engines and follow the instructions to register your Web page. Each search engine provides a link that says, "Add Your URL" or "Register Your Site." Clicking this link takes you to the registration page. Once on the registration page, you complete an online form with your site's URL, and then submit the form to the search engine's database. Within a few weeks, your site should be active on the search engine.

It's a good idea to test each search engine to ensure your site is properly registered. Go to each of the search engines where you registered your site, enter the appropriate keywords, and check to see that your site is included on the list of returns.

Register a Web Page

1   Log on to www.altavista.com, a popular search engine.

2   Click the Submit a Site link.

FIGURE 8.14

? If you have problems...

The instructions to register a site with AltaVista were accurate at the time of this writing. It is possible the registration process has changed. To ensure a successful registration, be sure you follow the on-screen instructions on AltaVista.

3   Follow the on-screen instructions for submitting a Web site.

You can submit individual Web pages. For instance, you can submit the home page, www.mysite.com, and each individual page's URL, such as www.mysite.com/about.htm. We recommend that you provide unique **`<meta>`** tags for each page within your Web site, and then register each page's URL with the search engines of your choice.

To Extend Your Knowledge...

CASE SENSITIVITY

Depending on the Web server, HTML file names may be case sensitive. Knowing how to name files correctly minimizes the possibility of links being broken due to incorrect file-naming conventions. We recommend that you use only lowercase file names.

Usernames and passwords are usually case sensitive. Check with your hosting provider to ensure that you understand their case requirements.

4	Repeat Steps 2 and 3 to register each page within your Web site.

5	Close the browser window.

SUMMARY

In Project 8, you learned that Web site creation includes much more than writing XHTML code. You learned that before you publish a Web site, you must prepare it in various ways. You discovered how to add comments to your code, which allow you to insert information and content throughout your Web site that does not display in the browser window. Comments allow you to provide additional information for those who view your source code, including contact information and copyright policies.

You learned that `<meta>` tags allow you to insert keywords and descriptions about your site, and that `<meta>` tags allows search engines to return your site in their search results. You learned that you must carefully consider the description you include on your page, since this description is what is returned to the user on the search results page.

You discovered that you must validate a Web page as an XHTML file before you can publish the document on the Web. Online validation services make it easy to check your code — and then correct any errors — before you publish your documents. You learned that you can register a domain name, and then upload your site to a reputable hosting service to "go live" on the Web. Finally, you discovered how to register your pages with search engines to ensure that the Web-viewing audience notices your site.

CAREERS IN DESIGN

THE DIFFERENT FACES OF WEB DEVELOPERS

Anyone reading this book who has had experience in the print industry understands the vast difference between the roles of creative personnel and production professionals. In that arena, designers are responsible for developing the look and feel that shapes the perceptions and experiences of the audience. Once the designer has finalized the layout of the piece, the production phase of the workflow begins. Print production professionals are responsible for ensuring the quality of the images, the clarity of the typography, and the other processes required to reproduce the design in quantity.

In the world of Web design, the same situation exists. Web designers are responsible for the look, feel, and effectiveness of the visitor's experience; their responsibility ends there. The next step in the process lies in the hands of Web developers — the programmers, database experts, and site maintenance professionals responsible for the "wiring" of the site.

The skills required for these two types of positions, while equally important, are dramatically different. This holds true in all aspects of professional communication. Creative talent ensures the quality of the user experience, while technical expertise ensures proper preparation and delivery of the content to the end user. As your career matures, it will become apparent on which side of the fence your talents lie — creative or technical.

KEY TERMS

ASCII value

Character entity

Comment tag

Comments

Description value

Document type definition (DTD)

Domain name

Domain registrar

File Transfer Protocol (FTP)

InterNIC

Keyword

Meta tags

Search criteria

Search engine

Storyboard

Upload

Validation

CHECKING CONCEPTS AND TERMS

MULTIPLE CHOICE

Circle the letter that matches the correct answer for each of the following questions.

1. How is the comment tag different than the other tags?
   a. There are no opening and closing tag commands.
   b. Comment tags begin with an exclamation point and two dashes.
   c. The comment tag displays content in the Title bar.
   d. None of the above.

2. What is the character entity for a non-breaking space?
   a. ©
   b.
   c. "
   d. None of the above.

3. Meta tags are container tags.
   a. True
   b. False

4. What meta value allows you to provide a description in a search engine results page?
   a. keywords
   b. description
   c. title
   d. author

5. Why should you assign descriptive titles to your documents?
   a. Sometimes search engines display the title as the actual link to the Web page.
   b. So readers know the exact page they are on.
   c. The title is one of the basic document tags.
   d. All of the above.

6. Why is it so important to validate your Web pages?
   a. You must ensure your XHTML source code meets the DTD requirements.
   b. You must ensure your XHTML source code meets the FTP requirements.
   c. You must ensure your XHTML source code meets the FCC requirements.
   d. None of the above.

7. What DTD is used for non-presentational code?

   a. Transitional

   b. Strict

   c. Frameset

8. What protocol uploads documents to a Web server?

   a. http

   b. mailto:

   c. smtp

   d. ftp

9. You are required to register every Web page.

   a. True

   b. False

10. Why is it best to use only lowercase file names?

   a. In case the server is case-sensitive, this helps prevent broken links.

   b. To ensure everything is in the same format.

   c. Adhering to one file-naming convention helps keep your files better organized.

   d. All of the above.

DISCUSSION QUESTIONS

1.   List at least three ways to take advantage of commenting code and content.

2.   When would you want to avoid using `<meta>` tags, and why?

3.   Discuss other ways to promote a Web site besides search engine registration.

SKILL DRILL

Skill Drills reinforce project skills. Each skill reinforced is the same, or nearly the same, as a skill presented in the lessons. Detailed instructions are provided in a step-by-step format. You should work through these exercises in the order provided.

1. Comment a Web Page

In this exercise, you provide comment lines for those who view your source code. You explain that other users are allowed to use the poems in their own collections.

1. Open index.htm from the WIP_08>PoetrySite folder.

2. Create a **<comment>** tag beneath the **<body>** tag.

3. For the content of the **<comment>** tag, add the following description.

   ```
   <!--This is a collection of my favorite poems. Please feel free to link to
   my Web page or use the poems for your own favorite collection. -->
   ```

4. Save the changes to index.htm.

5. Open the other documents within the PoetrySite folder. Add comment lines beneath the **<body>** tags to describe the documents. The comments can be brief descriptions about the poet featured on the page, or they can be copyright information.

6. Save your changes.

7. Open index.htm in a browser. Navigate through the site to ensure that the comments do not display on the pages.

FIGURE 8.15

8. Save your changes. Keep the file open for the next exercise.

2. Add <meta> Tags

You decide to include **<meta>** tags to increase the chances that your Web pages gain a high ranking on search engine results pages, as well as to provide a description of your pages to viewers.

1. From the PoetrySite folder, open emily.htm in the text editor and the browser.

2. Use **<meta>** tags to add keywords in the head of the document, such as "Emily Dickinson, famous poet, poetry, There is a Word."

3. Add the following description (using the **description=""** attribute) beneath the keyword **<meta>** tag in the head of the document.

   `"Emily Dickinson was born in Amherst, Massachusetts, on December 10, 1830."`

4. Provide the following descriptive title to the **<title>** tag: "Emily Dickinson, famous poetess."

```
emily - Notepad
File  Edit  Format  View  Help
<html>
<head>


<title>Emily Dickinson, famous poetess</title>
<meta name="description" content="Emily Dickinson was born in Amherst, Massachuetts on December
10, 1830.">
<meta name="keywords" content="Emily Dickinson, famous poet, poetry, There is a word.">

<body topmargin="0" bgcolor="#ffffff">


  <center>
  <table border="0" cellpadding="2">
    <tr>
      <td>
            <center>
            <img border="0" src="images/logo.gif" alt="My Favorite Poems" width="210"
height="23"></center>
            </td>
    </tr>
  </table>
  </center>
```

FIGURE 8.16

5. Save the changes to the file. Refresh the document in the browser.

6. Close all open windows.

3. Add Character Entities

In this exercise, you provide the year for copyright and the author of the Web page.

1. Open emily.htm in the text editor.

2. Add quotes around the actual body of the poem (excluding the title).

3. Beneath the poem, add the text, "Copyright © 2004. Kelly Valqui."

4. Save the changes to the file. Open the document in a browser.

5. Modify the rest of the poet pages by adding quotes around the poems, and adding the copyright information at the bottom of the page, directly beneath the poem.

6. Save the changes to the file. Test the Web site in your browser.

FIGURE 8.17

7. Close all open windows.

4. Validate the Web Site

The final step is to ensure your pages conform to the XHTML standard. You decide to use the Web site validator at www.htmlhelp.com.

1.   Open index.htm in the text editor.

     The file is located in the PoctrySite folder.

2.   Remove the alt name-value pair from all the image tags.

3.   Save the changes to the file. Launch your browser.

4.   Navigate to http://www.htmlhelp.com/tools/validator/. Validate the page by following the instructions for uploading a document from your hard drive.

     Errors display on the results page because image tags require the **<alt>** tag.

5.   Return to the text editor that contains index.htm. Add the **alt=""** attributes (with values) to all the images.

6.   Save the changes to the file. Re-upload the document to http://www.htmlhelp.com/tools/validator/.

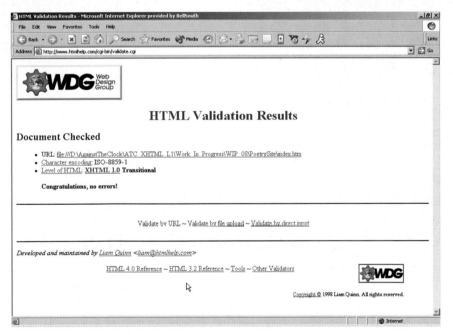

FIGURE 8.18

7.   Close the file in both applications.

CHALLENGE

Challenge exercises expand on, or are somewhat related to, skills presented in the lessons. Each exercise provides a brief introduction, followed by instructions presented in a numbered-step format that are not as detailed as those in the Skill Drill exercises. You should work through these exercises in the order provided.

1. Comment Out Sections of Body Content

Now that you've prepped the poetry site for final publication, complete the project by adding content, obtaining a hosting account, and validating the rest of the Web site.

1. From the WIP_08>PoetrySite folder, open emily.htm in the text editor.

2. Beneath the poem, add the following poem:

```
The Forgotten Grave
After a hundred years
Nobody knows the place, --
Agony that enacted there,
Motionless as peace.

Weeds triumphant ranged,
Strangers strolled and spelled
At the lone orthography
Of the elder dead.

Winds of summer fields
Recollect the way, --
Instinct picking up the key
Dropped by memory.
```

FIGURE 8.19

3. Save the changes. Open the file in a browser to display the new poem.

4. Comment out the poem you just inserted on the page.

5. Above the commented poem, add another **`<comment>`** tag and include the following: "Next poem to be featured."

6. Save the changes to index.htm. Refresh the document in the browser.

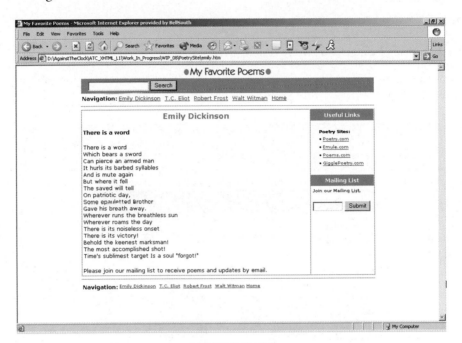

FIGURE 8.20

7. Save the file and leave it open for the next exercise.

2. Prepare for Search Engines

Before you publish you documents on the Web, you should provide additional information for search engine indexing. In this exercise, you use **`<meta>`** tags to add keywords and a description.

1. From the WIP_08>PoetrySite folder, open each poet's XHTML document in a text editor.

2. Provide 10 meta keywords for each page.

3. Provide a meta description for each page.

4. Change each title to one that is more descriptive.

5. Think of other ways to provide content for the site to increase search engine ranking, such as descriptive headings.

FIGURE 8.21

6. Save your changes. Test the document in the browser.

7. Leave the file open for the next exercise.

3. Find Free Hosting

In this exercise, you search the Web for free hosting service providers, and set up an account so you can publish your documents.

1. Launch a browser and go to www.google.com.

2. Type in "free Web hosting" in the Search field.

    You should receive a long list of free Web hosting services.

3. Find a service that suits your needs, such as the one found at www.free.prohosting.com (shown below). Create an account with the hosting provider.

FIGURE 8.22

4. To test the service, upload the entire content of the PoetrySite folder to their server.

5. Navigate through the Web site to ensure all the links work.

4. Validate an Entire Site

Even though you can validate documents on the Web by providing a URL, in this exercise you upload your document to the online validator, and then correct any errors that are returned.

1. Log on to the free online validation service.

2. Upload WIP_08>PoetrySite>emily.htm. Validate the document.

   You should receive a long list of errors that includes capital commands, missing quotes, and missing ending tags.

3. Using the error results page, navigate through the source file and make the necessary corrections.

4. Save the changes to the file. Re-upload the file to the validation service. Correct any errors that remain.

5. Repeat this process with the rest of the documents in the PoetrySite folder.

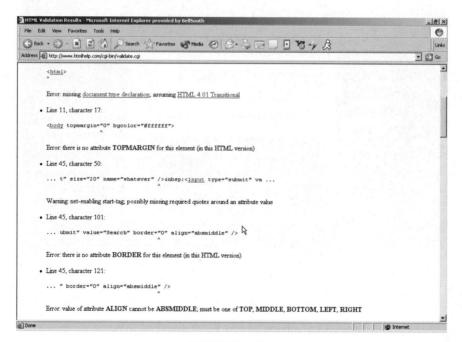

FIGURE 8.23

6. Close all open files and applications.

PORTFOLIO BUILDER

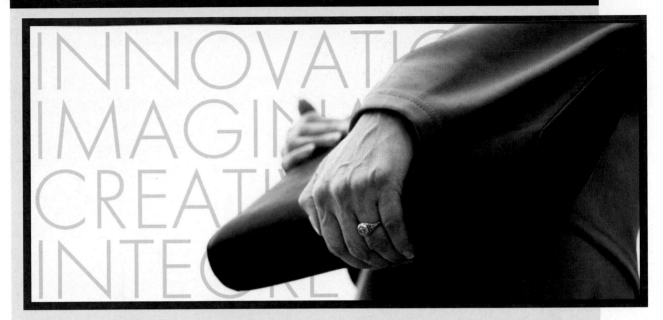

Publish a Portfolio Web Site

A published Web portfolio provides a very effective way to show your work to potential clients — all they need is an Internet connection to view your entire collection of pieces. Before you can publish an online portfolio of your work, however, you need to create the files, which should have been done in Project 4. If you did not complete the Portfolio Builder in Project 4, please do so now, and then you can complete this exercise.

To publish your portfolio site:

- Examine your source code to determine which document type definition is best for your pages. Validate your documents against that DTD.

- Depending on your specific needs, you can decide if you need to purchase a domain name of your own, or if you can use the domain name of your Web hosting service.

- After you decide whether to host your site with a free service or pay for a service, create a hosting account.

- If you choose to use a free Web hosting service, find out if the service will place any kind of advertisement on your page. You must consider how advertisements will affect your site's design.

- Upload your pages using whatever FTP method your hosting provider suggests.

- Make sure you include **<meta>** tags for each of your Web pages, regardless of whether you manually index your pages, or you use a service that indexes the pages for you.

- Register each of your pages with the search engines of your choice.

INTEGRATING PROJECT

This Integrating Project is designed to reflect a real-world XHTML programming job, drawing on the skills you learned throughout this book. The files you need to complete this project are located in the RF_XHTML_L1>IP folder.

Build the Backwater's Web Site

In this Integrating Project, you create a three-page Web site for a restaurant. The home page includes information about the restaurant; the menu page allows viewers to see the variety of foods offered at the restaurant; and the form page allows users to submit inquiries to the owner of the restaurant. Once the site is complete, you prepare it for publishing by providing meta information for search engines, as well as validate the document.

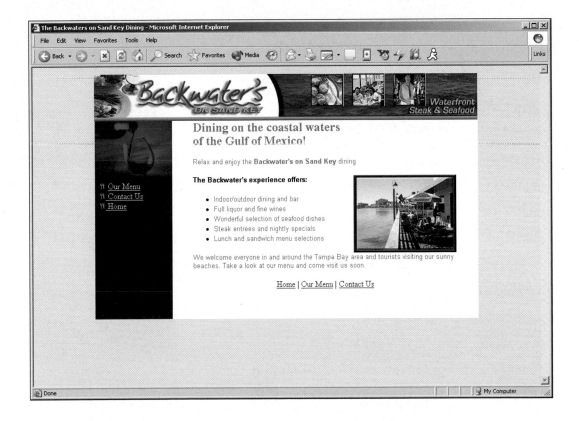

Plan a Site and Create a Home Page

1 Copy the RF_XHTML_L1>IP folder to your WIP_IP folder.

The images you need to complete this project are in the RF_XHTML_L1>IP folder. If you were hired to complete an actual project such as this one, the client or a graphic artist would provide the necessary images.

2 Open your text editor. Create a new XHTML document by adding the following document tags to the text file.

```
<html>
<head>
<title></title>
</head>
<body>
</body>
</html>
```

3 Save the file as "index.htm" in your WIP>IP>BackWater_Web folder.

Index.htm is the home page.

4 Open your browser. Navigate to the WIP>IP>BackWater_Web folder and open index.htm.

Index.htm displays in the browser as a blank document.

5 Switch to the text editor. Position your cursor between the **<title></title>** tags, enter the title, and then add the content shown beneath the **<body>** tag, as follows:.

```
<html>
<head><title>The Backwaters on Sand Key Dining</title></head>
<body>
<p>Dining on the coastal waters <br>of the Gulf of Mexico!</p>
<p>Relax and enjoy the Backwater's on Sand Key dining</p>
The Backwater's experience offers:<br />
Indoor/outdoor dining and bar<br />
Full liquor and fine wines<br />
Wonderful selection of seafood dishes<br />
Steak entrees and nightly specials<br />
```

```
Lunch and sandwich menu selections<br />

<p>We welcome everyone in and around the Tampa Bay area and tourists visit-
ing our sunny beaches.

Take a look at our menu and come visit us soon.</p>

</body>

</html>
```

6   Save the changes to index.htm. Refresh the document in your browser.

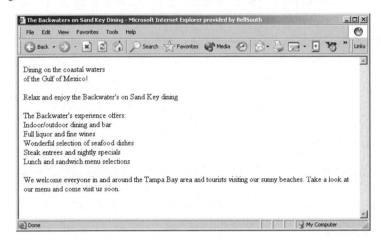

The text displays in paragraphs with single line breaks. Now you are ready to format the content.

7   Leave both applications open for the next exercise.

Format the Home Page

1   In the open document, switch to the text editor window.

2   Format the document by adding and replacing tags, as follows:

```
<html>

<head><title>The Backwaters on Sand Key Dining</title></head>

<body>

<h2> Dining on the coastal waters <br>of the Gulf of Mexico! </h2>

<p>Relax and enjoy the <b>Backwater's on Sand Key</b> dining</p>

<b>The Backwater's experience offers: </b>
```

```
<ul>
   <li>Indoor/outdoor dining and bar</li>
   <li>Full liquor and fine wines</li>
   <li>Wonderful selection of seafood dishes</li>
   <li>Steak entrees and nightly specials</li>
   <li>Lunch and sandwich menu selections</li>
</ul>
<p>We welcome everyone in and around the Tampa Bay area and tourists visit-
ing our sunny beaches.
Take a look at our menu and come visit us soon.</p>
</body>
</html>
```

3   Save the changes in the text editor. Refresh the document in the browser.

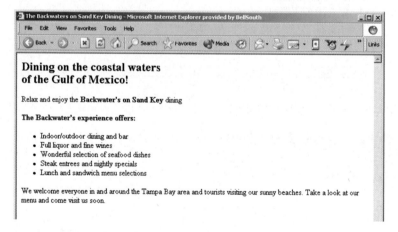

The formatting changes the display dramatically.

4   Switch to the text editor. Change the color and font style, as follows:

```
<html>
<head><title>The Backwaters on Sand Key Dining</title></head>
<body>
<h2><font color="#808080">Dining on the coastal waters <br>of the Gulf of
Mexico!</font></h2>
<p><font size="2" face="Arial" color="#808080"> Relax and enjoy the
<b>Backwater's on Sand Key</b> dining</font></p>
```

```
<b><font size="2" face="Arial" color="#000000">The Backwater's experience
offers:</font> </b>

<ul>

  <li><font size="2" face="Arial" color="#808080">Indoor/outdoor dining and
bar</font></li>

  <li><font size="2" face="Arial" color="#808080">Full liquor and fine
wines</font></li>

  <li><font size="2" face="Arial" color="#808080">Wonderful selection of
seafood dishes</font></li>

  <li><font size="2" face="Arial" color="#808080">Steak entrees and nightly
specials</font></li>

  <li><font size="2" face="Arial" color="#808080">Lunch and sandwich menu
selections</font></li>

</ul>

<p><font size="2" face="Arial" color="#808080">We welcome everyone in and
around the Tampa Bay area and tourists visiting our sunny beaches.

Take a look at our menu and come visit us soon.</font></p>

</body>

</html>
```

5 Save the changes in the text editor. Refresh the document in the browser.

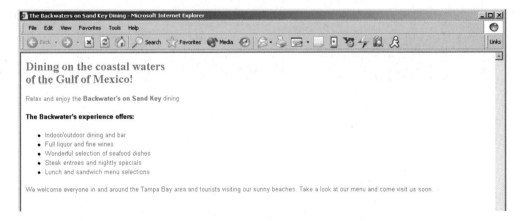

The font style displays as Arial, and the color as gray. The size of the text displays as XHTML Level 2.

6 Leave both applications open for the next exercise.

Place an Image and Provide a Background

1 In the open document, switch to the text editor window.

2 Add an image to the main page.

```
<html>

<head><title>The Backwaters on Sand Key Dining</title></head>

<body>

<h2><font color="#808080">Dining on the coastal waters <br>of the Gulf of
Mexico!</font></h2>

<p><font size="2" face="Arial" color="#808080">Relax and enjoy the
<b>Backwater's on Sand Key</b> dining</font></p>

<img border="0" alt="Backwaters Dining"  src="images/outside.jpg"
width="200" height="149" />

<b><font size="2" face="Arial" color="#000000">The Backwater's experience
offers:

</font> </b>

<ul>

...
```

3 Save the changes to the text file. Refresh the document in the browser.

The image displays in the default location on the page.

4 Switch to the text editor. Right-align the image to the text on the Web page.

```
...

<head><title>The Backwaters on Sand Key Dining</title></head>

<body>

<h2><font color="#808080">Dining on the coastal waters <br>of the Gulf of
Mexico!</font></h2>

<p><font size="2" face="Arial" color="#808080">Relax and enjoy the
<b>Backwater's on Sand Key</b> dining</font></p>

<img border="0" alt="Backwaters Dining"  src="images/outside.jpg"
width="200" height="149" align="right" />

<ul>

   <li><font size="2" face="Arial" color="#808080">Indoor/outdoor dining and
bar</font></li>

   <li><font size="2" face="Arial" color="#808080">Full liquor and fine
wines</font></li>

...
```

5 Include a background image for the Web page.

```
<html>

<head><title>The Backwaters on Sand Key Dining</title></head>

<body background="Images/bkg.gif">

<h2><font color="#808080">Dining on the coastal waters <br>of the Gulf of
Mexico!</font></h2>

<p><font size="2" face="Arial" color="#808080">Relax and enjoy the
<b>Backwater's on Sand Key</b> dining</font></p>

...
```

6   Save the changes to the text file. Refresh the document in the browser.

The background image displays, and the main image aligns on the right side of the Web page.

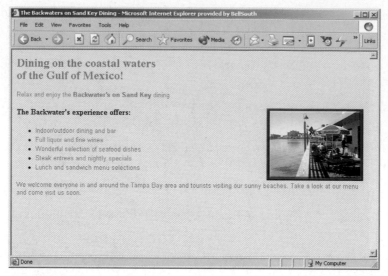

7   Leave both applications open for the next exercise.

Create a Navigational System

1   In the open file, add navigational links to the bottom of the page.

```
...

   <li><font size="2" face="Arial" color="#808080">Lunch and sandwich menu
selections</font></li>

</ul>

<p><font size="2" face="Arial" color="#808080">We welcome everyone in and
around the Tampa Bay area and tourists visiting our sunny beaches.

Take a look at our menu and come visit us soon.</font></p>

<p align="center">

<a href="index.htm">Home</a>   |

<a href="menu.htm">Our Menu</a>   |

<a href="contact.htm">Contact Us</a>

</p>

</body>

</html>
```

Before you begin creating a Web site, you typically know how many pages to include, as well as the names of the pages (Home, About, Contact). Once you know this information, you can begin building the navigational system, as well as the links to documents that you'll create later. Designers often include text links along the bottom of the page to provide an alternative navigational system.

2 Save the changes to the text file. Refresh the document in the browser.

The links display at the bottom of the page, even though they do not yet link to anything.

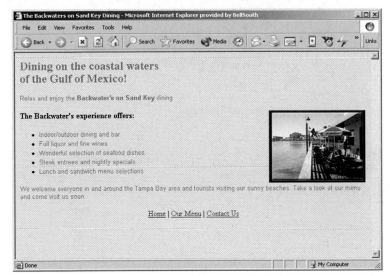

3 Switch to the text editor. Add names to all of the links.

```
...

<p>We welcome everyone in and around the Tampa Bay area and tourists visit-
ing our sunny beaches.

Take a look at our menu and come visit us soon.</p>

<p align="center">

<a href="index.htm" title="Our home page">Home</a>   |

<a href="menu.htm" title="Our Menu">Our Menu</a>   |

<a href="contact.htm" title="Feel free to contact us.">Contact Us</a>

</p>

</body>

</html>
```

4   Save the changes to the text file. Refresh the document in the browser. Hover your cursor over the links.

A yellow tool tip displays the text contained in the **title=""** attributes.

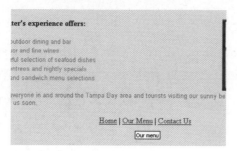

5   Leave both applications open for the next exercise.

Use Tables for the Layout

1   In the open file, create a table at the top of the page, above the existing content.

```
<html>
<head><title>The Backwaters on Sand Key Dining</title></head>
<body background="Images/bkg.gif">
<table width="747" border="0" cellpadding="0" cellspacing="0">
    <tr>
    <td rowspan="2">
    <img src="images/tophead_01.jpg" width="81" height="83" /></td>
    <td rowspan="2">
    <img src="images/tophead_02.gif" width="256" height="83" /></td>
    <td rowspan="2">
    <img src="images/tophead_03.gif" width="86" height="83" /></td>
    <td>
    <img border="0" src="images/3top.jpg" width="63" height="63" /></td>
    <td>
    <img src="images/tophead_05.jpg" width="16" height="63" /></td>
    <td>
```

```
<img border="0" src="images/1top.jpg" width="63" height="63"></td>

<td>

<img src="images/tophead_07.jpg" width="16" height="63" /></td>

<td>

<img border="0" src="images/2top.jpg" width="63" height="63" /></td>

<td>

<img src="images/tophead_09.gif" width="100" height="63" /></td>

</tr>

<tr>

<td colspan="6">

<img src="images/tophead_10.gif" width="324" height="20" /></td>

</tr>

<tr>

<td colspan="9">

<img src="images/tophead_11.gif" width="747" height="7" /></td>

</tr>

</table>
<h2><font color="#808080">Dining on the coastal waters <br>of the Gulf of
Mexico!</font></h2>
<p><font size="2" face="Arial" color="#808080">Relax and enjoy the
<b>Backwater's on Sand Key</b> dining</font></p>

...
```

This table displays a top header that consists of some images. Study the rows and cells in this advanced table to see how the table creates an image layout.

2 Save the changes. Refresh the document in the browser.

The table displays on the left side of the page, above the rest of the content. Next, you format the table so it aligns with the rest of the content.

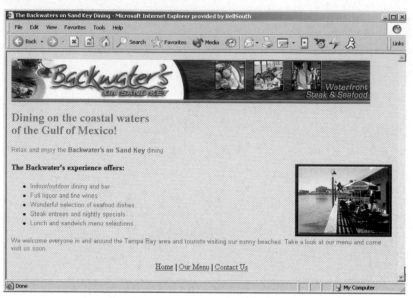

3 Switch to the text document. Center-align the table.

```
<html>

<head><title>The Backwaters on Sand Key Dining</title></head>

<body background="Images/bkg.gif">

<table width="747" border="0" cellpadding="0" cellspacing="0"
align="center">

<tr>

      <td rowspan="2">

      <img src="images/tophead_01.jpg" width="81" height="83" /></td>

      <td rowspan="2">

...
```

4 Save the changes to the text file. Refresh the document in the browser.

The table center-aligns on the Web page. The page would look more appealing if the content were the same width as the table.

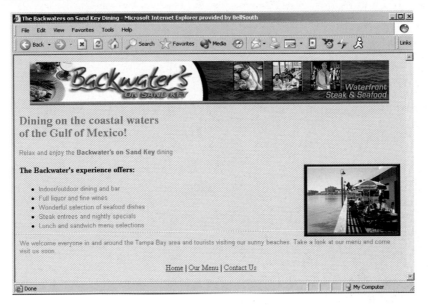

5 Leave both applications open for the next exercise.

Nest and Format Tables

You need to create another table below the header table — use the section on the left for the menu, and use the section on the right for the body content.

1   Add a new table and cell.

```
...

      <td colspan="9">

      <img src="images/tophead_11.gif" width="747" height="7" /></td>

      </tr>

</table>

<table width="747" border="0" cellpadding="0" cellspacing="0"
align="center">

<tr>

<td width="150" valign="top" bgcolor="#001b49">

<img src="images/wine3.jpg" alt="Backwaters Dining" border="0" width="150"
height="112" />

<h2><font color="#808080">Dining on the coastal waters <br>of the Gulf of
Mexico!</font></h2>

<p><font size="2" face="Arial" color="#808080">Relax and enjoy the
<b>Backwater's on Sand Key</b> dining</font></p>

      ...
```

The new table contains an image. This image displays above the menu.

2   Create a table within this new cell and table of links.

```
...

<table width="747" border="0" cellpadding="0" cellspacing="0"
align="center">

<tr>

<td width="150" valign="top" bgcolor="#001b49">

<img src="images/wine3.jpg" alt="Backwaters Dining" border="0" width="150"
height="112" />

<table border="0" cellspacing="0" cellpadding="0">

<tr>
```

```
            <td rowspan="6">

            <img src="images/spacer.gif" width="8" height="1" alt="Backwaters
Dining" border="0" /></td>

            <td valign="top">

            <img src="images/spacer.gif" width="1" height="2" alt="Backwaters
Dining" border="0" /><img src="images/fork1.gif" alt="Backwaters Dining"
border="0" alt="Backwaters Dining" width="12" height="12" />

            </td>

            <td> <a href="menu.htm"><font color="#FFFFFF">Our
Menu</font></a></td>

    </tr>

    <tr>

            <td valign="top">

            <img src="images/spacer.gif" width="1" height="2" alt="Backwaters
Dining" border="0"><img src="images/fork1.gif" alt="Backwaters Dining"
border="0" name="ab" width="12" height="12" />

            </td>

            <td><a href="contact.htm"><font color="#ffffff"> Contact
Us</font></a></td>

    </tr>

    <tr>

            <td valign="top">

            <img src="images/spacer.gif" width="1" height="2" alt="Backwaters
Dining" border="0" /><img src="images/fork1.gif" alt="Backwaters Dining"
border="0" name="ac" width="12" height="12" />

            </td>

            <td><a href="index.htm"><font
color="#ffffff"> Home</font></a></td>

    </tr>

    </table>

    </td>

<blockquote>

<h2><font color="#808080">Dining on the coastal waters <br>of the Gulf of
Mexico!</font></h2>

<p><font size="2" face="Arial" color="#808080">Relax and  enjoy the
<b>Backwater's on Sand Key</b> dining</font></p>

    ...
```

3   Open a new cell in the table. Enclose the body content within it.

```
...

      <img src="images/spacer.gif" width="1" height="2" alt="Backwaters
Dining" border="0" /><img src="images/fork1.gif" alt="Backwaters Dining"
border="0" name="ac" width="12" height="12" />

      </td>

      <td><a href="index.htm"><font
color="#ffffff"> Home</font></a></td>

</tr>

</table>

</td>

<td bgcolor="#FFFFFF">

<h2><font color="#808080">Dining on the coastal waters <br>of the Gulf of
Mexico!</font></h2>

<p><font size="2" face="Arial" color="#808080">Relax and enjoy the
<b>Backwater's on Sand Key</b> dining</font></p>

<b><font size="2" face="Arial" color="#000000">The Backwater's experience
offers:

</font> </b>

...

<p align="center">

<a href="index.htm" title="Our home page">Home</a>   |

<a href="menu.htm" title="Our Menu">Our Menu</a>   |

<a href="contact.htm" title="Feel free to contact us.">Contact Us</a>

</p>

<br />

</blockquote>

</tr>

</td>

</table>

</body>

</html>
```

4   Save the changes in the text file. Refresh the document in the browser.

The new nested tables provide a layout for the entire page.

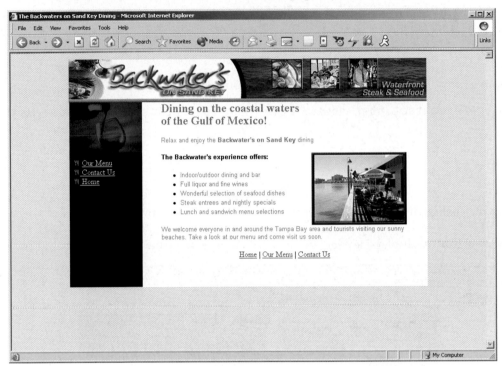

5   Leave both applications open for the next exercise.

Create a Form

1   With index.htm still open in the text editor, use the Save As feature to save a new XHTML document. Name the file "contact.htm".

2   Replace the content with form tags.

```
...
<td><a href="index.htm"><font color="#ffffff"> Home</font></a></td>

</tr>

</table>

</td>

<td bgcolor="#FFFFFF">

<blockquote>

<h2><font color="#808080">Contact &amp; Comments </font></h2>

<p><font color="#808080">Help us serve you better. Let us know what you
think.
```

```
<br />

Please take a moment to fill out our contact form. </font></p>

<p><font color="#808080">* required fields </font></p>

<p align="center">

<a href="index.htm" title="Our home page">Home</a>  |

<a href="menu.htm" title="Our Menu">Our Menu</a>  |

<a href="contact.htm" title="Feel free to contact us.">Contact Us</a>

</p>|

...
```

3   Save the changes in the text file. Refresh the document in the browser.

The new content displays, leaving the layout of the page the same as the home page.

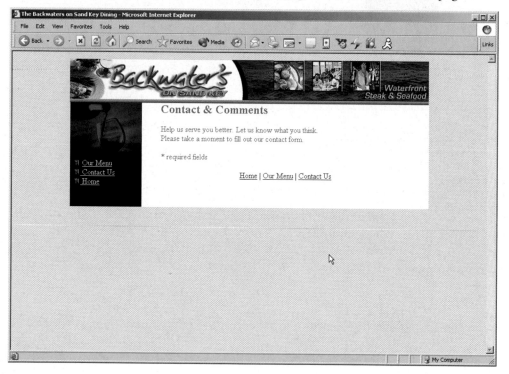

4   Create the following form.

...

```html
<h2><font color="#808080">Backwater's Contact &amp; Comments </font></h2>
<p><font color="#808080">Help us serve you better. Let us know what you
think.
<br />
Please take a moment to fill out our contact form. </font></p>
<p><font color="#808080">* required fields</font></p>
<p>
<form action="mailto:test@yourdomain.com" method="post">
<input type="text" size="24" name="firstname" /> First Name <br />
<input type="text" size="24" name="lastname" /> Last Name <br />
<input type="text" size="24" name="email" /> Email Address <br />
<input type="text" size="24" name="phone" /> Phone Number <br />
Comments:<br />
<textarea rows="5" cols="24" name="comments"></textarea>
</form>
</p>
<p align="center">
<a href="index.htm" title="Our home page">Home</a>  |
<a href="menu.htm" title="Our Menu">Our Menu</a>  |
<a href="contact.htm" title="Feel free to contact us.">Contact Us</a>
</p>
```

...

5　Save the changes to the text file and refresh the document in the browser.

The form displays below the text you entered in Step 2. Use your own email address so you can test the form.

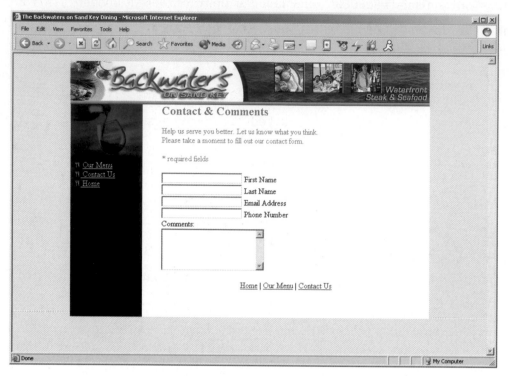

6　Close the file in both applications.

Add Meta Information and Comment Lines

1　Open index.htm in both the text editor and browser.

2　Provide keywords for the file.

```
<html>

<head><title>The Backwaters on Sand Key Dining</title></head>

<meta name="keywords" content="Dining, seafood, fine, fine dining, eat,
backwaters steak and seafood, indoor and outdoor dining" />

...
```

3 Provide a description for the document.

```
...

<title>The Backwaters on Sand Key Dining</title></head>

<meta name="keywords" content="Dining, seafood, fine, fine dining, eat,
backwaters steak and seafood, indoor and outdoor dining" />

<meta name="description" content="Dining on the coastal waters of the Gulf
of Mexico!">

...
```

4 Provide comments for each section of the document.

```
<body background="images/bkg.gif">

<!--TOP HEADER BANNER-->

<table width="747" border="0" cellpadding="0" cellspacing="0"
align="center">

        <tr>

                <td rowspan="2">

...

<!--LEFT NAVIGATION MENU-->

<table width="747" border="0" cellpadding="0" cellspacing="0"
align="center">

...

</table>

</td>

<!--CONTENT-->

<td bgcolor="#FFFFFF">

<blockquote>

<h2><font color="#808080">Dining on the coastal waters <br>of the Gulf of
Mexico!</font></h2>

<p><font color="#808080">Relax and enjoy the <b>Backwater's on Sand Key</b>
dining</font></p>

...
```

5 Save the changes. Refresh the document in the browser.

6 Leave both applications open for the next exercise.

Include DTD and Validate the Document

1 Switch to the text editor of the open document.

2 You used presentational elements in this Web site, so you must include the XHTML Transitional DTD at the top of the page, before the **<html>** tag.

```
<!DOCTYPE html

PUBLIC "-//W3C//DTD XHTML 1.0 Transitional//EN"

http://www.w3.org/TR/xhtml1/DTD/xhtml1-transitional.dtd />

<html>

<head>

<title>The Backwaters on Sand Key Dining</title></head>

...
```

3 Save index.htm in the text editor.

4 Log on to http://www.htmlhelp.com/tools/validator. Follow the instructions for uploading and validating the page.

The validator returns a list of errors. The errors may differ from one person to the next, depending on how well each person followed the steps in this project.

5 Address each error according to the XHTML Transitional standards. Continue to validate until all the errors are resolved.

6 Test all links and images.

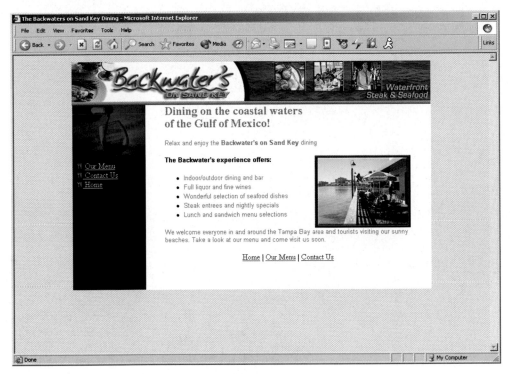

7 Close all applications.

XHTML TAG REFERENCE

Element	Strict	Transitional	Frameset	Basic	XHTML1.1	Empty
a	X	X	X	X	X	
abbr	X	X	X	X	X	
acronym	X	X	X	X	X	
address	X	X	X	X	X	
applet		X	X			
area	X	X	X		X	X
b	X	X	X		X	
base	X	X	X	X	X	X
basefont		X	X			X
bdo	X	X	X		X	
big	X	X	X		X	
blockquote	X	X	X	X	X	
body	X	X	X	X	X	
br	X	X	X	X	X	X
button	X	X	X		X	
caption	X	X	X	X	X	
center		X	X			
cite	X	X	X	X	X	
code	X	X	X	X	X	
col	X	X	X		X	X
colgroup	X	X	X		X	
dd	X	X	X	X	X	
del	X	X	X		X	
dfn	X	X	X	X	X	
dir		X	X			
div	X	X	X		X	
dl	X	X	X	X	X	
dt	X	X	X	X	X	
em	X	X	X	X	X	
fieldset	X	X	X		X	
font		X	X			
form	X	X	X	X	X	
frame			X			X

Element	Strict	Transitional	Frameset	Basic	XHTML1.1	Empty
frameset			x			
h1	x	x	x	x	x	
h2	x	x	x	x	x	
h3	x	x	x	x	x	
h4	x	x	x	x	x	
h5	x	x	x	x	x	
h6	x	x	x	x	x	
head	x	x	x	x	x	
hr	x	x	x		x	x
html	x	x	x	x	x	
i	x	x	x		x	
iframe	x	x	x		x	
img	x	x	x	x	x	x
input	x	x	x	x	x	x
ins	x	x	x		x	
isindex		x	x			x
kbd	x	x	x	x	x	
label	x	x	x		x	
legend	x	x	x		x	
li	x	x	x	x	x	
link	x	x	x	x	x	x
map	x	x	x		x	
menu		x	x			
meta	x	x	x	x	x	x
noframes			x			
noscript	x	x	x		x	
object	x	x	x	x	x	
ol	x	x	x	x	x	
optgroup	x	x	x		x	
option	x	x	x	x	x	
p	x	x	x	x	x	
param	x	x	x	x	x	x
pre	x	x	x	x	x	
q	x	x	x	x	x	
rb					x	

Element	Strict	Transitional	Frameset	Basic	XHTML1.1	Empty
rbc					X	
rp					X	
rt					X	
rtc					X	
ruby					X	
s		X	X			
samp	X	X	X	X	X	
script	X	X	X		X	
select	X	X	X	X	X	
small	X	X	X		X	
span	X	X	X		X	
strike		X	X			
strong	X	X	X	X	X	
style	X	X	X		X	
sub	X	X	X		X	
sup	X	X	X		X	
table	X	X	X	X	X	
tbody	X	X	X		X	
td	X	X	X	X	X	
textarea	X	X	X	X	X	
tfoot	X	X	X		X	
th	X	X	X	X	X	
thead	X	X	X		X	
title	X	X	X	X	X	
tr	X	X	X	X	X	
tt	X	X	X		X	
u		X	X			
ul	X	X	X	X	X	
var	X	X	X	X	X	

GLOSSARY

absolute path   The location of a file or Web page beginning with the root. Includes all necessary information to find the file or page. In the case of a Web page, called "absolute URL." See *relative path*.

accessibility   The ability for a disabled user to use a Web site.

action   The location that receives data from a form.

algorithm   A specific sequence of mathematical steps to process data. A portion of a computer program that calculates a specific result.

alignment   Positioning content to the left, right, center, top, or bottom.

alt text   Alternate Text. In Web page design, text that can be displayed in lieu of an image.

anchor   In a Web page, a type of hyperlink destination in which the destination is a specific location on a page.

animated GIF   A type of sequential file format where multiple bitmap images are displayed one after another.

animated graphics   Images of any type that move.

anonymous FTP   FTP protocol that allows users access to files for downloading. The user ID is anonymous, and the password is any valid e-mail address.

ARPANET   Advanced Research Projects Agency Network. Developed by the U.S. Department of Defense during the cold war to survive nuclear attacks, authority was distributed over a number of geographically dispersed computers. This concept was the basis of the Internet.

ASCII   American Standard Code for Information Interchange. Worldwide, standard ASCII text does not include formatting, and therefore can be exchanged and read by most computer systems.

ASP   Active Server Pages. A specification for a dynamically created Web page that contains either Visual Basic or JavaScript code. When a browser requests an ASP page, the Web server generates a page with HTML code. Only available on NT servers.

asset   An image, sound, video, or other file that may be used in a Web page.

attribute   Information included in the start tag of an element.

background   A static object or color that lies behind all other objects.

bandwidth   The transmission capacity, usually measured in bits per second (see *BPS*), of a network connection.

banner   Common form of Web advertisement. Most banner ads are animated GIFs.

basefont   The default size of the text that is displayed in a document window.

baud   The speed of a modem. Although not technically accurate, baud rate is commonly used to mean bit rate (the number of bits transmitted per second).

bitmap image   An image constructed from individual dots or pixels set to a grid-like mosaic. The file must contain information about the color and position of each pixel, so the disk space needed for bitmap images can be very large.

blank   When using frames, a value for the target attribute. This value causes the browser to create a new window for the linked content when the user follows the associated link.

boldface   A heavier, blacker version of a typeface.

border   A continual line that extends around an element.

BPS   Bits Per Second. A measurement of how fast data is moved from one place to another, usually in thousands of bits per second (Kbps) or million of bits per second (Mbps). A 28.8 modem can transport 28,800 bits per second.

browser   Software program that allows you to surf the Web. The most popular browsers are Netscape Navigator and Microsoft Internet Explorer. The very first browsers, such as Lynx, only allowed users to see text. Also called "Web browser."

browser compatibility   A term that compares how a Web page functions on different browsers. Incompatibilities often exist due to how a browser interprets the HTML. The differences may be very slight or significant.

bullet   A marker preceding text, usually a solid dot, used to add emphasis; generally indicates the text is part of a list.

button   An element a user can click to cause an effect, such as the submission of a form.

caps   An abbreviation for capital letters.

caps and small caps   A style of typesetting in which uppercase letters are used in the normal way, while the type that would normally be in lowercase is changed to uppercase letters of a smaller point size. A true small-caps typeface does not contain any lowercase letters.

Cascading Style Sheets (CSS)   Part of a Web page file listing properties that affect the appearance of content, the content to which those properties apply, and their values.

CD-R/CD-RW   A recordable CD disc and drive, also known as a "burner." A CD-R drive can write to a CD-R disc once; afterward, the disc cannot be erased or rewritten. CD-RW allows a CD-RW disc to be erased and rewritten. A CD-RW drive can also "burn" a CD-R disc.

CD-ROM   A device used to store approximately 600 MB of data. Files are permanently stored on the device and can be copied to a disk, but not altered directly.

cell   A unit of information within a table.

cellpadding   The margin around the inside of a table cell.

cellspacing   The margin between table cells.

CGI   Common Gateway Interface. Interface that allows scripts to run on a Web server. CGI scripts can be used to put the content of a form into an email message, to perform a database query, or to generate HTML pages on the fly.

CGI script   A CGI program used to process a form or provide other dynamic content.

CGI-bin   The most common name of a directory on a Web server in which CGI scripts are stored.

check box   A square the use can click to cause the form to send a name-value pair to the action; a form element that allows a user to choose zero or more choices.

client   A computer system or application that requests a service of another computer system on the network.

client-side   Scripting or other actions that take place within the browser, as opposed to the server.

clip art   Collections of predrawn and digitized graphics.

clipboard   The portion of computer memory that holds data that has been cut or copied. The next item cut or copied replaces the data already in the clipboard.

column   1. A vertical area for type; used to constrain line length to enhance design and readability. 2. A series of cells arranged vertically.

comment   A line in a piece of programming code that is intended to be read, not executed.

contrast   The relationship and degree of difference between the dark and light areas of an image.

cookie   Information a Web server writes to your computer hard disk via your browser, containing data such as login information and user preferences. This data can be retrieved so Web pages can be customized before they are sent to the visiting browser.

copyright   Ownership of a work. Permits the owner of material to prevent its use without express permission or acknowledgement. Copyrights may be sold, transferred, or given up contractually.

default   A specification for a mode of computer operation that occurs if no other is selected. The default font size might be 12 point, or a default color for an object might be white with a black border.

deprecated   The status of a tag or attribute that can still be used, but will eventually be removed, and so should be avoided, if possible.

DNS   Domain Name Server or Domain Name System. Maps IP numbers to a more easily remembered name. When you type http://www.somedomain.com into a browser, the DNS searches for a matching IP address (228.28.202.95).

DOCTYPE   Specification of the DTD that applies to a page.

document   The general term for a computer file containing text and/or graphics.

document root   The main directory for a Web site.

domain name   A unique name that is used to identify a Web site, FTP site, and/or email server. A domain name always points to one specific server, even though the server may host many domain names.

download   Transferring data from a server to your computer's hard disk.

DSL   Digital Subscriber Line. A means for gaining high-speed access to the Internet using phone wiring and a specialized phone connection.

dynamic   Content that changes according to client-side or server-side scripting.

e-commerce   Electronic Commerce. Conducting business online, including product display, online ordering, and inventory management. The software, which works in conjunction with online payment systems to process payments, resides on a commerce server.

element   The smallest unit of a graphic, or a component of a page layout or design. Any object, text block, or graphic might be referred to as a design element.

email address   An electronic mail address. Email addresses are in the form of user@domain.com (for example, chris@webguest.net).

email alias   Email address that points to another email address. All messages sent to an email alias are automatically redirected (forwarded) to the specified email address.

embedding   Including a complete copy of a text file or image within a document, with or without a link. See *linking*.

empty element tag   A tag that has no closing element tag.

empty tag   A tag that has no text between the opening and closing tags. Empty tags carry all information in attributes. There is no content to enclose, so empty tags are abbreviated with a "/" within the opening tag and have no closing tag.

encryption   Procedure that scrambles the content of a file before sending it over the Internet. The recipient must have software to decrypt the file. PGP (Pretty Good Privacy) is a commonly used encryption program.

end user   The person/s who will view and use your Web pages and designs.

file   A specific collection of information stored on the computer disk, separate from all other information. Can be randomly accessed by the computer.

file extension   The suffix used to identify file types under the Macintosh and Windows operating systems, separated from the rest of the file name by a period.

file:///   A protocol used by browsers to access information available on the local computer.

flow chart   A block diagram representing the major steps of an event. Used by computer programmers to translate events into computer logic.

font   The complete collection of all the characters (numbers, uppercase and lowercase letters, and in some cases, small caps and symbols) of a given typeface in a specific style; for example, Helvetica Bold.

font family   In Web design, a grouping of (supposedly) similar fonts, which will be used to display text in the Web page, See *Cascading Style Sheets*.

form   A page that enables a user to enter information and send it to a site via form elements, such as text boxes, radio buttons, and pull-down menus.

form validation   The process of making certain a Web form contains all required data and no invalid data.

frame   A section of the browser window displaying content; independent of all other areas within the browser window. This window-within-a-window can be referenced by links in other frames.

frameset   The document defining the layout on a framed page and breaking it into one or more frames.

GIF   Graphics Interchange Format. A popular graphics format for online clip art and drawn graphics. Graphics in this format are acceptable at low resolution. See *JPEG*.

hard disk   A magnetic storage medium consisting of specially coated metal disks, and associated mechanical and electronic equipment. Found inside most personal computers; can store a tremendous amount of information, and is sometimes removable or portable.

hardware   The physical components of a computer and its auxiliary equipment.

header information   Information at the beginning of a Web page file that defines the content and characteristics of the page.

hex values   Numbers specified in the hexadecimal system, commonly used for specifying colors on Web pages.

hidden field   Data not shown to the user, but submitted with the rest of the form data.

home page   Main page of a Web site. A Web site containing only one page is also called a home page.

HREF   Hyperlink Reference. HTML code that specifies a URL as the linked resource.

HTML   Hypertext Mark-Up Language. A tagging language that allows content to be delivered over the World Wide Web and viewed by a browser.

HTTP   Hypertext Transfer Protocol. The method used by browsers and Web servers to communicate, such as to request and deliver content, respectively.

hyperlink   An HTML tag that directs the computer to a different anchor or URL. A hyperlink can be a word, phrase, sentence, graphic, or icon. A hyperlink can also cause an action, such as opening or downloading a file.

hypertext   An organization of content that enables the user to select related content.

hypertext reference attribute   The location of the information to which a browser should link.

interface   The design with which users interact.

Internet   A global system of interconnected computers.

Internet Explorer   A common Web browser, developed by Microsoft.

InterNIC   Internet Network Information Center. The entity that keeps track of domain names. Recently, the right to register domain names has been widely granted to private companies, so the cost and services associated with obtaining a new domain can vary.

IP   Internet Protocol. The rules that provide basic Internet functions. IP allows computers to find each other.

IP address   A unique, 32-bit Internet address consisting of four numbers, separated by dots and sometimes called a "dotted quad" (90.0.0.95). Every client computer and every server computer connected to the Internet has a unique IP number that is assigned by the ISP.

JavaScript   A scripting language, designed by Netscape, that can be embedded into HTML documents.

JPEG   A compression algorithm that reduces the file size of bitmapped images. Named for the Joint Photographic Experts Group, which created the standard. JPEG is "lossy" compression; image quality is reduced in direct proportion to the amount of compression.

keywords   A word or words that identifies the content of a Web page and can be used by search engines as part of their process of determining the results of searches.

layout   The arrangement of text and graphics on a page, usually produced in the preliminary design stage.

left alignment   Text having a straight left edge and a ragged or uneven right edge.

linking   The act of placing a reference to one file (sound, graphic, or video) into another file. When the referenced file is modified, the placed reference is automatically (or manually, depending on the application) updated.

list   A series of items.

location   The address of a particular Web page or file.

mailto: A protocol used to tell the browser to create a new email message.

meta tag   An optional HTML tag that is used to specify information about a Web document. Some search engines index Web pages by reading the information contained within the meta tags.

monospace   A font in which all characters occupy the same amount of horizontal width regardless of the character.

Mosaic   The first Web browser (developed by NSCA) with the ability to display graphics. The Mosaic browser caused a major breakthrough in the way people could access the resources of the World Wide Web.

named target   A frame that has a designated name, allowing links to specify that content should be displayed within that frame.

name-value pair   A combination of two elements: a name that identifies the information, and a value (the actual information).

nested frameset   A frameset that is the content of the frame of another frameset.

nested tag   A tag contained within another tag.

nesting   Placing graphic files or tables within other graphic files or tables.

Netscape Navigator   A common Web browser.

no frames section   Content provided for browsers that does not support frames contained within a noframes element.

one-line text box   This field allows the viewer to insert a single line of data, such as a name or address. This form element is commonly used to gather basic demographic information from a user, or to act as a password field.

online   Currently connected to a computer network.

opening tag   The indication of the start of an element containing the name of the element and any attributes.

operating system (OS)   The software that allows your computer to function. Examples of operating systems are Mac OS X and Microsoft Windows.

page properties   In Web design, the characteristics of a layout page, including default background and text colors, page width, and background image.

page title   Text that appears in the Title bar of the user's browser when the page is viewed.

parent   The master element to which secondary "child" elements are related. Can refer to styles, graphic elements or objects, layers, folders, and Web site frames.

password box   A text box that replaces all characters with a bullet or asterisk to hide their identity.

Perl   Practical Extraction and Report Language. A powerful computer language, especially used for writing CGI scripts that handle input/output actions on Web pages.

PHP   A server-side, HTML-embedded scripting language used to create dynamic Web pages. The strength of PHP lies in its compatibility with many types of databases. PHP can talk across networks using IMAP, SNMP, NNTP, POP3, or HTTP.

pixel   Picture element. One of the tiny rectangular areas or dots generated by a computer or output device to constitute images. A greater number of pixels per inch results in higher resolution on screen or in print.

PNG   Portable Network Graphics. PNG is a new graphics format similar to GIF. It is a relatively new file format, and is not yet widely supported by most browsers.

POP   Post Office Protocol. Internet protocol used by ISPs to handle email for its subscribers. A POP account is a synonym for an email account.

pull-down menu   A menu that displays additional options.

radio button   A single round button a user can click to cause a form to send a name-value pair to the action.

radio group   A group of radio buttons with the same name. Only one radio button may be selected at a time within a radio group.

RAM   Random access memory. The "working" memory of a computer that holds files in process. Files in RAM are lost when the computer is turned off, whereas files stored on the hard drive or floppy disks remain available.

redirect   To cause the browser to load a different page without intervention from the user. A particular HTML code in the heading of a Web page that can seamlessly redirect the visitor to another Web page.

refresh   To reload a Web page.

reset button   A button that, when clicked, causes a form to return to the state it was in when the page was first loaded.

resolution   The density of graphic information expressed in dots per inch (dpi) or pixels per inch (ppi).

RGB   1. The colors of projected light from a computer monitor that, when combined, simulate a subset of the visual spectrum. 2. The color model of most digital artwork.

right alignment   Text having a straight right edge and a ragged or uneven left edge.

script   Instructions that tell the computer what to do.

scripting   The process of adding programming capabilities to a program (e.g., AppleScript), file (e.g., ActionScript), or Web page (e.g., JavaScript).

search engine   A Web site that allows users to search for keywords on Web pages. Every search engine has its own strategy for collecting data.

select list   A list of potential choices, displayed as a menu that appears when the user clicks it, or as a box with its own scroll bar.

select option   A potential choice listed in a select list.

selection   The currently active object/s in a window. Often made by clicking with the mouse or dragging a marquee around the desired object/s.

_self   When using frames, a value for the target attribute. This value causes the browser to place the linked content into the frame containing the current document when the user follows the associated link.

SGML   Standard Generalized Markup Language. The predecessor to Hypertext Markup Language; a means for creating universally available content using tagging.

site   See *Web site*.

site root directory   The parent folder that contains all other files and directories for a Web site.

SMTP   Simple Mail Transfer Protocol. Primary protocol to send and receive email between servers on the Internet.

source   The actual text that makes up the Web page received by the browser, including HTML/XHTML, client-side scripting, and other information.

spider   Program, also known as an orbit or a bot, used by some search engines to index Web sites. Spiders search the Web to find URLs that match the given query string.

storyboard   A series of sketches of the key visualization points of a Web page.

string   A unit of text.

submit button   A button that, when clicked, causes the browser to send form data to the server.

tags   An indication of the start and end of an element.

target   The page or part of a page to which a link points.

TCP/IP   Transmission Control Protocol/Internet Protocol. A suite of communications protocols that defines how information is transmitted over the Internet.

template   A document file containing layout, styles, and repeating elements (such as logos) by which a series of documents can maintain the same look and feel. A model publication you can use as the basis for creating a new publication.

text   The characters and words that form the main body of a publication or Web page.

text attribute   A characteristic applied directly to a letter or letters in text, such as bold, italic, or underline.

text box   A box into which users can type.

text editor   An application used to create or make changes to text files.

text effects   Means by which the appearance of text can be modified, such as bolding, underlining, and italicizing.

text string   Any sequence of alphanumeric characters that are not code commands.

text wrap   The ability of a browser to automatically continue text on the next line.

TIFF   Tagged Image File Format. A common format used for scanned or computer-generated bitmapped images.

top   When using frames, a value for the target attribute. This value causes the browser to place the linked content into the current browser window, rather than an individual frame, when the user follows the associated link.

transparency   The quality of an image element that allows background elements to partially or entirely show through.

type family   A set of typefaces created from the same basic design but in different variations, such as bold, light, italic, book, and heavy. 2. In Web design, a list of fonts that will be used to display text in a Web page. See *Cascading Style Sheets*.

type size   Typeface as measured (in points) from the bottom of descenders to the body clearance line, which is slightly higher than the top of ascenders.

typeface   A unique and distinctive design of a font alphabet; the combined group of all the letters, figures, and punctuation of a specific font.

uploading   The process of sending a file from one computer to a remote server.

uppercase   The capital letters of a typeface as opposed to the lowercase (small) letters. When type was hand composited, the capital letters resided in the upper part of the type case.

URL Uniform Resource Locator. Address of any resource on the Web.

usability The ease with which a user can access, navigate, and achieve goals on a Web site.

user ID Unique identifier you must enter every time you want to access a particular service on the Internet. The user ID is always accompanied by a password.

validate To analyze a file to ensure the structure, tag names, and attributes are correct, according to the DTD selected.

validation Making certain input fields, particular types of information, or information in a specific format mandatory for a form to be successfully submitted.

W3C The World Wide Web Consortium. The group responsible for defining HTML Standards (http://www.w3c.org).

WAI An acronym for the Web Accessibility Initiative.

Web Accessibility Initiative A project at the W3C to create guidelines for actions that developers should take to increase the accessibility of their sites and applications.

Web designer An individual who is the aesthetic and navigational architect of a Web site, determining how the site looks, how it is designed, and what components it contains.

Web developer A person who builds the technical architecture of Web sites, providing the programming required for a particular Web product to work.

Web directory A site that contains categorized listings of Web sites.

Web host A company that provides access to a server on which you can place your Web site content. This server is connected to the Internet, allowing the general public to access your Web site.

Web page A single file or Web address containing HTML or XHTML information. Web pages typically include text and images, but may include links to other pages and other media.

Web site A collection of HTML files and other content that visitors can access by means of a URL and view with a Web browser.

Webmaster The person who is responsible for the Web server (usually the sysadmin).

Web-safe color A color palette used for images that will be displayed on the Internet. The Web-safe color palette is a specific set of colors that can be displayed by most computer-operating systems and monitors.

World Wide Web Client/server hypertext system for retrieving information across the Internet.

wrap Type set on the page so it wraps around the shape of another element.

WYSIWYG Web-page editor A Web-page editor that allows an author to directly manipulate items on a page, so that What You See Is What You Get.

XForms An emerging specification defining advanced functionality for Web forms.

XHTML An acronym for eXtensible HyperText Markup Language. The reformulization of HTML 4.01 in XML.

XHTML Elements An emerging specification for defining the handling of events on a Web page.

XHTML Frameset A version of XHTML that includes all tags that are part of HTML 4.01, including those involving frames.

XHTML Strict A version of XHTML that does not include any presentational tags or attributes.

XHTML Transitional The most common version of XHTML. Includes all tags and attributes that are part of HTML 4.01, except those involving frames.

XML An acronym for eXtensible Markup Language.

INDEX

&   313
    99, 102, 313
"   313, 314
<a>   130, 131, 132, 138
<b>   3, 42, 45
<base>   144–146, 282, 283
<blockquote>   21, 22, 23, 24
<body>   7, 8, 53, 55, 137, 262, 294

   15, 16, 17, 58, 60, 92, 95
<comment>   310–311
<dd>   61, 62
<dl>   61, 62
<dt>   61, 62
<em>   45
<font>   45, 48
<form>   212, 213
<frameset>   262, 264, 294
<head>   7, 8
<hr />   105
<html>   7, 8
<i>   3, 42, 45
<img />   84, 85, 86, 89, 91, 96, 138
<input />   213
<li>   57, 58, 59, 60
<line>   17
<meta>   308, 315, 316–317, 322, 327, 328
<noframes>   294–295
<object>   91
<ol>   59, 60
<option>   234, 237
<p>   10, 12, 13, 15, 17, 58, 60, 92
<pre>   162
<s>   40
<section>   21
<select>   234
<strong>   45
<table>   164, 165, 176, 192
<tbody>   188, 190
<td>   164, 166, 169, 192
<textarea>   240
<tfoot>   188, 191
<th>   169, 173
<thead>   188, 189
<title>   7, 8
<tr>   164, 166, 169, 178, 192
<u>   40, 42, 45
<ul>   56, 58

A

absolute URLs   129, 142–143, 144, 216
action=""   216–218, 222, 223
Active Server Page (ASP)   65, 216, 242
adding hyperlinks   130–133, 138–139
Adobe Illustrator   99
Adobe Photoshop   99
align=""   13, 25, 91–92, 93, 94, 105, 173, 183–187
aligning paragraphs   13–14
alink=""   140
alt=""   89, 90
alternate text   89–90
anchor tag   130
anchors   134–137
animation   83
AOL   162
ASCII value   312
assets   140
attribute-value pair   13

B

background   53
background color   192
backward compatibility   2
bandwidth   89
banners   82
base target   282–284
bgcolor=""   55, 192, 193, 194
blank target   284, 286–287
blockquotes   21
body tags   7, 8
body text   53–56
bold tag   3
bolding   43
border attribute   140
border=""   87, 88, 140, 168, 275, 278
bordercolor=""   192, 194
borders   140–141, 275–278
browser   2, 5
browsers   45
bullets   57
buttons   244–246

C

Cascading Style Sheets (CSS)   10, 40, 42, 48, 55, 66, 140, 192, 199, 211, 215, 264, 271, 274, 319
case sensitivity   328
cellpadding   195–197
cells   163
cellspacing   195–197
certification   246
Certified Internet Webmaster (CIW)   246
CGI   211, 216, 222
character   2
character codes   312–315
character entity   99, 312
check boxes   226–233
checked=""   226, 271
cite=""   24
clear=""   92, 95
closing container tags   13
ColdFusion   65, 242
color names   45, 46
color=""   45, 47
cols=""   262
colspan=""   170, 172–174
column span   170, 171
columns   163, 177
comments   308, 309–311
controlling frames   271–274
controlling images   91–95
copyright   313
Corel WordPerfect   5
creating Web pages   5–7

D

default text   40, 50
definition lists   61–63
deprecated features   10
deprecated tags   14, 17
description value   315
destination   130
document tags   7–9
Document Type Definitions (DTD)   10, 318–319
domain names   142, 324–325
domain registrar   324
downloads   128